from POLITICAL ECONOMY *to* ECONOMICS

And Back?

from POLITICAL
ECONOMY
to
ECONOMICS

And Back?

Edited by
James H. Nichols, Jr.,
and Colin Wright

With an Epilogue by
Allan Bloom

ICS Press

Institute for Contemporary Studies
San Francisco, California

The Institute for Contemporary Studies is a nonpartisan, nonprofit public policy research organization. The analyses, conclusions, and opinions expressed in ICS Press publications are those of the authors and not necessarily those of the Institute, or of its officers, directors, or others associated with, or funding, its work.

Inquiries, book orders, and catalogue requests should be addressed to ICS Press, Institute for Contemporary Studies, 243 Kearny Street, San Francisco, CA 94108. (415) 981-5353. FAX (415) 986-4878.

Distributed to the trade by National Book Network, Lanham, Maryland.

— Library of Congress Cataloging-in-Publication Data —

From political economy to economics—and back? / edited by James H.
  Nichols, Jr., and Colin Wright; with an epilogue by Allan Bloom.
     p.   cm.
     Papers from a conference held at Claremont McKenna College in
Nov. 1987.
     Includes index.
     ISBN 1-55815-113-3 (cloth)
     1. Economics—Congresses. 2. Political science—Congresses.
  I. Nichols, James H., 1944–   II. Wright, Colin.
HB74.P65F76   1990
330—dc20   90–42824
                                          CIP

Contents

CONTENTS

Foreword

Economists look at the world in an entirely different manner from everyone else. From their technical vocabulary to their basic assumptions, economists are increasingly a breed apart even from their close cousins, political scientists.

Today economics is coming under fire as some of its root assumptions are questioned. One of the fundamental disagreements concerns the microeconomic doctrine of the completely rational and self-interested individual with fixed and stable preferences. One rarely meets such a person, and the assumption that he exists precludes some of life's most interesting and essential questions: Where do preferences come from? How do they change? Why?

To ask these questions is not to denigrate the great achievements of modern economics. The Institute's respect for the science of economics is attested by the many books on macroeconomic issues we have published over the years—books that have had a substantial influence on national policy.

But it is clear that a huge gap exists between economic and political thought—and that a reconciliation of these disciplines is, as Irving Kristol writes, one of the great challenges of our age. In the spirit of inquiry we offer these essays by renowned thinkers in both fields.

Robert B. Hawkins, Jr., President
Institute for Contemporary Studies

Preface

The first beginnings of this volume arose from the collaboration of the editors—an economist and a political scientist—in designing and team-teaching a course entitled "Foundations of Political Economy." Over some years we had grown increasingly dissatisfied with the separation between the academic study of economics and that of politics. We judged that our capacity to understand what goes on in society would be strengthened and deepened by efforts to rejoin economics and political science in a revived study of political economy. We noted with interest and some sense of encouragement that this judgment seemed to be more widely shared than it had been, say, twenty or thirty years earlier.

The economist, who for many years specialized in public finance and development, had rekindled an earlier interest in welfare economics, economic history, and questions of economic justice. The political scientist, specializing in the area of political philosophy, had acquired a healthy respect for the usefulness of economic approaches in analyzing some deep-seated tendencies in the political structures of representative democracy and various problems of public policy. He had also developed a growing interest in how modern views of political economy emerged from certain themes found in the work of earlier political philosophers.

Our work together on an interdisciplinary course emerged naturally from these converging interests. We are grateful to our academic institution, Claremont McKenna College, for considerable support in this endeavor. We wish to express our sincere gratitude to the Lynde and Harry Bradley Foundation for financial support that advanced our work further, especially in making possible a conference at Claremont McKenna College in November 1987, where most of the material here published was presented. Chapters 2–3 and 5–9 were prepared for the conference; Chapters 1 and 4 were written especially for this volume; Chapter 10 is an edited version of comments delivered orally at the end of the conference.

James H. Nichols, Jr.
Colin Wright
Claremont McKenna College

One

James H. Nichols, Jr.

Introduction: Political Economy and the Problems of Political Philosophy

Today the relations between politics and economics, and between the study of politics and that of economics, present a confusing spectacle. On the one hand, politics and economics seem separate, even opposed. Politicians frequently promote proposals apparently in blind disregard of reasonable considerations of economic efficiency, while economists who have propounded elegant, economically efficient solutions to problems of public policy are often left shaking their heads in bewilderment or disgust at the carryings-on in the political system. Economics, at least in its mainstream, makes plausible claims to be in every sense a science, with generally accepted technical terms and methods of inquiry and demonstration; its technically sophisticated, sometimes recondite, language sounds strange to the ears of ordinary consumers, citizens, and wage earners or businesspeople, who converse, bargain, or deliberate in quite different ways. Political science, by contrast, while customarily applying the term "science" to its activity or product, cannot claim to have attained any general agreement on how politics should be studied or what terms of discourse should be used. It is, rather, an arena in which a multiplicity of approaches—behavioral, philosophical, historical—to the study of politics contend. The various approaches tend to develop their own special terminologies that differ from one another as much as they differ from the language commonly used by citizens and statesmen.

On the other hand, strong currents within both political science and economics seek to join together once more the studies of these two areas of our social activity. Most evidently, important efforts have for some decades been under way in economics to apply its assumptions and methods to the study of politics, indeed of social life in all aspects; and a goodly number of influential voices within political science have adopted and adapted this approach. From political science, investigations into the economic dimensions of politics have multiplied: the political influence of economic power has been and remains a topic of political research frequently visited during the past several decades; public policy studies rely heavily on the cost-benefit analysis developed by economists; and an area called political economy (predominantly concerned with such matters as international economic issues, terms of trade, and the involvement of the political structures in modernization) has recently emerged as an important subfield of the discipline of political science.

Things were not always so confusing. If one looks to Adam Smith—by general agreement the founder of economics or political economy as (from the broadest historical perspective) we know it—the relation of politics and economics is clear. Smith describes political economy as

> a branch of the science of a statesman or legislator [that] proposes two distinct objects: first, to provide a plentiful revenue or subsistence for the people, or more properly to enable them to provide such a revenue or subsistence for themselves; and secondly, to supply the state or commonwealth with a revenue sufficient for the public services. It proposes to enrich both the people and the sovereign.[1]

In this key respect Smith remains in apparent agreement with the classical tradition descending from Aristotle, for whom political science was the comprehensive study of human affairs, within which political economy is clearly subordinate.

In comparing Smith and Aristotle on the relation between politics and economics, however, one immediately discerns striking and crucial differences. For Aristotle, economy is management of the household, including the acquisition of such material goods as are required by a virtuous way of life for that household. Political economy deals with comparable matters in the life of the political community; or to put it another way, political economy treats economic needs as political issues—how can necessary provisions, such as foodstuffs, an adequate supply of healthful water, and materials for implements of war, best be supplied to the political community? The subject of political economy has a distinctly secondary interest for Aristotle, and he treats it briefly, almost contemptuously. He casts considerable doubt on the dignity and even the moral propriety of sophisticated arts of acquisition, especially the more refined devisings of finance; he concedes with apparent reluctance that many cities (that is, independent political communities) do need to be concerned with these dubious practices in order to raise adequate revenues; and he notes grudgingly that "some even of those engaged in politics are concerned only with these matters."[2]

How different is the picture when we turn to Smith! Political economy is not treated sketchily and tangentially, but is the fully developed subject of his largest book, elaborated in vast, if not precisely loving, detail. Moreover, as Marc Plattner argues in the first part of his chapter in this volume, Smith's political economy is concerned with the ultimate goals of jurisprudence and therefore of political society as such.

It is true that we still find traces of the older skepticism concerning the worth of money-making activities. In a famous passage, Smith characterizes the unjust exploitation of which businessmen are fond: "People of the same trade seldom meet together, even for merriment and diversion, but the conversation ends in a conspiracy against the public, or in some contrivance to raise prices."[3] Consider another memorable example, where Smith describes the feudal nobility's turn from warlike pursuits, hospitality, and political leadership to acquiring money for the sake of luxurious consumption:

> For a pair of diamond buckles, perhaps, or for something as frivolous and useless, they exchanged the maintenance, or what is the same thing, the price of the maintenance of a thousand men for a year, and with it the whole weight and authority which it could give them. . . . Thus, for the gratification of the most childish, the meanest and the most sordid of all vanities, they gradually bartered their whole power and authority.[4]

The context in which Smith expresses this traditional moral tone, however, is a narration of how the rise of commerce and the dissolution of the feudal order paved the way to a development of opulence in Europe that had previously been blocked from its natural course by particular political and legal institutions. Likewise, Smith partly maintains a traditional moral stance in discussing the basic and widespread human drive "to better oneself." The most common, but by no means the highest, form taken by this drive is the effort to improve one's economic condition—not so much to meet strict necessities, or even to provide bodily comforts, but, typically, to be looked upon more favorably by one's fellows. Smith's critical analysis partakes of the older moral view, but he does not seek to discourage, limit, or transform the passion in question. He takes it as a given and refrains from mounting any overall endeavor, such as would be typical of the older tradition, to show how the moral and political order should try to moderate or elevate—in short, to educate—that passion. Rather, Smith takes cheer, or at least comfort, in elaborating how freedom for the activities motivated by this human passion, within the appropriate legal structures to ensure order and property rights, can provide the basis for a commercial society of growing prosperity.

How did this remarkable change in the view toward commerce, acquisition, liberal commercial society, and political economy come about? A question of this sort points down several possible avenues of historical explanation. Smith himself in *The Wealth of Nations* (differing in this respect from his manner in *The Theory of Moral Sentiments*) speaks relatively little about his intellectual predecessors, but provides an extensive economic history of Europe from the fall of the Roman Empire to his own day, with emphases on political and legal institutions, modes of land ownership, and commerce. Nathan Rosenberg's chapter in this volume takes a similar approach to developments in political economies since Smith's day (with an additional emphasis on technological and other innovations). In the present context, however, where we are concerned with the most general relations between political science and economics (as well as between polity and economy), the record of comprehensive philosophical reflections on these matters promises to be especially revealing.

In this perspective, the key figure appears to be John Locke. Locke's crucial contribution to the new view of political economy has recently been given a notably concise formulation by Thomas Pangle. In contrasting Christians or Stoics who hold "that the supply of wealth in the world is fixed and we must all rest content with what God or Fortune has allotted us" with post-Machiavellian mercantilists who say "that the supply of wealth in the world is fixed and we must strive to increase our country's share at the expense of others," Pangle observes: "The science of economics could not disencumber itself of its moral bad odor until a theoretical basis was found for combining commitment to 'growth' with commitment to justice. Locke was the discoverer of that basis."[5] Traces of what Smith would call mercantilism, to be sure, are to be found in Locke's thought (such as a tendency to measure national wealth in terms of precious metals), which Smith expunged from his more fully developed and perfected political economy; but the crucial foundation for the new political economy was laid in Locke's new conceptions of human happiness, liberty, property, labor, and the good society.

Two of the chapters that follow agree on the special importance of John Locke's thought for bringing about the moral reorientation needed for Smithian political economy, a reorientation so successful, according to Plattner, that it tends now to be taken for granted. In "The Concept of Private Property in the History of Political Economy," Abram Shulsky deals mainly with Locke's complex treatment of property. He offers a close analysis of how Locke first argued for private property's origin in the state of nature, limited by the two conditions of spoilage and sufficiency for others; and of how Locke then showed the way to overcome these limitations so that a legitimate natural right to unlimited acquisition of private property emerged. Shulsky explores how, indeed whether, this natural-right conception of property can be meaningful in a civil society that establishes and regulates property with positive laws and in which no more unowned land is available. From these considerations Shulsky goes on to draw inferences about what kind of society (and political economy) Locke hoped to promote. Having argued that Locke legitimated the unlimited acquisition of property ultimately on the basis of overall benefit to society rather than on that of natural right, Shulsky suggests Locke's strategic reasons for presenting his doctrine of property in terms of natural rights. On the one hand, Locke confronted dominant views opposed to his own, which he sought either to persuade or at least to placate for the time (in hopes, soon realized, of eventually supplanting them). On the other hand, he seems to have considered his way of formulating property (and other) rights as a valuable means within society's political and moral self-understanding for making such rights more secure in the future.

In "Natural Rights and the Moral Presuppositions of Political Economy," Plattner agrees with Shulsky that the crucial foundations for Smithian political economy were laid by Locke, whose political philosophy brought about a decisively changed moral orientation toward labor, commerce, money making, accumulation, and opulence, as well as toward their appropriate roles and places in political society as a whole. Setting forth from Locke's conception of property rooted in natural right, Plattner identifies two distinct traditions of political economy. One, exemplified in the thinking of leading American founders, places fundamental reliance on natural rights, natural liberty, and justice that originates in accordance with nature from social contract. The other tradition, utilitarianism, looks to arguments of overall social benefit as decisive for evaluating laws, institutions, and policies. At every level of argument, Plattner gives more weight than Shulsky does to the explicit natural-right basis of property in Locke. He argues that the individual's natural right to the product of his labor, despite the numerous complications that such a right must undergo in established civil orders, nonetheless retains *prima facie* moral force and remains, as Locke thought, a crucial basis for a people's acceptance of the justice of a free society. Plattner's conclusion makes one wonder how long citizens' understanding of and attachment to a free society with a liberal economic order could survive a loss of belief in the underlying justice of that society's system of property rights. After all, the restrained and sober James Madison predicted that people will pursue justice until they have it or liberty be lost in the pursuit.

Allan Bloom's epilogue, "Philosophical Issues in Political Economy," underlines Locke's crucial importance for political economy and sheds light on it from another point of view by comparing Locke with Hobbes and the reactions of modern economists to Locke with their reactions to Hobbes. Economists, Bloom notes, tend to find in Hobbes a kindred spirit, but tend to dismiss Locke as wordy, confused, and irrelevant to their concerns. The economists' affinity to Hobbes is surely understandable: his clearly stated assumptions about human passions and human reasoning, his scientific attempt to model the artificial construction of a viable political society, his lively debunking of religious or philosophical authorities' claims to superior judgment of human goods and ills—all these things evoke sympathetic resonance in minds formed by hypotheses of rational, utility-maximizing individuals. By contrast, Locke's complexity and intentional obscurity on some points (motivated in part by considerations of political rhetorical strategy) seem murky; in consequence he receives less careful study, and wins less respect.

Bloom argues, however, that economists need to recognize and understand Locke's crucial contribution if they are to be fully aware of the roots, both theoretical and practical, of their own discipline. After all, Locke's doctrine, not Hobbes's, won public respectability and prevailed politically. Hobbes elaborated his teaching in the menacing Machiavellian shadow of the danger of war, civil or international, where political factors of violence and fraud are ever present to the actors' (and the observers') minds. To construct what he considers the necessary unity of society, Hobbes fashions a sovereign power that towers starkly supreme over any and all rights of property and of liberty; no property exists by nature, and actual property rights are totally the creature of the political sovereign, wholly dependent on the sovereign's will. Not Hobbes but Locke provides an appealing basis —in a generally peaceful teaching about politics—for property and economic activity that are in some sense independent of the political sovereign (or the leading center of government, as the tamer Lockean sovereign might be better described) and hence for a more securely free market. David Gauthier's chapter in one way and Viktor Vanberg and James Buchanan's in another seek to develop a Hobbesian mode of reasoning and presentation to obtain a Lockean result in the form of secure civil liberties, a free market, and a bourgeois ethic of rational industriousness and trustworthy reliability.

To restate: Locke argues for a realm of property, of economic activity, of a market, that in an important sense is liberated from political control. The act of thus freeing the economy from previous misguided political restraints is itself, of course, a political act, but Locke appears to hope that it could be what one might call a constitutional political act, which need not be repeated on any regular basis. In basic agreement with Locke, Smith introduces the additional wrinkle (perhaps prefigured in Locke's more or less anthropological sketch of political and economic development) that certain historical processes involving the market may work to corrode overly constrictive political institutions (best illustrated by his story of the decline and transformation of feudalism) and hence tend toward the choiceworthy political economy, the system of natural liberty, whose full establishment would nonetheless require acts of intelligent statesmanship.

Although Smith's political economy maintains connections with the older tradition, in which political science or philosophy includes political economy as a subordinate part, he takes long strides toward viewing the economy as an entity in some sense independent of political rule; this innovation prepares the way for the reasonable expectation that a science of political economy might well be developed independently of political science. To quote again part of a key passage from Smith: "Political economy, *considered as a branch of the science* of a statesman or legislator, proposes . . . first, to provide a plentiful revenue or subsistence for the people, *or more properly to enable them to provide* such a revenue or subsistence *for themselves.*"[6] It is customary to say (as I have done above) that Smith defines political economy as a branch of political science; but his actual assertion—that it is *considered* a branch of that science—raises the possibility that one could instead consider it as something more autonomous. Similarly, his assertion that political economy should more properly make the people able to provide for themselves points emphatically toward limiting the political aspect of political economy to providing a general enabling framework within which people's economic activity would enjoy substantial independence.

Colin Wright's chapter, "Competing Conceptions of Political Economy," begins with a historical sketch of how Smith's political economy was eventually transformed by his successors into economics. The way for this transformation, I have suggested, was prepared by the new conception of political economy just now limned; it proceeded, as Wright shows, along with, and partly as a consequence of, the evolving distinctions between science and art, between theoretical science and applied science, and eventually between positive and normative science or between fact and value. Along the way, economics both broadened and narrowed: it came to deal with a broader scope of human actions than had the earlier political economy; but, developing as positive science, it excluded a range of questions involving goals and purposes from its scientific purview, and pushed concern with such matters to a fringe area of economics. Donald McCloskey and John Nelson contend in their chapter that the conception of economics as positive science with a clearly defined and widely accepted methodology is open to serious challenge; but they also make clear that that conception is still the more or less official self-understanding of economics as an academic discipline.

The area on the fringe of mainstream economics is sometimes called political economy; the second part of Wright's chapter tries to analyze and categorize just what "political economy" means to economists of various persuasions today. The chapter ends with some reflections on the significance of the continuing difference between economics and political economy (in whichever way conceived). Despite important disagreements among the various groups of economists on how they conceive of political economy in itself and in relation to economics, Wright suggests that one fact about political economy is common to the several conceptions: its arising from, building on, or incorporating the original purpose for the study of all human actions—to guide actions better toward reasonable goals. In short, the renewal of interest in political economy today reflects the fact that the chief motivation for sciences of human affairs is to find more knowledgeable ways of pursuing the human good or goods.

Although economics developed ever greater technical sophistication, with substantial benefits for the understanding of certain areas and problems, its separation from politics entailed costs as well. Political actors and political scientists became more likely to ignore the real costs and conditions of policies they favor; and economists increasingly overlooked the political and moral conditions of peaceful free society (including free markets) and increasingly lost their ability to make economic arguments prevail in political contexts.

All this, if true, provides ample motivation to continue the effort of recreating or revivifying political economy. But how can this best be done? What is or should be involved in an attempt to rejoin politics and economics in a renewed study of political economy? The questions that arise are numerous and urgent. When economics has pretty much detached itself from politics, how does it account for its activity, its conception of human nature and life, its role or purpose in society as a whole? Are there important aspects of political life that tend to elude the scrutiny of this newer economics? If so, what are they, and how could one deal with them without relinquishing the benefits of sophisticated economics? On what terms, with what conception of human beings and of human action, with what view of civil life (including economic, moral, and political dimensions) can the studies of politics and of economics once more be put together? Do the needed basic conceptions and approaches come from the current practices of economics, or must they come from elsewhere? If so, from where, and what are they? The remaining chapters in this volume all address some aspect of these questions.

In "Economists on Tastes and Preferences," Steven E. Rhoads works within the context of political economy understood as economics applied to designing, analyzing, and implementing public policies. He examines in particular how economists treat tastes and preferences and finds that the dominant tendency in economics goes contrary to political and moral common sense. From a scientifically neutral stance that tries to avoid controversial moral assertions, economists generally assume tastes and preferences to be fixed and treat all tastes and preferences as equally worthy of consideration and equally needing to be included in the aggregates of utility that determine costs and benefits. Rhoads argues, however, that such assumptions are anything but uncontroversial; with the support of a wide range of examples, he seeks to show that they fly in the face of

9

well-founded and deeply held political and moral convictions. He suggests that when economists develop cost-benefit analyses of public policies, for example, they need to remedy the political and moral shortcomings of the standard *homo economicus* model with considerations drawn from a more comprehensive prudence. Earlier political economists like John Stuart Mill seem to exemplify the broader mode of thinking that Rhoads calls for.

In "Economic Man and the Rational Reasoner," by contrast, David Gauthier seeks to defend the vitality, validity, or utility of the conception of rationality that economics characteristically uses—that is, rationality as the individual's calculated maximization of utility. To this end, he argues for a more extensive conception of maximization than is commonly used. In particular, he argues that rationality can extend to the choice of a maximizing plan that may require one to make certain choices along the way that are not the most preferred in the immediate situation. Thus, one might rationally choose to act as though one had a fixed disposition of character—for instance, the disposition to keep one's agreements. Gauthier's chapter, besides contrasting with Rhoads's essay, also invites close comparison with that of Vanberg and Buchanan, as I have already suggested. With quite similar suppositions and modes of argument, Gauthier deals with the individual's thought processes in an effort to show that the rationality of maximization can support (or perhaps produce or replace) what are traditionally discussed as moral virtues like keeping faith or justice; Vanberg and Buchanan seek to explain similar consequences by analyzing how patterns of social action emerge.

In an effort to understand the conditions for economic innovation and growth, Nathan Rosenberg examines a crucial intersection of politics and economics in "Economic Experiments." He investigates what forms of economic associations, of business enterprises, and of other economic structures are permitted and facilitated by a political community's legal order. Through analyzing the historical record of Western economic growth, he finds that a key factor, often underestimated or overlooked, is the freedom to engage in experimentation with new forms of economic organization. Contrary to an opinion widely held, not least by those under Marx's influence, giant firms do not always prevail; both now and in the past, extremely varied types and sizes of business enterprises have flourished and made innovations crucial to increased production and to other aspects of economic progress. Many writers have emphasized scientific and technological developments as causes of economic growth; Rosenberg distinctively argues that investments in science and technology may generally fail to provide much reward in economic productivity unless the key feature of freedom to experiment is present in the legal-political-economic system.

In "The Rhetoric of Political Economy," Donald N. McCloskey and John S. Nelson present a postmodernist analysis of the orthodoxy within economics (and to a lesser degree within political science and other social sciences) that would prescribe definitive rules of method for genuinely scientific inquiry. Such modernist methodological strictures, they argue, have outlived whatever usefulness they may for a time have had in economics or political economy. Rather than providing sound guidance for good economics or political science, such narrowing rules of would-be science keep practitioners from a precise and full awareness of what they could be, or actually are, doing in the way of theorizing and research. We should not strive to follow such insufficient and inadequately grounded rules, McCloskey and Nelson argue, but instead should recognize that every field of inquiry is a realm of discourse where certain kinds of arguments and evidence are considered appropriate; moreover, the standards of appropriateness change over time and in response to changing circumstances, problems, and concerns. Thus theory, argument, and research can only be judged by the criteria of evolving discursive traditions. Our rejection of rigid rules of scientific procedure (which are honored more in the breach than the observance in political economy and economics anyway) should be accompanied by an awareness of the necessarily rhetorical character of all human inquiry and argument. By questioning any permanent grounding for the divisions among academic disciplines such as economics and political science, McCloskey and Nelson prepare the way for increased openness to political economy (and to any other disciplinary minglings for which a persuasive case could be stated). Like Rhoads's chapter, this one suggests a critical stance toward the familiar simplifying hypothesis of *homo economicus:* by no means to reject it altogether, indeed to maintain it for whatever purposes prove genuinely useful to our understanding, but to deny it any canonical status in the discipline of economics.

Viktor Vanberg and James M. Buchanan in "Rational Choice and Moral Order" seek to explore how rational, utility-maximizing individuals might interact over time so as to develop stable patterns of behavior equivalent to effectively followed rules that constitute a moral order. Their argument proceeds from several key distinctions.

11

In place of the familiar division between private interest and common good (or individual will and general will), they use a distinction between the individual's constitutional or rule interest and the individual's action or operational interest. The problem of moral and social order is thus reformulated as the problem of how the action interest can come to correspond with the constitutional interest. They distinguish further between constructivist (archetypically Hobbesian) ways to effect compliance, and spontaneously arising incentives that tend to produce compliance (exemplified in suggestions made by David Hume, Adam Smith, and others). Their special concern is to investigate how and in what kinds of situations spontaneous ordering tends to occur. They note a difference between the easier case of coordination problems and the harder case of prisoner's dilemma problems (where perverse incentives create a special difficulty). Concerning these latter, they further note an important difference between the cases of trust rules (like keeping explicit agreements) and of solidarity rules (like not polluting or like contributing one's fair share of effort to the performance of a common task).

Their analysis seems to end in this position: the logic of rational individuals' social interaction, probably aided in an important measure by a genetically evolved tendency to reciprocal behavior, spontaneously favors, in some areas and to some degree, the development of social rules that enjoy effective compliance. Where such spontaneous ordering falls short (as apparently it always must, especially in the realm of solidarity rules), constructed incentives to ensure compliance and the punishment of rule breaking remain necessary. The solution to the problem of the social ordering of rational, utility-maximizing individuals thus comes from spontaneous tendencies together with political-legal constructions that make good the inadequacies, for the purpose of social ordering, of that spontaneity. Those constructions have been more or less well designed for the purpose; in the best case they would be rationally designed in the light of adequate economic analysis. Applied economic science or art must perfect spontaneity or nature.

When developed to completion in the directions in which Vanberg and Buchanan point, this kind of explanation may fully account for the emergence and stable perseverance of good laws, moral norms, and institutions. To the extent that the explanation succeeds, the gap between individualistic economics and moral political order will be bridged; if the explanation falls short, the elaboration of its shortcomings could help us to clarify what additional ways of thinking are needed to articulate the proper relation between individualist economic theory and the requirements of a good moral-political order.

Bloom's epilogue, besides discussing Locke and Hobbes, presents an analysis and critique of Vanberg and Buchanan's chapter, together with some general reflections on issues about political economy raised both by the chapters and by the comments and discussion at the conference. Bloom indicates that Vanberg and Buchanan in one way, and Gauthier in another, seek to deal with the fundamental problems of society that political philosophy has addressed over the centuries, on the basis of the fundamental economic premise of rational self-interested individuals. If this approach to the problems should prove ultimately successful, one could only welcome it as the social science, the political economy, indeed the political philosophy that we need, erected on the foundations of the contemporary economic approach to studying human action.

Bloom argues, however, that such an approach cannot bridge the gap between rationally calculating self-interested individuals and moral human beings in a choiceworthy political society. He argues further that the model of self-interested individuals cannot really make sense of certain human types: the proud man, like Achilles, whose anger from affronted pride cannot be guided by any calculus of pleasures and pains; the devoted citizen, ready cheerfully to risk death in battle for his country's defense or glory; the pious man, for whom the relation to the author of our being is overwhelmingly more important than any considerations of ordinary advantage.

If Bloom's argument holds up, the intellectually appealing simplifications of economic analysis could never fully explain some of the most interesting human types, nor could it explain a key moral dimension of a good society. If this is the case, political economy must continue to wrestle with recurrent dilemmas about where economic approaches are useful and appropriate and where considerations of a different sort—and what sort are they?—must prevail. In other words, political economy can never free itself from the perennially controversial issues of political philosophy.

Two   Abram N. Shulsky

The Concept of Private Property
in the History of Political Economy

The term "political economy" has a somewhat old-fashioned ring to
it; it hearkens back to the days of Adam Smith, and beyond, before
economics emerged as an independent social science that uses sophisticated mathematical models and is definable, in rather abstract
terms, as the science of the allocation of scarce resources so as to maximize the attainment of desired ends. For Smith, indeed, political
economy, rather than being a separate social science, was "a branch
of the science of a statesman or legislator" directed to two ends:
"First, to provide a plentiful revenue or subsistence for the people, or
more properly to enable them to provide such a revenue or subsistence for themselves; and secondly, to supply the state or commonwealth with a revenue sufficient for the public services."[1] Thus,
although political economy dealt with much the same subject matter
as does the technical economics of today, it did so in a different manner; it did so in the context of an equally practical (and normative)
political science meant to inform statesmen about practical affairs
and to guide their political activity.

   Although the concept of private property is obviously central to
Smith's work, he does not examine it closely in terms of its origin or
justification; rather, he seems to take its existence and legitimacy for
granted,[2] much as he takes for granted the intrinsic goodness of liberty.[3] In his lectures on jurisprudence, for example, Smith begins his

15

treatment of the subject by stating that "the first and chief design of every system of government is to maintain justice; to prevent the members of a society from encroaching on one another's property, or seizing what is not their own. The design here is to give each one the secure and peaceable possession of his own property."[4]

The reason for the lack of an explicit defense of private property appears to be that Smith did not write a treatise on political science corresponding to *The Wealth of Nations,* his major work on political economy. However, it is not too difficult, if only because of his frequent reference to "natural liberty," to place him in the modern political theory tradition of Hobbes, Spinoza, and Locke. Since it is in the work of John Locke, in particular in his *Second Treatise of Government*, that the idea of private property is most forcefully explicated, it is that work, and the discussion of private property in its well-known fifth chapter, that I will consider first.

Locke's Theory of the Origins of Private Property

The origin of private property for Locke is seen in a person's labor, in which necessity leads, or prods, him to engage. This in turn is based on the notion that a person (in some sense) owns, or has property in, his own body, and hence is entitled to the yield of his body's actions or exertions: "Though the earth and all inferior creatures be common to all men, yet every man has a property in his own person; this nobody has any right to but himself. The labor of his body and the work of his hands, we may say, are properly his" (sect. 27).[5] Thus, the notion of private property has an important connection with that of human equality: because human beings are equal, no one can have a valid claim to another person's labor without that person's consent; the fundamental distinction is between human beings on the one hand, and all other, inferior, creatures on the other. This same equality is the basis of the characterization of individuals' relationship to one another in the state of nature, "there being nothing more evident than that creatures of the same species and rank, promiscuously born to all the same advantages of nature and the use of the same faculties, should also be equal one amongst another without subordination or subjection" (sect. 4).

Thus Locke takes issue with one of the best-known features of Aristotle's discussion of economics in the First Book of his *Politics;* that is, the doctrine of "natural slavery," by which he asserts the existence of a group of individuals who, lacking the foresight to conduct their own affairs, are naturally in a position of subordination to others who know how to make use of their bodily labor. While Locke feels the need to give some account of slavery, which existed in the English colonies of his time, he is careful to deprive it of a basis in any natural differences among people; rather, it is "the state of war continued between a lawful conqueror and a captive" (sect. 24). It is thus something inherently foreign to civil society and, one would suppose, a constant threat to the attainment of its peaceful purposes.

In Locke's first instances of private property, namely the gathering of acorns or apples (sect. 28), the actual exertion is minimal or nonexistent, as is the contribution of the person's labor to the final product; the acorn or apple is unchanged by the person's act of gathering it. Indeed, in this case, the real title seems to be need rather than labor: if the "consent of all mankind" had been necessary before the gatherer could rightfully eat the apples or acorns, "man had starved, notwithstanding the plenty God had given him" (sect. 28). Instead of concluding that the notion of property is simply irrelevant in this case, however, Locke uses this example to argue that only the labor of gathering could give the gatherer a title to the apples or acorns.

Having used this trivial case to establish the principle, Locke can turn to more interesting cases, such as agriculture, where the labor involved is substantial. In the course of the chapter, Locke twice reappraises the contribution to the final agricultural product that is due to labor as opposed to land; the estimate increases from nine-tenths (sect. 37) to ninety-nine one-hundredths (sect. 40), then to nine-hundred-ninety-nine one-thousandths (sect. 43).

This analysis identifies labor as the origin of private property in the sense that it is something that must be understood to belong exclusively to an individual, rather than to mankind in common. It does not, however, explain why one individual, as opposed to another, is entitled to "mix" his labor, as Locke says, with a particular group of gatherable acorns or apples, or a particular plot of cultivable land, and thereby establish his claim to the entire product resulting from the mixture of the labor, which was exclusively his, and the "raw materials," which belonged to mankind in common.

To vindicate what would otherwise look like an unjustifiable appropriation of commonly held objects or land for private use, Locke introduces two conditions or limitations: first, one may not take more than one can make use of before it spoils (the "spoilage" limitation); and second, one must leave "enough and as good" for others (the "sufficiency" limitation). In the primitive condition of human beings in the "state of nature,"[6] these limitations are not onerous. In fact, they are, so to speak, self-enforcing, since one would have no motive to gather foods which would spoil before one could eat them; nor, given the low population density characteristic of such a time, could one possibly appropriate so much land as not to leave "enough and as good" for others.[7]

Locke introduced the first of these limitations, the spoilage limitation, in order to answer the objection that "if gathering the acorns, or other fruits of the earth, etc., makes a right to them, then any one may engross as much as he will" (sect. 31). The possibility of infinite accumulation by one person would seem to be the antithesis of the original community of property; the spoilage limitation helps to bridge the manifest gap between the original situation and the resulting private property of individuals. In this connection, Locke asserts that God and nature intend certain purposes with respect to human beings, and that the limitation can be deduced from an understanding of those purposes.

Thus, the spoilage limitation is supported by the following reasoning:

> The same law of nature that does by this means [i.e., gathering] give us property does also bound that property, too. "God has given us all things richly" (I Tim. 6:17), is the voice of reason confirmed by inspiration. But how far has he given it us? To enjoy. As much as any one can make use of to any advantage of life before it spoils, so much he may by his labor fix a property in; whatever is beyond this is more than his share and belongs to others. (Sect. 31)

Locke's approach to this issue is, at first glance, not too dissimilar from that of Aristotle; according to the latter, the various modes of acquisition (such as, hunting, agriculture, and commerce) may be divided into two categories, natural and unnatural. Those modes of acquisition which merely take from nature what she stands ready to provide are natural, whereas those that make possible the accumulation of money without having direct recourse to the natural sources of useful things are unnatural.

This division rests on the fundamental tenet that nature provides the things that man needs to survive. Aristotle's general statement, by way of a conclusion to his discussion of natural acquisition, is:

One must suppose both that plants exist for the sake of animals and that the other animals exist for the sake of human beings—the tame animals, both for use and sustenance, and most if not all of the wild animals, for sustenance and other assistance, in order that clothing and other instruments may be got from them.[8]

Aristotle asserts that there is a natural limit on this sort of acquisition. Ultimately it is a limit set by the material requirements of the good life; any goods possessed in excess of that optimal amount are of no use, and hence cannot be considered true wealth. However, Locke's and Aristotle's understandings of this sort of "natural" limit on acquisition differ in fundamental ways that have important consequences for the further development of their doctrines.

For Aristotle, the natural limit results from a more comprehensive consideration of the good life, and of the material requirements for it; since these requirements are not infinite, infinite acquisition makes no sense.[9] For Locke, on the other hand, the source of the limitation appears to be more legalistic in nature; since Locke's original question was how any private property could come into being given the original community of wealth in the state of nature, the purpose of the limitations is primarily to bolster the case that the appropriation of common property by one individual does not harm the rights of other individuals.

(This is obviously true with respect to the "enough and as good" limitation noted above; it may, however, seem inaccurate with respect to the spoilage limitation, which derives from the nature of some forms of property, in particular, food. Even in this regard, however, Locke points out that "it was a foolish thing, as well as *dishonest*, to hoard up more than he could make use of" [sect. 46; emphasis supplied].[10] The reason why it is important to stress the injustice involved in the "perishing of anything uselessly" in one's possession [sect. 46] is discussed later.)

Since, for Locke, the rationale for the spoilage limitation is not linked directly to an overarching end of human life, it becomes possible for him to imagine ways in which it might be sidestepped or totally overcome. Thus, if someone "bartered away plums that would have rotted in a week for nuts that would last good for his eating a whole year, he did no injury; he wasted not the common stock, destroyed no part of the portion of the goods that belonged to others" (sect. 46). Carrying this argument to its extreme, one might exchange perishable food for a piece of metal (if one were "pleased with its color"), a "sparkling pebble," or a diamond; of these durable items, one might accumulate as much as one wished. Thus, the "invention" of money, that is, the tacit agreement that "a little piece of yellow metal which would keep without wasting or decay should be worth a great piece of flesh or a whole heap of corn" (sect. 37), is the mechanism by which infinite accumulation becomes not only possible but lawful.

In addition to being durable, gold and silver (and other precious metals or gems) have the advantage, from the point of view of Locke's argument, of being "little useful to the life of man" (sect. 50). Thus, even though they are rare (as they have to be to serve conveniently as money) and hence "enough and as good" will not be left for others, one individual's amassing of a large quantity of them does not deprive others of any of the "truly useful but perishable supports of life" (sect. 47). In this manner, the spoilage limitation becomes the crucial one; the sufficiency limitation is allowed to fall by the wayside.

Locke's argument is thus exposed to the following objection. It appears to depend on an absolute distinction between useful but perishable goods that can only be consumed in limited quantities, and durable but useless ones that are capable of infinite accumulation. Such a distinction is obviously incomplete; there clearly are goods that are both useful and durable, such as those used for clothing and shelter. The emphasis on spoilage as the limit on accumulation suggests that the infinite accumulation of such goods would be lawful in the state of nature, independently of whether or not others had greater need of them. Thus, the natural rationing on which Locke appears to rely becomes much less convincing. The sufficiency limitation is observed only with respect to perishable food, where it is identical to the spoilage limitation.[11]

When one looks at the question of how the land itself becomes the private property of an individual, this difficulty becomes even greater. At first, Locke argues, an individual's appropriation of land could cause no problems, since the amount of land involved would be inherently limited: A man could appropriate no more than he could work, since his labor was his sole title to the land; furthermore, he could lawfully enclose no more land than he could make use of the product of. Thus, "whatsoever [a man] tilled and reaped, laid up and made use of before it spoiled, that was his peculiar right; whatsoever he enclosed and could feed and make use of, the cattle and product was also his" (sect. 38). Properties governed by such limitations would, in practice, be so small, Locke contends, that no one could reasonably complain about another's appropriating land that originally belonged to everyone. For anyone who wanted to work the land, "there was as good left as that already possessed, and more than he knew what to do with, or his industry could reach to" (sect. 34).

Once money comes into use, however, the situation is quite different. Just as money enables one to accumulate movable wealth indefinitely, it allows one to increase one's land holdings as well. By "inventing" money, people

> found out a way how a man may fairly possess more land than he himself can use the product of, by receiving in exchange for the overplus gold and silver which may be hoarded up without injury to any one, these metals not spoiling or decaying in the hands of the possessor. (Sect. 50)

Once this happens, however, there is no longer enough land for everyone.[12] In this case, the natural rationing scheme breaks down completely.

An even more important objection, however, has to do with the goal of this accumulation. Elsewhere in the *Second Treatise,* Locke appears to accept a somewhat older, moralistic view, according to which the "desire of having more than man needed" (sect. 37) was condemned as "covetousness" (sect. 75) and *"amor sceleratus habendi, evil concupiscence"* (sect. 111).[13] In chapter 5, however, Locke is clearly intent on legitimizing rather than condemning or restraining that desire.

Regardless of this intention, Locke does not give in this context an intelligible account of the desire to have more than one needs. Instead, he appears to belittle it; he even implies at times that the motive for accumulation is almost infantile—someone wishes to accumulate gold because he is "pleased with its color" or gems because he is captivated by a "sparkling pebble" (sect. 46).[14] The indefinite accumulation of wealth seems to serve no meaningful end; Locke explains and defends its lawfulness, but not its purpose, as far as the individual accumulator is concerned. Locke remains almost completely silent about the plausible reasons (desire for security and luxury) why one would be interested in accumulating a large amount of gold and silver.

In defending the position that an individual has a title not only to the product of his labor, but also to the land he works, Locke says that "God gave the earth to men in common; but since he gave it them for their benefit and the *greatest conveniences of life they were capable to draw from it,* it cannot be supposed he meant it should always remain common and uncultivated" (sect. 34; emphasis supplied). Generally, in the course of chapter 5, Locke introduces the theme of "conveniences of life" or "comfort" alongside the earlier theme of preservation as being the fundamental law of nature.[15] (In this connection, Locke tends to refer, as in the quotation above, to God rather than to nature as the source of a person's right to seek comfort and convenience as well as preservation.)

Locke, however, does not directly attribute accumulation to a desire for greater comfort; in fact, what is needed at the beginning of the accumulation process is frugality rather than luxury. Instead, Locke concentrates on the advantages the accumulator confers on others, that is, on his fellow human beings and on his "prince."

In general, Locke argues that the enclosing and appropriating of land, so far from being a threat to the interests of others, is actually a benevolent action:

> He who appropriates land to himself by his labor does not lessen but increase the common stock of mankind; for the provisions serving to the support of human life produced by one acre of enclosed and cultivated land are . . . ten times more than those which are yielded by an acre of land of an equal richness lying waste in common. And therefore he [that lives off of ten acres of cultivated land rather than one hundred acres of waste land] may truly be said to give ninety acres to mankind. (Sect. 37)

Although an individual is motivated to work an amount of land larger than that required for his own support by the desire to possess the produce of it, he must, if he is to make any use of that produce before it spoils, trade it to others for something more durable. Thus, one way or another, the perishable product of his labor winds up in the hands of others. Locke puts forward as plausible (although he clearly does not believe it himself) the contention that in Spain a person may farm land to which he has no other title than his making use of it; furthermore, "the inhabitants think themselves beholden to him who by his industry on neglected and consequently waste land has increased the stock of corn which they wanted" (sect. 36).

Thus, whoever produces and hence owns the additional food that is produced when a person lays claim (by means of his labor) to larger land holdings, those who consume it are, in a sense, the beneficiaries of whatever arrangements led to its being produced. Nevertheless, it remains unclear why, if there is "enough and as good" land left over, any one would have to buy food rather than produce his own.[16]

Locke does not provide an explicit answer to this question. An implicit answer may be found, however, in the long catalogue of the different kinds of labor which are necessary to produce something as simple and common as bread (sect. 43). In order for people to take advantage of the fact that "invention and arts had improved the conveniences of life" (sect. 44), some form of division of labor was necessary; hence the coming into being of a continual trade between the agricultural and manufacturing sectors.

Locke does not address the politically more interesting question of the origin of the division—quite thoroughgoing in Locke's time— between those who own the land and those who work it. At one point, Locke seems to imply that the differing possessions among people are due to "differing degrees of industry" (sect. 48). However, this is hardly consonant with the observable facts of Locke's time— many of the landowners were members of an aristocratic class that prided itself on doing no work at all. Indeed, given the feudal origins of the great land holdings throughout Europe, one suspects that, despite God's intention, the world belonged more to the "quarrelsome and contentious" than to the "industrious and rational" (sect. 34).

Before considering this issue further, we must note another curious feature of Locke's account of the origin of property in labor, which is that it appears to apply only to the state of nature and to have no relevance whatsoever to property in civil society. There, as Locke makes clear, labor does not give a title to property,[17] and it is possible to own land even though there is not "enough and as good" left for others.[18] (Indeed, once money is introduced, it can "scarce happen" that "there are still great tracts of land to be found which . . . lie waste" [sect. 45].) In civil society, property is determined by positive law only: "In governments, the laws regulate the right of property, and the possession of land is determined by positive constitutions" (sect. 50).

At the beginning of chapter 5, Locke had posed the following objection to his views, which the chapter was intended to answer: "But this [i.e., that God has given the earth to mankind in common] being supposed, it seems to some a great difficulty how any one should ever come to have a property in anything" (sect. 25). In response, Locke proposed "to show how men might come to have a property in several parts [of the earth] without *any express compact of all the commoners*" (sect. 25; emphasis supplied). It now appears that this effort was unnecessary since, in the interesting case (that is, in civil society), property is regulated by positive law, which is to say, by a law that does ultimately derive its force from consent.[19]

In general, however, Locke emphasizes that the natural law remains valid in civil society: "The law of nature stands as an eternal rule to all men, legislators as well as others. The rules that they make for other men's actions must, as well as their own and other men's actions, be conformable to the law of nature" (sect. 135). Thus, in particular, "the fundamental law of nature being the preservation of mankind, no human sanction can be good or valid against it" (sect. 135).

This would seem to imply that, even in civil society, no property right can be valid if it prevents a starving person from having food that is not needed by others.[20] Locke, however, seems to argue that this situation need never arise in the case of any able-bodied person, since a day laborer in England is better off materially than a "king in America"; in other words, a person in civil society who owns no property whatsoever is still able to live better than the "richest" person in the primitive state preceding the use of money and the intensive application of human labor to the "almost worthless materials" provided by nature.

It is not only the individual members of the commonwealth, including the poorest of them, who stand to benefit from these developments. After arguing that "labor makes the far greatest part of the value of the things we enjoy," Locke interrupts his argument to address the princes of the world:

> This shows how much numbers of men are to be preferred to largeness of dominions; and that the increase of lands and the right employing of them is the great art of government; and that prince who shall be so wise and godlike as by established laws of liberty to secure protection and encouragement to the honest industry of mankind, against the oppression of power and narrowness of party, will quickly be too hard for his neighbors. (Sect. 42)

Thus, Locke promises that the liberation of acquisitiveness by means of "the honest industry of mankind" will produce benefits both for individuals, including those who appear to fare worst by it, and for the state. It is in accord with the "fundamental law of nature," in that the preservation of the human race (in presumably increasing numbers) depends not on the scanty gifts of nature but on the ability of human labor to transform nature's "almost worthless materials" into the means of preservation, and even comfortable preservation, for human beings.

From a present-day perspective, it would seem that these practical arguments should have been sufficient for Locke, who need not have bothered trying to prove that unlimited accumulation of private property was legitimate in the state of nature. There are, however, at least two reasons why Locke may have felt it advantageous to make that argument, despite the fact that, technically, it settles nothing with respect to the regulation of property within civil society.

First, Locke had to deal with a set of older ideas (opposed to his and based, at least in part, on moral arguments) that arguments from mere utility could not effectively counter. Both Aristotle and Christianity taught that unlimited acquisitiveness was, at best, a diversion from the true ends of life; it was unnatural or spiritually impoverishing. Despite Locke's citation of the Bible to the effect that "God has given man all things richly to enjoy,"[21] he must inculcate a distrust of divine or natural care for human beings in order to encourage them to take the actions necessary for their own well-being. By asserting, and then overcoming, the spoilage limitation, Locke creates the impression that he has given the older view its due; his attitude toward it appears respectful, and to the extent that his difference with it becomes visible, it appears to be more one of degree than of kind.[22]

Second, Locke may be looking forward as well as back. The fact that unlimited acquisitiveness is in everyone's long-term interest is not enough to guarantee that people's actions with respect to it will in fact be governed by that long-term interest. Shorter-term interests, to say nothing of envy, are likely to lead both princes and populaces to take liberties with the "established laws of liberty," which should protect and encourage the "honest industry of mankind." Giving even unlimited acquisition of private property a basis in nature is one way of counteracting this tendency.

The notion that private property precedes civil society, and can have a legitimate basis outside of it, provides additional political strength to the argument that one cannot arbitrarily change rules governing property rights, or take away someone's property without compensation. As section 42 makes clear, the real purpose has to do with establishing public confidence in property rights in the future, so as to strengthen the individual's incentive to accumulate property. The need to protect property derives from a prior purpose of promoting the acquisition of property. As James Madison so precisely puts it, "From the protection of different and unequal faculties of acquiring property, the possession of different degrees and kinds of property immediately results."[23] It is the protection of these "faculties," not of the resulting property, that Madison says is the "first object of government."

Thus, strictly speaking, it does not really matter how the current property holders acquired their property; one protects it not because one regards their past acquisitive practices as legitimate, but in order to give confidence to those who, by their current labor, seek to accumulate property in the future. This is all to the good, since, as noted above, in the England of Locke's time the great land holdings were not the result of prior labor and frugality and were not held at that time by people who represented those values.

To some extent, according to Locke, this problem will solve itself. The "men [who] live lazily upon the product of the land" and who grow poor by virtue of their "squandering and waste" are eventually forced to sell their land to "industrious and thriving men" who have made money in trade and want to invest it in something more permanent.[24]

Nevertheless, difficulties can arise by virtue of the fact that the people who own land are not necessarily the "industrious and rational" to whose use, according to Locke, God gave it (sect. 34). The problem is described in a letter of Thomas Jefferson in which he reflects on the "numberless instances of wretchedness" he has observed in France:

> I asked myself what could be the reason so many should be permitted to beg who are willing to work, in a country where there is a very considerable proportion of uncultivated lands? These lands are undisturbed only for the sake of game. It should seem then that it must be because of the enormous wealth of the proprietors which places them above attention to the increase of their revenues by permitting these lands to be labored. . . .
> Whenever there are in any country uncultivated lands and unemployed poor, it is clear that the laws of property have been so far extended as to violate natural right. The earth is given as a common stock for man to labor and live on. If for the encouragement of industry we allow it to be appropriated, we must take care that other employment be provided to those excluded from the appropriation. If we do not, the fundamental right to labor the earth returns to the unemployed.[25]

Jefferson believes that "it is too soon yet *in our country* [emphasis supplied] to say that every man who cannot find employment, but who can find uncultivated land, shall be at liberty to cultivate it, paying a moderate rent," but it is not clear that he would be so cautious in the case of France. Nevertheless, he does think that "legislators cannot invent too many devices for subdividing property, only taking care to let their subdivisions go hand in hand with the natural affections of the human mind." Thus, he recommends the abolition of primogeniture and (somewhat less clearly in accordance with the principle just stated) progressive taxation of landed estates.

For our purposes, the main interest of this letter is that it shows how one might, given certain conditions, make an argument for land reform on a thoroughly Lockean basis. The practical question would be only whether such land reform, involving an exception to the established laws, would encourage or discourage "the honest industry of mankind" in the future. Given the feudal origin of the large landholdings involved, one could make a strong argument that the former would be the case; however, this depends on there being some means of assuring people that "bourgeois property" will be respected in the future.

More generally, the insistence on the prepolitical nature of property rights makes the more basic point that economic arrangements are governed by certain laws of nature and are hence not reasonably, or at all, subject to the arbitrary choice of the political rulers of a society. For Aristotle, the nature of the regime is the basic political fact, and all economic arrangements (such as the distribution of property, and the existence or absence of slavery) have to be understood and judged in the light of the regime. The regime itself is, to some extent, a matter of human choice, although all sorts of other factors, including historical accidents of many different kinds, have a major influence in determining its nature. At any rate, the example of Sparta seems to indicate that, under some circumstances, a regime can come into existence that pursues its own goals to a very high degree and seemingly remolds human nature, oblivious to the constraints that appear to apply to other regimes.

For Locke, on the other hand, there would appear to be no such leeway for political choice. His *Considerations*,[26] for example, begins with the question of whether regulation of interest rates is possible, a question which he answers in the negative; the self-interest of individuals is so strong that the force of law will be insufficient to make them lend and borrow at the legal, as opposed to the natural, rate of interest. More importantly, to judge from his advice to princes concerning "established laws of liberty,"[27] he may have believed that the international competition and rivalry among states may force each ruler to adopt wise policies lest the others become "too hard" for him. In other words, once one country harnesses the self-interest of its people to a policy of unlimited economic growth, the others may have no choice but to follow suit. In this sense, then, the law of nature would be fully operative even within civil society, and would permit the unlimited acquisition of private property.

In a sense, however, this development came to full fruition only after Locke's time, in the work of Adam Smith. Locke's emphasis is on the accumulation of wealth, by which he seems to mean primarily money (in the circumstances of his time, gold and silver). There appears to be an innate human desire to accumulate wealth in this way, but it is constantly, and often successfully, opposed by sloth (the desire to avoid the pain of labor) and self-indulgence and vanity (the desire for luxury). In his *Considerations*, Locke inveighs at length against the taste for imported luxuries which he believes is impoverishing England:

> And if the virtue, and provident way of living of our ancestors (content with our native conveniences of life, without the costly itch after the materials of pride and luxury from abroad) were brought in fashion and countenance again amongst us; this alone would do more to keep, and increase our wealth, and enrich our land, than all our paper helps about interest, money, bullion, etc. which however eagerly we may catch at, will not, I fear, without better husbandry, keep us from sinking, whatever contrivances we may have recourse to. (Pp. 117–18)

Although Locke does not, in this work, recommend that the government act to solve this problem by legislation (he may have believed that measures such as sumptuary laws or prohibitive tariffs on luxury goods would be no more effective than laws regulating interest rates), he does elsewhere favor vigorous government action, for example to make sure the able-bodied indigent work instead of beg, and to help establish the linen trade in Ireland (to prevent it from competing with England's wool trade).[28]

Adam Smith, on the other hand, softens the tension between man's acquisitiveness, on the one side, and his laziness and self-indulgence, on the other. For the desire to accumulate wealth, in the form of gold and silver, he substitutes the constant desire to better one's condition.[29] The real wealth of a nation, according to Smith, does not depend on the size of its accumulated stockpile of gold and silver (as Locke thought); rather, as a nation's annual production of useful goods (determined by other factors) increases, an amount of gold and silver sufficient to support its trade will automatically flow toward it. Thus, the need for an active governmental policy is lessened, and the people's wealth, and their enjoyment of it, may be allowed to increase simultaneously and automatically.

The Psychological Basis of Economic Activity

As the preceding section makes clear, one cannot meaningfully discuss the societal import of respect for private property rights without examining the motivations that determine the behavior of the property holders. Before examining Locke's understanding of this situation, I will look briefly at current economic theory, which posits the existence of the "ideal type" *homo economicus,* who evaluates the available alternatives in terms of some *numéraire* (utility) and then (inevitably) chooses that which rates highest in these terms.[30] In some sense, then, homo economicus pursues what the classical philosophic tradition calls the *summum bonum,* or highest good, with this major difference: the evaluation of the alternatives made by homo economicus has no validity for anyone other than himself.

The history of utility theory is in a sense the coming to terms with the impossibility of grounding this notion in psychology or physiology, that is, of finding some objective measure of an item's utility, such as its ability to produce mental or physical pleasure or pain. In the end, therefore, it was necessary to limit oneself entirely to "revealed" preferences, that is, to trying to calculate relative utilities from the observed behavior of individuals in choosing, for example, to buy n_1 units of item x_1 and n_2 units of item x_2 (when these items are available at prices p_1 and p_2, respectively).

This is not the place to discuss the technical complexities of this approach.[31] One particular detail of this approach, however, is important for understanding the Lockean attitude toward private property: what must be compared is not only the individual's relative preference for goods x_1 and x_2, but his preference for present, as compared with future, consumption. Given positive real interest rates (the normal situation)—in other words, an individual choosing to abstain from present consumption can gain the means to consume more in the future—it follows that "at the margin" there is a preference for present over future utility ("positive time preference"). The degree of time preference varies from individual to individual, depending not only on the individual's character but also on his current income and wealth and his expectations for the future.

Within the framework of positive economics, the degree of time preference exhibited by any one individual in a given set of circumstances is regarded as arbitrary. There can be no implication, for instance, that a lesser degree of time preference, that is, a greater concern for the future, is any more rational than a greater degree of time preference. There is nothing inherently irrational in the behavior of the archetypical profligate heir, who squanders a large inheritance in a year and is thereafter reduced to poverty.

Locke's own starting point with respect to these matters is quite different from that of current economic theory. Most striking is his denial that human beings seek a *summum bonum*, a greatest good of any kind; instead, they are moved by a present discomfort (which can be a desire—the consciousness of lacking some good thing—as well as the presence of some evil), which they try to alleviate: "[What determines the will with respect to our actions] is not, as is generally supposed, the greater good in view; but some (and for the most part the most pressing) *uneasiness* a man is at present under" (Locke's emphasis).[32]

While a good not possessed can become (via desire) the basis of a present uneasiness, Locke makes clear that the will, understood in this mechanistic sense, is much more likely to be determined by the uneasiness caused by some present pain or discomfort; in most cases, alleviating the present pain will take precedence over taking steps to secure the future good.

> All present pain, whatever it be, makes a part of our present misery: but all absent good does not at any time make a necessary part of our present happiness, nor the absence of it make a part of our misery. If it did, we should be constantly and infinitely miserable; there being infinite degrees of happiness which are not in our possession.[33]

Nevertheless, Locke does not leave it at this mechanistic explanation of human behavior. He allows for a kind of freedom, which consists of a person's being able to suspend his will for the moment, to consider the longer-term effects of his actions. (More precisely, a person is able to focus his mind on the future pains or pleasures which might either be caused, or be avoided or foreclosed, by a proposed present course of action, thereby enabling them, along with the present pains or pleasures, to influence the determination of his will. The same mechanistic determination of the will occurs, but a larger number of factors are brought to bear on it, and the final result reflects a wider range of considerations.)

Thus, although Locke's basic relativism remains,[34] there is a certain standard of rationality that he applies to human choices, and therewith a certain need for moral education as well. In discussing why people, although they seek happiness, often fail to attain it, Locke attributes a major share of the blame to their mistake in unreasonably preferring present to future pleasures (and, presumably, avoiding present at the expense of suffering future pains):

> But that this [preferring present to future pleasure] is a wrong judgment, everyone must allow, let his pleasure consist in whatever it will: since that which is future will certainly come to be present; and then, having the same advantage of nearness, will show itself in its full dimensions, and discover his willful mistake who judged of it by unequal measures.[35]

Thus, Locke seems to believe that a certain amount of moral self-restraint is necessary for people to be able to make rational choices. Although he does not discuss what economics now calls "time preference" in any detailed way, it is clear that he is willing to regard it as fundamentally irrational, as being caused by an inability or unwillingness to suspend one's will long enough to allow consideration of the future pains one's actions will bring down on one, or the future pleasures that one will be denied. The economic problem that Locke attributed to overindulgence in luxuries thus has a moral component to it; and it is to be corrected as much (if not more) by proper moral education as by regulatory legislation. The kind of rational maximization of utility that modern economics regards as the ordinary basis of consumer behavior is for Locke the "great principle and foundation of all virtue and worth."[36]

Private Property and the Common Good

As we have seen, the true basis for the protection of private property rights is the incentive that such protection provides for "industrious and rational" activity that increases the economic well-being of the entire community. It is this activity that, according to Locke, overcomes natural scarcity and enables the preservation of the largest number of human beings (which Locke refers to as the "fundamental law of nature").

The individual, on the other hand, is presumably motivated by self-interest—the desire for economic security on the one hand, and for comfort and convenience (or, as we would say, a higher standard of living) on the other. Locke does not rely on the individual's willingness to work selflessly toward the preservation of the largest number; he seems to assume that, in the absence of a self-regarding incentive (which comes into being with the use of money), an individual will not produce more than is needed for his or her immediate consumption.

This distinction between the presumed motives for individual behavior and the overall goal sought by the system raises an obvious question: Will this all work automatically or is some sort of governmental intervention required? There are various types of problems that might require governmental action.

First, there is the question of whether the government must regulate the currency in order to preserve the benefits that accrued from the original introduction of money. Locke, viewing money as virtually identical with precious metals (gold and silver), sees the government's role as purely ministerial; that is, the minting of coins is a convenience to trade, which obviates the need to weigh and assay them with each transaction. Indeed, since the value of money is determined entirely by the amount of gold or silver it contains, any attempt by government to control it is futile.

Perhaps because of the growing importance of banks and banknotes in the intervening years, Smith's view seems to be more complex. He recommends government regulation of banking practices, even if it is necessary to violate "natural liberty" (or, as we might say, freedom of contract).[37] As Smith's long digression on the Bank of Amsterdam makes clear, maintaining confidence in paper currency is not a simple matter; his praise of the Dutch in this regard is justified by their having succeeded in doing this so brilliantly that it is a "universal article of faith" (in a city noted for its religious tolerance and diversity!) that the bank always has enough specie on hand to meet all its obligations.[38]

Second, there is the question of whether the government must intervene to promote overall prosperity. I have noted the difference between Locke and Smith on the question of mercantilism and its implications for such policies as sumptuary laws and tariffs on luxury goods. Jefferson's conditional defense of land reform discusses the same issue: What should be done if the extravagance of the rich is so extreme that it defeats the fundamental purpose of private property rights, the incentive they provide for increased production?

Finally, there is the issue that lies at the basis of most modern attacks on free-market economics: the question of equality. Although it was not a very great practical problem for Locke and Smith (especially as compared to potential aristocratic opposition, since the aristocracy was more likely to be in a position to do something about it), it is perhaps theoretically important, because of the great stress laid on human equality in terms of natural rights.

Once the notion of inheritance is accepted, it is clear that the original equality of the state of nature leaves no trace with respect to the distribution of property in civil society. Furthermore, although the working of the free-market system as a whole may produce the most productive economy that can be achieved, there are within it many specific activities (of the "program trading" variety) that do not in themselves seem very productive, at least not in proportion to the handsome way in which they are compensated. Thus, political pressure for some revision in the distribution of wealth effected by the market can be expected to be a relatively common occurrence.

An additional issue is the means by which the government might operate to effect this distribution of property. Jefferson describes the means of subdividing property he favors as "silently lessening the inequality of property."[39] In a similar vein, James Madison favors "the silent operation of laws, which, without violating the rights of property, reduce extreme wealth toward a state of mediocrity, and raise extreme indigence toward a state of comfort."[40] This is in keeping with Madison's distinction (for example, in *Federalist* 10)[41] between the "rights of . . . citizens" and the "permanent and aggregate interests of the community" as the goals of government. "Good" government must seek the latter, but respect for the former is the *sine qua non* of a government's justice, which is a more essential characteristic:

> The public good is the ordinary, practical object of government's concerns, and the good which can be attained goes beyond the preservation of rights to the promotion of interests. However, a public which does not secure rights but is otherwise prosperous contradicts the purpose for which it was created.[42]

Subsequent developments in economic thought have called into question the assertion that there is a community interest separate from protection of the rights of citizens. In some sense, this is a logical outgrowth of a theory that saw the community come into existence in order to protect preexisting rights. However, it remains to be seen whether the notion of a "permanent and aggregate" interest can be dispensed with in the realm of public policy.

Three   Marc F. Plattner

Natural Rights and the Moral
Presuppositions of Political Economy

Adam Smith is widely and properly regarded as the founder of scientific economics and as the classic exponent of capitalism and a free market economy. John Locke, who wrote almost a century earlier than Smith, is regarded with equal justice as the founder of the modern theory of property embodied in capitalism, as well as of the wider liberal tradition to which free-market capitalism belongs. Central both to Locke's teaching about property and to his broader political teaching—as reflected, for example, in the American Declaration of Independence—is the doctrine of natural rights.

The goal of this chapter is to clarify some of the key moral presuppositions of modern political economy. I see this task as twofold: first, to identify the shared tenets that distinguish both Smith and Locke from premodern (or from anticapitalist) thought; and second, to explore the ways in which the tradition of economic thought that traces its lineage to Smith diverges from the natural-rights version of liberalism founded by Locke.

Adam Smith's Political Economy

Before the eighteenth century, economics was either a practical subject discussed chiefly by men of affairs, or, insofar as it was treated in a more theoretical fashion, a subordinate part of political philosophy. This earlier subordination is recalled not only in the term "political economy," but also in the definition Adam Smith gives the new science in *The Wealth of Nations*. Political economy, he states, is

> a branch of the science of a statesman or legislator [that] proposes two distinct objects: first, to provide a plentiful revenue or subsistence for the people, or more properly to enable them to provide such a revenue or subsistence for themselves; and secondly, to supply the state or commonwealth with a revenue sufficient for the public services. It proposes to enrich both the people and the sovereign.[1]

This statement makes it clear what the goal of political economy is—namely, riches, for both the individual and the government. It does not indicate, however, the relation of political economy and its goal to the other branches of legislative science. At the conclusion of his treatise on moral philosophy, *The Theory of Moral Sentiments* (1759), Smith laments the failure of philosophers to establish "a system of what might properly be called natural jurisprudence, or a theory of the general principles which ought to run through, and be the foundation of the laws of all nations." He then states his own intention to write "another discourse, endeavor[ing] to give an account of the general principles of law and government, and the different revolutions they have undergone in the different ages and periods of society, not only in what concerns justice, but in what concerns police, revenue, and arms, and whatever else is the object of law."[2]

Smith subsequently published his work on political economy, *The Wealth of Nations* (1776), but not a comprehensive discourse on natural jurisprudence. There are available to us, however, two records of notes taken from the lectures Smith gave on jurisprudence in his post as Professor of Moral Philosophy at Glasgow University. As reported in both of these accounts, Smith defined "jurisprudence" in the same broad manner as in the conclusion of *The Theory of Moral Sentiments*, and divided it into four parts in accordance with that definition: Justice, Police, Revenue, and Arms.

According to the fuller of the two accounts (1762–63), Smith in his opening lecture characterized the initial part of jurisprudence as follows:

> The first and chief design of every system of government is to maintain justice; to prevent the members of a society from encroaching on one another's property, or seizing what is not their own. The design

here is to give each one the secure and peaceable possession of his own property.[3]

He then went on to state:

> When this end, which we may call the internal peace, or peace within doors, is secured, the government will next be desirous of promoting the opulence of the state. This produces what we call police. Whatever regulations are made with respect to the trade, commerce, agriculture, manufactures of the country are considered as belonging to police.

With regard to revenue, the third branch of jurisprudence, Smith said he will

> consider the different methods which have been taken to raise the sum necessary for the expense of the state in different countries, and how far they are adapted to do this with the least loss or hindrance to the industry of the people, which ought to be the chief thing in view.

Finally, Smith explained the inclusion of the subject of arms by noting:

> Besides these three considerations of the security of property, the police, and the revenue of the kingdom or state, it must also be necessary to have some means of protecting the state from foreign injuries. Though the peace within doors be never so firmly established, yet if there be no security from injuries from without the property of individuals cannot be secure.

Comparing this account of the branches of jurisprudence with the definition of political economy in *The Wealth of Nations*, it becomes apparent that political economy comprises police and revenue, and that the remaining parts of the science of the legislator are justice and arms.[4] The latter two tasks of legislation, however, have as their goal the security of property. Thus, although internal justice and external defense may be the most basic and pressing concerns of the legislator, they seem in another sense to be ministerial or subordinate to the goals of political economy—namely, "to enrich both the people and the sovereign." Moreover, as between these two aims of political economy, Smith in the lectures makes it clear that the task of meeting the expenses of the sovereign ought to be carried out in the way that least hinders "the industry of the people"—in other words, that the end of revenue is subordinate to that of police.

For Adam Smith, then, the opulence of the people appears to be the ultimate aim of jurisprudence. To appreciate the significance of this view, it will be useful to inquire further into Smith's identification of the branch of jurisprudence concerned with enriching the people as "police." In the first of his lectures on police, he notes that this word "originally derived from the Greek *politeia*, signifying policy, politics, or the regulation of a government in general. It is now however generally confined to the regulation of the inferior parts of it." Smith indicates the range of police in the modern sense by recounting the instructions given to a newly appointed Intendant of Paris—"to provide for the *netteté* (cleanliness), *sûreté* (security) and *bon marché* (cheapness of goods) in the city."[5] The first two of these—keeping the streets clean and the "proper form and regulation of town guards"—are said to be subjects of "too mean a nature" to be treated in his course. But cheapness (which is "a necessary consequence of plenty" or opulence) is not considered too mean to be the subject of very many lectures, and subsequently of the greatest part of *The Wealth of Nations*.

In his comments on the science of natural jurisprudence at the close of *The Theory of Moral Sentiments*, Smith had noted that the *Laws* of Cicero and of Plato "are laws of police, not of justice."[6] Here Smith is clearly using the term "police" in its ancient sense, for Plato's *Laws* contains detailed regulations regarding the political and social institutions, education, religious beliefs, and way of life of the citizens. Among other things, these regulations impose the strictest bounds on the pursuit of wealth—for example, fixed and inalienable allotments of land, narrow limits on the accumulation of property, the banning of gold and silver, and the forbidding of "vulgar" commercial occupations. Riches are held to be incompatible with virtue and friendship among the citizens.[7]

By explicitly reducing the object of police to promoting the opulence of the people, Smith makes plain his rejection of the ancient view that the goal of legislation is to promote virtue and public spirit. Smith's contemporary, Jean-Jacques Rousseau, had deplored the fact that while "ancient political thinkers incessantly talked about morals and virtue, those of our time talk only of commerce and money."[8] With regard to this dichotomy, Smith clearly sides with modern political thought against Rousseau and the ancients. Once it is no longer believed that legislation must be guided by the requirements of civic virtue, the unlimited pursuit of wealth is free to emerge as the aim of both the individual and the nation. With this change, the way is paved for economics to be elevated from a subordinate or inferior part of political science to its capstone. And with the acceptance of the goal of maximization of wealth, economics can come into its own as an autonomous field of knowledge both worthy of and amenable to theoretical or scientific study.

Smith's specifically economic prescription for "accelerating the progress of the society toward real wealth and greatness" is embodied in what he called "the system of natural liberty":

> Every man, as long as he does not violate the laws of justice, is left perfectly free to pursue his own interest his own way, and to bring both his industry and capital into competition with those of any other man, or order of men. The sovereign is completely discharged from a duty, in the attempting to perform which he must always be exposed to innumerable delusions, and for the proper performance of which no human knowledge or wisdom could ever be sufficient; the duty of superintending the industry of private people, and of directing it toward the employment most suitable to the interest of society.[9]

It is clear, however, that Smith never believed that the free-market system he recommends would ever be fully implemented: "To expect, indeed, that the freedom of trade should ever be entirely restored in Great Britain, is as absurd as to expect that an Oceana or Utopia should ever be established in it."[10] Yet this by no means led Smith to despair regarding the future prospects of his country, for he did not regard economic or commercial policy as the crucial determinant of prosperity:

> The security which the laws in Great Britain give to every man that he shall enjoy the fruits of his own labor, is alone sufficient to make any country flourish, notwithstanding these [the corn laws] and twenty other absurd regulations of commerce. . . . The natural effort of every individual to better his own condition, when suffered to exert itself with freedom and security, is so powerful a principle, that it is alone, and without any assistance, not only capable of carrying on the society to wealth and prosperity, but of surmounting a hundred impertinent obstructions with which the folly of human laws too often incumbers its operations.

Thus Smith notes that although the three countries adopted similarly counterproductive mercantilist policies, Great Britain has grown rich while Spain and Portugal remain "beggarly."

> This bad policy is not in those countries counterbalanced by the general liberty and security of the people. Industry is there neither free nor secure, and the civil and ecclesiastical governments of Spain and Portugal, are such as would alone be sufficient to perpetuate their present

state of poverty, even though their regulations of commerce were as wise as the greater part of them are absurd and foolish.[11]

For Smith, then, the essential condition for prosperity is a political order that provides the people with liberty and security, and thus guarantees them the enjoyment of the fruits of their labor. This requires a government that not only prevents its citizens from oppressing or despoiling one another, but also is itself restrained from oppressing or despoiling them. When these conditions are met, people's "universal, continual, and uninterrupted effort to better their own condition" can be allowed free reign.[12] The stability and good order of the society do not require that the citizens be imbued with a strict sense of moral duty or a strong devotion to the public good. In a commercial society, people's self-interested and "vulgar" desire of "augmenting their fortune" is alone sufficient to produce that industriousness, sobriety, and frugality that Smith characterizes as "good conduct."[13] This self-interested good conduct in turn not only reinforces political stability but also, by promoting the steady accumulation of capital, leads to ever-increasing national wealth. This natural harmony between the individual's pursuit of his own economic advantage and the public good—understood as constituted by liberty, security, and prosperity for all—lies at the core of Smith's political thought. The idea that free competition is a more efficient commercial policy than government bounties and restraints is merely an extension and refinement of this more general view.

The Liberalism of John Locke

In viewing the security, liberty, and prosperity of the individual as the ends of civil society, Smith places himself squarely in the liberal tradition, whose great founder was John Locke. It is altogether fitting that Locke was the first eminent philosopher to write treatises wholly devoted to economic issues in the modern sense. In *Some Considerations of the Consequences of Lowering the Interest and Raising the Value of Money* and *Further Considerations Concerning Raising the Value of Money*, Locke espouses a mercantilist approach to questions of economic policy. In this regard, of course, he may be reckoned an opponent rather than a progenitor of Smith's "system of natural liberty." Yet as I have already indicated, the respects in which Smith follows Locke are much more fundamental. It is in Locke's political philosophy that we first find clearly enunciated not only the pre-eminence of economic motives in political life, but also the view that the individual's uninhibited pursuit of economic self-interest is both morally legitimate and conducive to the common good—a view directly contrary to that of both classical and biblical morality.

The legitimation of the pursuit of wealth by modern political philosophy may be viewed under a number of different, though interrelated, aspects. On the political plane, it was necessary to show, first, that endorsing and thereby unleashing the desire for gain need not produce a degree of selfishness and license that would make it impossible to maintain a stable political order. This argument, implicit in Locke, is spelled out in Smith's analysis, presented above, of how the desire to augment their fortune leads people to decent and orderly behavior—or what Tocqueville later characterized as "regularity of morals."

Second, again on the political plane, it was necessary to show that a polity devoted to the pursuit of individual wealth could maintain the martial abilities required to defend itself. On this question Locke declared that a ruler "who shall be so wise and godlike as by established laws of liberty to secure protection and encouragement to the honest industry of mankind against the oppression of power and narrowness of party will quickly be too hard for his neighbors,"[14] and Smith concluded, "In modern war the great expense of firearms gives an evident advantage to the nation which can best afford that expense; and consequently, to an opulent and civilized, over a poor and barbarous nation."[15]

The classical and biblical traditions, however, did not limit their critique of money-making to its potentially damaging political effects. They also viewed the passion for wealth as inimical to the cultivation of moral virtue and piety, which was regarded as the principal goal of civic life. The modern rehabilitation of economic self-interest therefore presupposed a critique of the classical and biblical understandings of virtue and its relation to political society. Most obviously, this critique consisted in a narrowing of the scope and the goals of the political community. Thus, John Locke, after arguing that "the care of each man's salvation belongs only to himself" and not to the magistrate, states the goals and limits of political power as follows: "Provision may be made for the security of each man's private possessions, for the peace, riches and public commodities of the whole people, and, as much as possible, for the increase of their inward strength against foreign invasions."[16]

It is fair to say, however, that the relegation of religion and virtue to the private sphere and the concomitant narrowing of the political sphere also reflected modern political philosophy's skepticism about the attainability and even the worth of the classical and biblical virtues. The political thought of Locke and Smith belongs to the modern tradition founded by Machiavelli and Hobbes, and shares its debunking view of the Utopian and unrealistic character of ancient and medieval moral and political teachings. In part, then, it is this implicit undermining of the higher moral virtues with which wealth getting was held to be in conflict that paves the way for the legitimation of economic self-interest. This legitimation had a positive as well as a negative aspect, however, and it is here that Locke's teaching about property is of absolutely central importance. Locke provides a new notion of justice that legitimizes the wealth seeking of the money-maker while calling into question the aristocratic virtues of ancient and feudal society.

In a well-known passage in his *Second Treatise of Government*, Locke states: "The great and chief end . . . of men's uniting into commonwealths, and putting themselves under government is the preservation of their property."[17] As this formulation makes clear, Locke holds that people came to possess property prior to their entry into civil society—that is, in the state of nature. In this respect, he directly contradicts the view of Thomas Hobbes, the originator of the modern doctrine of the state of nature. Hobbes held that in the state of nature there is "no propriety, no dominion, no *mine* and *thine* distinct; but only that to be every man's that he can get, and for so long as he can keep it."[18] Indeed, Hobbes describes his "first inquiry" into natural justice as asking "from whence it proceeded that any man should call anything rather his own than another man's." He concludes that "this proceeded not from nature, but consent (for what nature at first laid forth in common, men did afterward distribute into several impropriations)."[19]

Locke agrees with Hobbes that in political society the right of property is determined by the civil law, and he acknowledges that the security of property is extremely precarious in the state of nature. Yet he devotes his famous chapter "Of Property" in the *Second Treatise* to showing that men have a *natural* right to property that is morally valid in the precivil state and does not depend on the consent of other men. The basis of this natural right to property is labor. It is true that the earth has been given to all men in common, "yet every man has a property in his own person. This nobody has any right to but himself. The labor of his body, and the work of his hands, we may say, are properly his."[20] Therefore, when a person in the state of nature "mixes his labor," which is wholly his own, with what nature has given in common, he converts it into private property.

In the course of Locke's account of the origin of property, there appear to be two limitations on the validity of appropriation by means of labor. The first is an alleged provision of natural law that limits a person's property to what he can use before it spoils: "Whatever is beyond this, is more than his share, and belongs to others." This, to be sure, places some limits on the amount of apples or plums a person may pick and retain in his possession. But if he were to trade such perishable goods for

> a piece of metal, pleased with its color, or . . . a sparkling pebble or a diamond, and keep those by him all his life, he invaded not the right of others; he might heap up as much of these durable things as he pleased; the exceeding of the bounds of his just property not lying in the largeness of his possession, but the perishing of anything uselessly in it.

It is clear that, in the context of civilized society, this antispoilage provision constitutes not a limitation on accumulation of wealth but rather a justification for amassing as much money as one pleases. Thus Locke concludes that "a man may fairly possess more land than he himself can use the product of, by receiving in exchange for the overplus gold and silver, which may be hoarded up without injury to anyone, these metals not spoiling or decaying in the hands of the possessor."

The second limitation on acquisition through labor in the state of nature is that there must be "enough, and as good left in common for others." Thus in the most primitive stage of the state of nature, where human beings satisfy their basic needs through appropriating the "spontaneous" products of the earth (through hunting and gathering), Locke argues that the amount appropriated by any individual could hardly make a dent in "the plenty of natural provisions there was a long time in the world." He quickly acknowledges, however, that man's desire for a more comfortable life and "the penury of his [primitive] condition" prompt him toward improving upon the spontaneous produce of the earth through agriculture, thus making the earth itself the most important object of property.

The legitimate natural title to landed property is also supplied by labor: "As much land as a man tills, plants, improves, cultivates and can use the product of, so much is his property. He by his labor does, as it were, enclose it from the common." But how can the appropriation of land be squared with the condition that there must be enough and as good left for others? Prior to the invention and acceptance of money, Locke argues, the scope of men's appropriation of land was limited by their ability to make immediate use of its products; therefore the amount of available land exceeded people's needs, as continued to be the case in the wilds of seventeenth-century America. Yet this justification clearly can no longer apply once men, prompted by the use of money, have begun to enlarge their possessions, and land accordingly has become scarce.

Thus, Locke subtly begins to shift the grounds on which he legitimizes property in land. He argues that

> he who appropriates land to himself by his labor does not lessen but increase the common stock of mankind. For the provisions serving to the support of human life produced by one acre of enclosed and cultivated land are (to speak much within compass) ten times more than those which are yielded by an acre of land of an equal richness lying waste in common. And therefore he that encloses land and has a greater plenty of the conveniences of life from ten acres than he could have from a hundred left to nature, may truly be said to give ninety acres to mankind.

Rather than diminishing what is left for others, the appropriation and cultivation of land results in an increase of the useful products available to others. Consequently, "a king of a large fruitful territory [in America] feeds, lodges and is clad worse than a day laborer in England."

In the early stages of the state of nature, labor could be a valid title to property because of the plenty of natural provisions. Locke subsequently makes it clear, however, that the plenty provided by "unassisted nature" consists of acorns to eat, water to drink, and leaves, skins, or moss to wear. It is "wholly owing to labor and industry" that instead of these primitive goods, people in agricultural societies routinely enjoy the use of bread, wine, and cloth. Thus Locke argues that it is not "so strange, as perhaps before consideration it may appear, that the property of labor should be able to overbalance the community of land. For it is labor indeed that puts the difference of value on everything." The value of the products that man enjoys from agriculture—not to mention the other arts—"must all be charged on the account of labor, and received as an effect of that; nature and the earth furnished only the almost worthless materials as in themselves." Therefore, "that which made up the great part of what he applied to the support or comfort of his being, when invention and arts had improved the conveniences of life, was perfectly his own, and did not belong in common to others." Because it is the source of value, labor is also the natural source of property.

The great moral innovation of Locke consisted in his exaltation of the value of labor and his identification of labor as the source of a naturally valid title to property. In the *First Treatise,* he states that "justice gives every man a title to the product of his honest industry, and the fair acquisitions of his ancestors descended to him."[21] To labor for one's own (or one's family's) unlimited economic gain, and to enjoy the benefits of that labor, is just. Moreover, such productive labor contributes to the well-being of the society as a whole.

Locke's moral orientation is illuminated by his praise for the "industrious and rational," who devote themselves to labor, as opposed to the "quarrelsome and contentious," who "meddle with what was already improved by another's labor." The latter sort of person desires "the benefits of another's pains, which he ha[s] no right to."[22] Elsewhere, in explaining why men must form political societies in order to preserve their property, Locke speaks of "the pravity of mankind being such that they had rather injuriously [i.e., unjustly] prey upon the fruits of other men's labors than take pains to provide for themselves."[23] Injustice, in other words, comes to be identified not with other forms of selfishness but only with forcefully taking away what others have earned by their labor. Justice, then, consists not in helping others or in public-spiritedness but in respecting the legitimate rights—and especially the property rights—of others. This Lockean view is clearly mirrored in Adam Smith's definition of justice quoted earlier: "The first and chief design of every system of government is to maintain justice; to prevent the members of a society from encroaching on one another's property, or seizing what is not their own."

To be sure, not taking what legitimately belongs to others had always been regarded as a key component of justice. But Locke's teaching that labor or industry is both the natural title to property and the proper focus of human endeavor effects a transvaluation of the classical view of these matters. Plato's *Laws,* for example, proposes a polity in which

> great money-making is impossible, and the consequence is that there should not and cannot be anyone who makes money in any way from illiberal pursuits. No one need seek in any way to accumulate money

from the sort of occupation that receives the contemptible epithet "gross vulgarity" and that can distort the character of a free man.[24]

When Aristotle in the *Nicomachean Ethics* deals with the virtue related to wealth, he discusses liberality, which principally concerns the right use of wealth rather than its acquisition. He concludes that "it is not easy for a liberal man to be rich, since he is not good either at getting money or at keeping it, while he is profuse in spending it and values wealth not for its own sake but as a means of giving."[25] And in the *Politics*, Aristotle condemns the kind of wealth getting that involves trade, money, and exchange and that aims at unlimited riches.[26]

As the discussion of household management in Aristotle's *Politics* makes clear, the treatment of economic matters by the ancients was powerfully influenced by the institution of slavery. The leisure that enabled the gentleman to devote himself to the cultivation of virtue (including liberality), to politics, and to philosophy was made possible by the wealth production of slaves. Obviously, an economy based upon slavery is incompatible with the principle that human beings possess a natural right of property founded upon labor and therefore each man is entitled to enjoy the fruits of his own labor.

Moreover, it is impossible for a teaching that acknowledges the legitimacy of slavery to condemn as unjust by nature the forcible seizure of things produced by the labor of others. Thus Aristotle, in a passage much remarked upon by modern political philosophers, includes brigandage along with shepherding, agriculture, fishing, and hunting among the natural modes of human acquisition, a category from which he excludes exchange and trade. The contrast between the morality associated with a commercial way of life and the martial virtues characteristic of noncommercial societies is powerfully drawn by Montesquieu:

> The spirit of trade produces in the mind of a man a certain sense of exact justice, opposite, on the one hand, to robbery, and on the other to those moral virtues which forbid our always adhering rigidly to the rules of private interest, and suffer us to neglect this for the advantage of others. The total privation of trade, on the contrary, produces robbery, which Aristotle ranks in the means of acquiring; yet it is not at all inconsistent with certain moral virtues. Hospitality, for instance, is most rare in trading countries, while it is found in the most admirable perfection among nations of vagabonds.[27]

A preference for commerce and industry over the war and violence attributed to ancient and medieval society is a persistent theme in modern political philosophy. Thus Hobbes notes that

> the militia was of old reckoned in the number of the gaining arts, under the notion of booting or taking prey. . . . And great commonweals, namely, that of Rome and Athens, by the spoils of war, foreign tribute, and the territories they have purchased by their arms, have sometimes so improved the commonwealth, that they have not only not required any public monies from the poorer sort of subjects, but have also divided to each of them both monies and lands. *But this kind of increase of riches is not to be brought into rule and fashion.*[28]

In a similar vein, Hamilton in the *Federalist* states:

> The industrious habits of the people of the present day, absorbed in the pursuits of gain and devoted to the improvements of agriculture and commerce, are incompatible with the condition of a nation of soldiers, which was the true condition of [the ancient] republics.[29]

It is necessary to consider in this light Locke's discussion of conquest in the *Second Treatise*. Locke not only argues that conquest, as opposed to "consent of the people," cannot provide a legitimate foundation for government; he also goes to great lengths to demonstrate that the just conqueror's rightful claim to any property of the conquered is limited to "reparation for the damages received and the charges of the war, and that too with reservation of the right of the innocent women and children." Even a just war cannot be a legitimate means of acquiring wealth. Indeed, even a person's natural right to life is more easily forfeited than his natural right to property:

> For it is the brutal force the aggressor has used that gives his adversary a right to take away his life and destroy him if he pleases, as a noxious creature; but it is damage sustained that alone gives him title to another man's goods. For though I may kill a thief that sets on me in the highway, yet I may not (which seems less) take away his money and let him go; this would be robbery on my side. His force, and the state of war he put himself in, made him forfeit his life, but gave me no title to his goods.[30]

Even in the state of war—except perhaps for cases of the most extreme want—property cannot rightfully be acquired by forcible taking from others.

In the course of his chapter on conquest, Locke ridicules those who "found absolute monarchy upon the title of the sword" and claims that the Norman conquest provides a foundation for absolute monarchy in England.[31] Locke's teaching is similarly antithetical to any attempt to found a right to property upon the "title of the sword." It thereby implicitly raises questions about the origins of large aristocratic landholdings in England—questions that were to be made explicit by Locke's successors. In John Stuart Mill's words:

> The social arrangements of modern Europe commenced from a distribution of property which was the result, not of just partition, or acquisition by industry, but of conquest and violence; and notwithstanding what industry has been doing for many centuries to modify the work of force, the system still retains many large traces of its origin.[32]

Locke's doctrine of the natural right to property undermines the morality of what Mill termed the "predatory classes" and supports the way of life of the "productive classes."[33] The good man seeks to accumulate property for himself and his family through his own industry, while peaceably respecting the rights of others. Locke supplies the theoretical underpinnings of what may be called the bourgeois ethic.

The Utilitarians

The success of the moral reorientation advocated by Locke has been enormous; indeed, it has been so great that today it is utterly taken for granted. The goal of maximizing individual wealth through labor and industry remains the bedrock of liberalism and the unquestioned premise of modern economics. Yet the key theoretical foundations of Locke's teaching have been wholly abandoned by contemporary liberalism and by present-day economic thinkers. Liberal political economy's rejection of the Lockean framework of natural rights is by no means a recent development. In fact, its roots can be discovered at the origins of modern political economy, in the thought of Adam Smith and his contemporaries.

One noteworthy sign of Smith's divergence from Locke is the fact that Smith, in his lectures on jurisprudence, follows David Hume in rejecting Locke's theory of the social contract.[34] Both Hume and Smith argue that in fact princes and subjects in almost all political societies do not base the duty of obedience on any notion of a social contract. Their opposition to this aspect of Locke's teaching derives

in part from a conservative wariness about the revolutionary implications of making the consent of the people the sole foundation of
legitimate government. Instead of contract or consent, Smith holds
that "authority" and "utility" are the two principles of allegiance to
the civil magistrate.

Those thinkers who reject the doctrine of the social contract typically also reject the associated Lockean doctrines of the state of nature and the natural rights of man. Thus Hume labels the state of
nature a "mere philosophical fiction, which never had, and never
could have any reality," and does not speak of natural rights.[35]
Smith's position is somewhat more ambiguous. Although he speaks
in the lectures of the natural rights to life and liberty, he seems to
deny the Lockean view that the right to property is natural and to
question the usefulness of discussions of the state of nature.[36] The
clearest expression within eighteenth-century liberalism of this rejection of key elements of Locke's teaching is found in the thought of
Jeremy Bentham. Bentham denies that there is a clear demarcation
between the state of nature and the state of political society; he labels
the social contract a "chimera" ("effectually demolished by Mr.
Hume"), and offers in its place the Humean principle of utility; and
he ridicules the idea of "natural imprescriptible rights" as "rhetorical
nonsense—nonsense on stilts."[37]

One may distinguish, then, two branches of liberalism deriving
from the thought of John Locke: the natural rights tradition and the
utilitarian tradition. The natural rights tradition would include the
physiocrats and the French revolutionaries who composed the Declaration of the Rights of Man and the Citizen, Tom Paine and certain
other early British radicals, the American Founders, John Marshall
and other American jurists of the nineteenth century, and perhaps
Herbert Spencer. Today this tradition, although it continues to exert a
lingering influence over American popular opinion, is largely moribund among intellectuals; apart from the followers of Leo Strauss,
only Robert Nozick and a few other libertarians might plausibly
claim to be its heirs.

In the utilitarian tradition, the most prominent figures are Hume,
Adam Smith (though in less clear-cut fashion), Bentham, James Mill,
and John Stuart Mill. This is clearly the branch of liberalism in which
political economy—and, more distantly, present-day economics—
has its theoretical roots. The importance of Smith and J. S. Mill for
political economy goes without saying; and although the significance of Bentham's strictly economic writings may be slight, his

decisive impact on the subsequent course of economic thought is attested by no less an authority than Alfred Marshall, who identifies Bentham as "on the whole the most influential of the immediate successors of Adam Smith."[38]

Despite jettisoning the natural rights foundation of Locke's teaching, the utilitarian tradition remained committed to such Lockean goals as individual liberty, the security of private property, and the emancipation of economic self-interest as a means of enriching both the individual and the nation. No less than the adherents of natural rights, the utilitarians of the eighteenth and early nineteenth centuries affirmed the bourgeois ethic. They regarded labor as the source of value and the ultimate basis for private property, and were wholly dedicated to the proposition that the laws should seek to ensure to men the fruits of their own labor. Where the two traditions differed was regarding the grounds on which men ought to be rewarded with the fruits of their labor. Locke himself had supplemented his defense of the individual's natural right to property—that is, to the fruits of his labor—with the argument that securing this right would promote an increase in societal wealth ultimately benefiting all. It was this latter justification that the utilitarians seized upon and made the chief basis of their case for the security of private property.

The rejection of natural rights by utilitarians like Bentham by no means led them to waver in their support for the existing distribution of property. Indeed, some radical versions of the natural rights doctrine were much more hostile to the prevailing economic order, particularly with respect to land ownership; a doctrine that founded the natural right to property upon labor could readily be interpreted and applied in a way that challenged the disproportion between productive labor and wealth in contemporary civil societies. For this and other reasons the natural rights teaching came to be associated in many quarters with Jacobinism. Thus Albert Venn Dicey has argued that "the unlimited scorn entertained by every Benthamite for the social contract and for natural rights" helped make Benthamism attractive to moderate English opinion by serving as "a guarantee against sympathy with Jacobinical principles."[39]

Bentham's own teaching, it is true, reckoned material equality as one of the four "subordinate objects" of legislation (subordinate, that is, to the general end—"the happiness of the body politic"). He argued that greater wealth brings greater happiness, and, "the more nearly the actual proportion approaches to equality, the greater will be the total mass of happiness." Yet Bentham remained resolutely opposed to the redistribution of property because of the overriding importance he attached to security: "When security and equality are in opposition, there should be no hesitation; equality should give way." And "the grand principle of security," according to Bentham, directs the legislator to "maintain the distribution [of property] which is actually established. This, under the name of justice, is with reason regarded as his first duty: it is a general and simple rule applicable to all states, adapted to all plans, even those which are most opposed to each other."[40]

Alfred Marshall attributes Bentham's "passionate desire for security" to the impression made upon his mind by "the terror of the French Revolution."[41] Yet the importance that Bentham places upon the security of property and the reasoning he employs to defend it are entirely consonant with the teaching of Adam Smith. Bentham holds that unless the laws afford the security of enjoying the fruits of one's labor, human industry is paralyzed. The conditions of savages and of peoples living under "the absurd despotism of the Turk" are adduced as examples of the poverty that prevails where security is lacking. Poverty is the "primitive condition of the human race"; the creation of wealth is made possible only when the security of property is assured. "The law does not say to a man, 'Work and I will reward you'; but it says to him, 'Work, and by stopping the hand that would take them from you, I will ensure to you the fruits of your labor, its natural and sufficient reward, which, without me, you could not preserve.'"[42]

Bentham appears to entertain no doubts, on purely utilitarian grounds, about the desirability—indeed, the justice—of laissez-faire capitalism. Nevertheless, his arguments reflect the lingering influence of those aspects of Locke's thought that he explicitly rejected. Despite his contempt for the doctrine of natural rights, he invokes the *naturalness* of ensuring to men the fruits of their own labor; and despite his reservations about the notion of the state of nature, his justification for the security of private property lays great stress on the contrast with a primitive or savage state of mankind in which no such security exists.

It is only when these Lockean ways of thinking lose their hold that there is a serious weakening of the connection between utilitarianism and the bourgeois ethic of capitalism. Such a weakening can be observed in the dominant economic work of the mid-nineteenth century, John Stuart Mill's *Principles of Political Economy*.

To be sure, Mill's massive treatise contains many echoes of the Benthamite viewpoint. He asserts, for example, that

> All laws or usages . . . which chain up the efforts of any part of the community, in pursuit of their own good, or stand between those efforts and their natural fruits—are (independently of all other grounds of condemnation) violations of the fundamental principles of economic policy; tending to make the aggregate powers of the community productive in a less degree than they would otherwise be.[43]

In several places he stresses the vital importance of security of property as a precondition of prosperity: "Industry and frugality cannot exist where there is not a preponderant probability that those who labor and spare will be permitted to enjoy."[44] His insistence on maintaining the connection between exertion and reward leads him to condemn trade union opposition to piecework as "one of the most discreditable indications of a low moral condition given of late by part of the English working classes . . . dislike to piecework in itself, except under mistaken notions, must be dislike to justice and fairness, a desire to cheat, by not giving work in proportion to pay."[45]

In an earlier passage of the *Principles,* however, noting that most of the French socialist manufacturing associations that had begun by sharing the remuneration equally had subsequently adopted a standard of piecework, Mill concludes:

> The original principle [i.e., equal remuneration] appeals to a higher standard of justice, and is adapted to a much higher moral condition of human nature. The proportioning of remuneration to work done is really just only in so far as the more or less of the work is a matter of choice: when it depends on natural difference of strength or capacity, this principle of remuneration is itself an injustice: it is giving to those who have; assigning most to those who are already most favored by nature. Considered, however, as a compromise with the selfish type of character formed by the present standard of morality, and fostered by the existing social institutions, it is highly expedient; and until education shall have been entirely regenerated, is far more likely to prove immediately successful, than an attempt at a higher ideal.[46]

Along these same lines, Mill elsewhere speaks of "the true idea of distributive justice, which consists not in imitating but in redressing the inequalities and wrongs of nature."[47]

The opposing viewpoints expressed in these two sets of quotations coexist uneasily within Mill's *Principles.* The first set seems to regard rewarding individuals with the fruits of their own labor not only as economically efficient, but also as both natural and just. The second, by contrast, defines distributive justice as emphatically opposed to nature and to the natural connection between labor and its fruits. It also implies that the proper standard for judging the distributional consequences of capitalist society is not the insecurity and poverty of a precivilized state, but some future and more enlightened era by whose higher and less selfish standard of morality capitalism will be found severely wanting.

This kind of shift in perspective would hardly be possible within the natural rights tradition. The central role of the state of nature in that tradition ensures that the precivilized past will remain as a key point of reference; and the very idea of a natural right to the fruits of one's labor requires that nature remain a guidepost for distributive justice. Within the utilitarian tradition, on the other hand, there is no intrinsic barrier to the adoption of the very different viewpoints that Mill seems to have absorbed from philosophy of history and from socialism. Thus, despite its Lockean ancestry and the intimate association of its Benthamite version with laissez-faire, utilitarianism proved highly susceptible to being turned in an anti-capitalist direction.[48]

Noting that Mill's *Principles of Political Economy* was "the most successful and influential treatise of that age," Joseph Schumpeter remarks:

> Nothing can be more revealing of the character of bourgeois civilization—more indicative, that is, of its genuine freedom and also of its political weakness—than that the book to which the bourgeois accorded such a reception carried a socialist message and was written by a man palpably out of sympathy with the scheme of values of the industrial bourgeoisie.[49]

Schumpeter probably goes too far in suggesting that the confused and often contradictory message of the *Principles* can be simply classified as socialist. Yet he is surely on the mark in observing that this classic of bourgeois political economy calls into question the basic ethical premises of capitalist society. Having abandoned the theoretical underpinnings of the doctrine of natural rights, the utilitarian tradition of political economy winds up more or less grudgingly acceding to the moral critique of capitalist justice offered by its egalitarian and "progressive" opponents.

The Modern Era

After Mill, it is difficult to find a distinguished political economist who does not share to some degree his ambivalence toward the capitalist ethic, and in particular his doubts about the justice of distribution in capitalist society. To be sure, most political economists reconciled themselves to the system of private property, but their objections to socialism tended to be practical rather than moral. Henry Sidgwick, for example, asserted: "I object to socialism not because it would divide the produce of industry badly, but because it would have so much less to divide."[50]

By 1923, the prominent American economist Frank H. Knight could write: "We find a fairly general agreement among serious writers that the principle of *need*, which would practically amount to equal sharing as a general rule, is the ideal basis of distribution."[51] Knight, a teacher of Milton Friedman, has been described by F. A. Hayek as "the American economist who has done most to advance our understanding of a free society."[52] Yet Knight's book, *The Ethics of Competition*, quoted just above, turns out to be an almost unqualified attack on the bourgeois ethic and on the justice of distribution under capitalism. Knight specifically challenges the notion that labor supplies an ethically valid title to income, and he does so principally on the same ground as Mill: he argues that from an ethical standpoint that "inherited [i.e., natural] capacity," which he identifies as the most important source of more productive labor, "represents an obligation to the world rather than a claim upon it."[53]

The view that greater productivity stemming from greater natural ability is not morally deserving of larger rewards is now virtually universal among economists who have addressed this question. For thinkers of an egalitarian bent, this argument has become a crucial element in the moral justification of government policies aimed at the redistribution of income. Thus Arthur Okun, for example, defending the case for redistribution in his *Equality and Efficiency*, asserts that "society should aim to ameliorate, and certainly not to compound, the flaws of the universe" by deciding to "restrict prizes that bestow vastly higher standards of living on people with . . . greater innate abilities."[54]

A still more striking elaboration of J. S. Mill's assertion that "the true idea of distributive justice . . . consists . . . in redressing the inequalities and wrongs of nature" is to be found in John Rawls's *A Theory of Justice*. The premise that natural ability, because it is unde-

served and hence "arbitrary from a moral point of view," cannot provide a moral claim to greater reward is the very foundation of
Rawls's entire theoretical structure.[55] That structure yields a "difference principle," which calls for redistribution to maximize the economic benefits to the least advantaged. The difference principle,
according to Rawls, represents an agreement to "regard the distribution of natural talents as a common asset."[56] In short, because individuals do not deserve their own natural talents, these talents should
in effect be collectivized and regarded as the common property of
society as a whole.

It is difficult to imagine a view that runs more directly counter to
the Lockean principle that the individual has a natural right to the
fruits of his labor. The foundation of this right according to Locke is
the fact that "every man has a property in his own person: this nobody has any right to but himself. The labor of his body, and the
work of his hands, we may say, are properly his."[57] From this perspective, the question of whether people deserve the particular body
and hands (and brain) with which they are endowed does not arise;
the individual's sole mastery and possession of his own person is the
irreducible starting point of moral reasoning about property. Consequently, differences in wealth that flow from people's unequal natural endowments are in no way unjust, and the individual's pursuit of
wealth is not rendered morally questionable by the fact that some are
more successful than others.[58]

By contrast, for those who question the morality of rewards accru-
ing to greater natural ability and therefore abandon the notion of a
right to the fruit of one's labor, the justice of economic inequality and
of the capitalist ethic is rendered highly problematic. This becomes
apparent even in the thought of such apostles of the free market as
Hayek and Friedman. Although both these authors reject the
redistributionist conclusions drawn from it by Okun and Rawls, they
fully endorse the argument that since individuals do not deserve the
natural abilities they inherit, neither do they deserve in an ethical
sense the rewards that flow from the exercise of these abilities.[59] As a
consequence, both Hayek and Friedman explicitly eschew any attempt to defend capitalism on grounds of distributive justice.[60] This
of course does not lead them to the view that capitalism is morally
indefensible. Instead, they seek to construct their case for a capitalist
order by attributing the supreme moral value to individual freedom.
It is in the name of freedom—and not of justice—that they defend the
economic inequality generated by capitalism.[61] Hayek even goes so

far as to say that a society based on the principle of distributive justice "in all essential respects would be the opposite of a free society."[62]

Individual freedom (or liberty) is of course an essential principle for the entire liberal tradition. But the radical divorce of freedom from justice represents a decisive departure from the teaching of John Locke, in which the rights to liberty and to property in the fruits of one's labor go hand in hand. This loss of belief in the justice of a liberal economic order even by its most eminent proponents is the ultimate consequence of the rejection of the doctrine of natural rights by the tradition of political economy.

Four   Colin Wright

Competing Conceptions of
Political Economy

The old and venerable term "political economy" designates an academic discipline. Having fallen into disuse and given way to "economics," it is now enjoying a revival, albeit with some variation in its usage. Although this variation suggests the importance and legitimacy of asking "What is political economy?" or "What are we to understand 'political economy' to mean?" it also suggests that any statement concise enough to be recognized as a definition would be stipulative and contentious.

As we shall see, some uses of the term "political economy" conflate topical designation with prescription—they not only refer to an area of study, but come bundled with an ideology. This of course happens, in varying degrees, to all disciplines within the social sciences. One reason for this complication is that the topical domain of these disciplines comprises such subjects as equality, freedom, and justice, and a concern for the good society. These difficult, controversial, and complex topics provoke strong and differing opinions among reasonable people. In the view of some, the domain of political economy includes such topics, and often even places them in a prominent position. For this reason, among others, I intend in this chapter not so much to offer a definition of political economy as to examine and comment upon its various uses; to see what common elements, if any, exist in these uses; and through this examination to come to a better appreciation of the richness and complexity of the concepts and issues that fall within the purview of political economy.

This chapter is organized as follows. First I sketch the history of how thinkers have defined the discipline that we now call economics, in order to lay a foundation for a better understanding of current uses of the term "political economy." I then classify these uses and relate this classification to certain aspects of the history and current characterization of economics. I conclude with some of my own views regarding the appropriate description and intellectual location of political economy.

Political Economy: Old and New

In this section I offer a short, selective history of how political economy changed its name to economics. The selectivity does not knowingly support a specific point of view, but seeks rather to highlight those instances that represent a significant change in the way the discipline defined itself.

We customarily date modern economics from the publication of Adam Smith's *An Inquiry into the Nature and Causes of the Wealth of Nations* in 1776. Smith referred to his discipline as "political economy," but he was not the first to do so—this honor apparently goes to Montchrestien in 1615. The most interesting pre-Smithian use appears in James Steuart's *An Inquiry into the Principles of Political Economy*, which, published a decade before Smith's *Wealth of Nations*, first used political economy in the title of an English text. Of great interest is the way Steuart connects the characterization of economics as household management found in Aristotle's *Politics* with the demands placed upon economic considerations by the rise of the modern state. Steuart writes that "economy, in general, is the art of providing for all the wants of a family, with prudence and frugality."[1] That is, economy is Aristotle's "household management." 6

Steuart continues:

What economy is in a family, political economy is in a state. . . . The statesman [this is a general term to signify the legislature and supreme power, according to the form of government] is neither master to establish what economy he pleases, or, in the exercise of his sublime authority, to overturn at will the established laws of it. . . .

The great art therefore of political economy is, first to adapt the great different operations of it to the spirit, manners, habits, and customs of the people; and afterward to mold these circumstances so, as to be able to introduce a set of new and more useful institutions.

The principal object of this science is to secure a certain fund of subsistence for all the inhabitants, to obviate every circumstance which may render it precarious; to provide every thing necessary for supplying the wants of the society, and to employ the inhabitants (supposing them to be free-men) in such a manner as naturally to create reciprocal relations and dependencies between them, so as to make their several interests lead them to supply one another with their reciprocal wants. . . .

It is the business of a statesman to judge of the expediency of different schemes of economy, and by degrees to model the minds of his subjects so as to induce them, from the allurement of private interest, to concur in the execution of his plan.[2]

In these few sentences Steuart lays out the essence of what political economy was initially considered to be: it was to the nation what economy (economics) was to the family. Since economics was the prudential management of the household economy, political economy was the prudential management of the national economy. Steuart suggests that although all men are motivated by self-interest, differences in circumstance will bring about differences in social history and forms of government, which in turn will require differences in political economy or national economic institutions. Statesmen, somehow knowing that better institutions might exist, have a responsibility for encouraging citizens to adopt them, through appeals to their enlightened self-interest.

This excerpt from Steuart gives a hint of what might be called institutional relativism, in that he recognizes no single best system for national economic management. The best depends upon the "spirit, manners, habits, and customs of the people." On the other hand, the statesman is presumed to know what are good and bad economic arrangements for a particular people and to be obliged to do what he can to achieve and develop good institutions. This role for the statesman clearly imparts a strong rationalistic and prescriptive element to Steuart's political economy. It also helps us see what John Stuart Mill meant in asserting that definitions of political economy like Steuart's (and subsequently Smith's) take political economy to be the science that "teaches nations how to become rich."[3]

A crucial matter of concern for Smith was the nature of national wealth and how best to increase it. Although he thought that civil government had some responsibility for the economic or material welfare of its citizens and thereby for increasing wealth, he considered that this was most efficiently accomplished by developing institutions that would enable individuals to provide most of their wants for themselves. To support these institutions, as well as to provide for what we now call collective or public goods, the government must acquire command over some resources, a task best accomplished through taxation. All of this is partly reflected or adumbrated in the most famous, if not the most original, definition of political economy, that of Smith:

> Political economy, considered as a branch of the science of a statesman or legislator, proposes two distinct objects: first to provide a plentiful revenue or subsistence for the people, or more properly to enable them to provide such revenue or subsistence for themselves; and secondly, to supply the state or commonwealth with a revenue sufficient for the public services. It proposes to enrich both the people and the sovereign.[4]

Drawing upon his views on human nature, Smith judged that the most desirable relationship between political and economic institutions is one that allows the "obvious and simple system of natural liberty" to flourish, for an individual is naturally motivated to "better himself," and

> every man, as long as he does not violate the laws of justice, is [should be?] left perfectly free to pursue his own interest his own way . . . the sovereign is completely discharged from a duty . . . of superintending the industry of private people, and of directing it toward the employments most suitable to the interest of the society.[5]

The Wealth of Nations may be interpreted as a treatise-tract because it integrates descriptive and prescriptive elements, positive and normative economics. Smith integrates discussions of how the economic system did and would work under different institutional arrangements (positive analysis) with discussions regarding preferred outcomes (normative analysis) and ways to achieve them. As a tract, it seeks to persuade its readers that the amorphous group that Smith christens the mercantilists were wrong about the nature of wealth and wrong in what they advocated for the economic role of government.

After Smith, and throughout most of the nineteenth century, "political economy" appeared in the titles of many texts, most of which began with a definition of political economy. The most widely read for a long time was Mill's *Principles of Political Economy: With Some Applications to Social Philosophy*, published in 1848, a text of broad scope that combined descriptive and prescriptive analysis. Elsewhere, in his essay "On the Definition of Political Economy: And on the Method of Investigation Proper to It," he develops his preferred definition of political economy by first dismissing other definitions and ruminating about problems in methodology. He dismisses the view that "Political Economy is a science which teaches . . . in what manner a nation may be made rich" on the grounds that it confuses "science" and "art"; he dismisses the view that "Political Economy . . . is to the state, what domestic economy is to the family" on the grounds that domestic economy is an art but political economy is a science, and thus the two cannot be compared.[6] After some preliminary definitions and some reflections on human nature and the nature of society, he suggests that political economy "considers mankind as occupied solely in acquiring and consuming wealth."[7] Even though this statement exemplifies a necessary simplification such as all sciences engage in, and though no political economist "was ever so absurd as to suppose that mankind are really thus constituted";[8] nevertheless it is not a bad assumption. He concludes that political economy should be defined as "the science which traces the laws of such of the phenomena of society as arise from the combined operations of mankind for the production of wealth, in so far as those phenomena are not modified by the pursuit of any other object."[9] In his desire to define political economy with care, Mill takes up several methodological issues, including the differentiation between science and art. He is concerned to define political economy in such a way as to make it a science; and in doing so he provides one of the earliest treatments of the role of simplifying assumptions in economic analysis. As in other areas, Mill's methodological approach to the discipline plays a transitional role between classical and neoclassical economics. His interest in methodology and his concern for separating science and art foreshadowed the modern separation of positive from normative economics. As we shall see, it was this eagerness for the discipline to be more scientific that led one of Mill's successors to change its name.

At this stage in the development of economics, political economy was not the name of a field within a discipline, but of the discipline as a whole. It included all of the analyses and techniques extant in the discipline, applications of this body of analysis to perceived problems, and normative arguments for and against particular solutions to economic and social problems. It was the all-encompassing name for this new discipline. Men like Ricardo, Mill, Jevons, and Sidgwick, to give just four prominent names in the period between Smith and Marshall, did not specialize in a corner of their discipline and use the term "political economy" in their titles; they were in command of and contributed to a broad range of topics within the discipline. They were the leaders of their discipline—the leading "economists" of their day.

To understand some aspects of how the use of the term "political economy" evolved, it is helpful to consider Sidgwick, for he refers to an intellectual climate that reached fruition in Marshall. Sidgwick was one of the last polymaths among economists. He wrote not only *The Principles of Political Economy* but also *The Principles of Politics* and *The Methods of Ethics*. This interest in the full and traditional domain of political economy—economics, politics, and ethics—doubtless influenced his brief statement in *The Principles of Political Economy* on the topical domain of political economy.[10] He notes in his own terms that for Smith, political economy included science and art; what we might call description and prescription. But economists more contemporary to Sidgwick tended to emphasize the science and eliminate the art. Sidgwick remained sympathetic to the Smithian view, though he preferred to speak specifically of the art and the science of political economy. For Sidgwick, the art of political economy deals especially with the prescribed relationships between government and the economy, whereas the scientific part deals with issues that can to some degree be isolated from study of the rest of society—although he suggested that it is well to leave the degree of separation between the science and art of political economy somewhat indefinite.

Alfred Marshall's *Principles of Economics,* published in 1890, replaced Mill's *Principles* as the discipline's standard text. It is here that we see the name change from political economy to economics. In the opening paragraph Marshall writes: "Political Economy or Economics is a study of mankind in the ordinary business of life; it examines that part of individual and social action which is most closely connected with the attainment and with the use of the material requisites for well being."[11] What at first looks like the casual substitution of one term for another appears on closer inspection to have been motivated by the desire to move the professional study of economics in a more scientific direction. As Keynes suggested:

> Marshall was the first great economist *pur sang* that there ever was; the first who devoted his life to building up the subject as a separate science, standing on its own foundations with as high standards of scientific accuracy as the physical or biological sciences. . . . He was the first

to take up this professional scientific attitude to the subject, as something above and outside current controversy, as far from politics as physiology is from the general practitioner.[12]

Reading this passage in the light of later logical positivism and the fact/value controversy in the social sciences, we might too hastily infer that Marshall intended to move the discipline in a more scientific direction by distinguishing between the study of facts and the study of values and by emphasizing that the appropriate domain of economics is primarily the study of facts. Indeed, several passages tend to support such an interpretation of Marshall. When he wrote *Principles*, the rudiments of the fact/value distinctions were developing, as was the notion that science should deal only with facts. His seeming agreement with this view is supported by the following passages, if we take his use of "practical" to be related to contemporary concern for "values":

> Economists must be greedy of facts. . . . Its purpose firstly to acquire knowledge for its own sake, and secondly, to throw light on practical issues. . . . The practical uses of economic studies should never be out of the mind of the economist, but his special business is to study and interpret facts. . . . The above [matters of fact] are the main questions with which economic studies have to deal directly. . . . The practical issues which, though lying for the greater part outside the range of economic science, yet supply a chief motive in the background to the work of the economists.[13]

Although these passages suggest that Marshall held the chief task of economics to be the study of facts, others suggest that he changed the name from political economy to economics because he thought that it should deal with a broader range of issues than political issues alone. Take, for example, the following: "Economics is thus taken to mean a study of the economic aspects and conditions of man's political, social and private life; but more specifically of his social life."[14] This statement quite clearly indicates a desire to broaden the domain of economics. In addition, we know that Marshall intended his work specifically to help understand business and commercial activities. He most probably would, for example, have strongly advocated making economics the center of MBA programs. It is reasonable to conclude that Marshall wanted to make the study of economics not only more scientific but also applicable to a broader range of subjects than it had heretofore been. He emphasized that "economic science" should deal with what we now call positive economics, but that it should still include normative economics, though perhaps as a secondary part; and that the term "economics" was preferable to "political economy":

> But though thus largely directed by practical needs, economics avoids as far as possible the discussion of those exigencies of party organization, and those diplomacies of home and foreign politics of which the statesman is bound to take account in deciding what measures that he can propose will bring him nearest to the end that he desires to secure for his country. It aims indeed at helping him to determine not only what that end should be, but also what are the best methods of a broad policy devoted to that end. But it shuns many political issues, which the practical man cannot ignore: and it is therefore a science, pure and applied, rather than a science and an art. And it is better described by the broad term "Economics" than by the narrower term "Political Economy."[15]

This passage reflects Marshall's desire that economics not serve primarily in daily political battles, but falls short of denying the economist any role in developing (normative) ends.

Pigou, a student of Marshall, defined economics in empirical terms consistent with a positivistic approach: "Economics deals with those aspects of human behavior that can be brought directly or indirectly under the measuring rod of money."[16] If you deal only with those aspects of human behavior that can be measured, you invite the use of quantitative techniques (which you may tend to equate with scientific methods). "Political" has been altogether dropped, and the trend is toward narrowing the scope while broadening the topical domain of economics.

Important aspects of this view were extended by Robbins in *The Nature and Significance of Economic Science*. His definition is the one used in most modern texts, in some form or other: "Economics is the science which studies human behavior as a relationship between ends and scarce means which have alternative uses."[17] He suggested that his definition was analytical, for it focuses attention upon a particular aspect of behavior—that which is caused or influenced by scarcity. He also said that "there are no limitations on the subject matter of Economic Science save this,"[18] where "this" refers to the presence of scarcity and the resulting necessity of choosing among alternative courses of action. This approach to the topical domain of economics has led to its being called, in some circles, the science of choice or the science of decision making.

Robbins, clearly influenced by Hume's pronouncements on moving from "is" to "ought," held strongly to the division of economics into positive and normative:

Economics is neutral as between ends. Economics cannot pronounce on the validity of ultimate judgments of value. . . . Between the generalizations of positive and normative studies there is a logical gulf fixed which no ingenuity can disguise and no juxtaposition in space or time bridge over. . . . It [economics] is fundamentally distinct from Ethics.[19]

The last definition that I wish to consider is offered by Gary Becker in *The Economic Approach to Human Behavior*. Seeking to characterize the activity he observed many economists increasingly engaging in, the investigation of nontraditional topics, Becker criticized previous definitions for emphasizing the scope rather than the approach of economics. He argued that "scope" definitions tended to limit economics to some list of eligible topics, whereas "approach" definitions encouraged economists to investigate whatever topics seemed amenable to their particular set of tools. Becker describes the economic approach as guided by these assumptions:

- Economics assumes "maximizing behavior more extensively and explicitly" than other disciplines do. (Utility or wealth maximization of individuals, profit maximizing behavior of firms, etc.)

- This maximizing behavior takes place over "stable preferences." (These are not preferences for oranges versus apples, or Chevy versus Ford, but basic aspects of life such as food, honor, prestige, health, envy, benevolence. It is also assumed that rich and poor, or people in different cultures, do not differ much on these basics.)

- Markets develop to coordinate, with varying degrees of efficiency, the actions of different participants.[20]

The reach of economics thus defined is broad. Although no one has claimed that it constitutes a unified social science, a generous and sympathetic observer might describe it as moving in that direction. Such generosity is not universal; some observers dismiss whatever unifying tendency one might see in the economic approach as imperialism—unification attempts under protest! In any event, this approach does not limit economics to the study of material wants or traditional markets. Some find this a liberating change in the way economics is conceived, for it permits any problem susceptible to this approach to come legitimately within the domain of economics

Economics or Political Economy?

Use of the term "political economy," which diminished in the late nineteenth century, is now reviving, as a casual perusal of new book titles and journal articles will confirm. On the basis of the preceding sketch of the discipline and from a perusal of the current literature, I classify practitioners into four groups according to their views of the distinction between political economy and economics:

I. Those who essentially make no distinction beyond saying that "political economy" is the old term and "economics" is the new.

II. Those who use "political economy" to refer to the study of the interrelationship between the economy and the state. This use suggests an interest in economic policy or in the economic content of public policy in general, and an interest in economic development.

III. Those who think that modern economics has become too abstract, too mathematical, too ignorant of the institutional, historical, and political constraints in which economic behavior functions; and as a consequence has become impractical and irrelevant. The kind of economics that is not guilty of such failings they refer to as political economy.

IV. Those who use the economic approach to study what some political philosophers call "political things," particularly political institutions.

These categories are not necessarily mutually exclusive or exhaustive; this classification is simply meant to be useful for thinking about the current state of the discipline.

The first view, that "economics" is the new and "political economy" the old name, is probably the most common. It is also the least helpful and, understandably, is held by those not personally interested in political economy. It nonetheless contains an important measure of truth. The first economists did use "political economy" as an all-encompassing reference to their discipline, and "economics" is similarly used today. This usage introduces some bias against political economy, and thereby tends to preclude even considering it as one of an increasing number of fields within economics. This bias remains dominant, as can be seen from the absence of "political economy" from the American Economic Association's subject classification system for articles and abstracts. The term has gone from the all-inclusive name of the discipline to one without official recognition even as a subdivision of economics.

Economists in the first group accept Robbins' definition of economics with its emphasis on science. They suggest that improvements are steadily being made in our understanding of the economic universe, through the use of scientific methods. The concept of scientific investigation reflected in this view asserts that economics can be divided into two nonintersecting parts, positive and normative; and that the positive is the only legitimate area of study for an economist qua economist. They argue for a value-free economics and tend to emulate the physical sciences (albeit, as critics suggest, in their nineteenth-century mechanistic and deterministic phase). This emulation leads to the use of mathematics and statistics as tools to discover the characteristics of the economic universe.

I shall refer to individuals in this group as Type I economists and what they practice as Type I economics. One might prefer to call them scientific or technical economists but doing so would introduce the unnecessary bias of suggesting that all others are unscientific and therefore inferior, and the additional problem of defining what we mean by "technical" or "scientific." "Modern" is likewise not a suitable adjective; so I fall back on a numbering system.

The second way of distinguishing economics and political economy—call it Type II economics—is also rooted in history. As noted in the earlier discussion of Steuart and Smith, economics comes from the Greek word *oikonomia*, which meant "household or domestic management" and included the "art of acquisition" as required by someone managing a household. In the seventeenth and eighteenth centuries scholarly attention increasingly focused on the best economic policies for the nation-state. To differentiate between management of the polis and management of the household, "political" was added to "economy" to yield "political economy."

The presence of the word "nations" in the title of Smith's *Wealth of Nations* reflects his central interest in national economic issues. He held economic growth to be good, discussed various kinds of economic policies, and advocated those he thought would best achieve certain objectives such as national opulence. Political economy, as the title for the emerging discipline, throughout most of the nineteenth century included within its purview the application of economic analysis to questions of economic policy. No separation between positive and normative was elaborated, and some economists thought it their responsibility to discover and apply immutable economic laws in the development of wise economic policy. Although Mill and Sidgwick begin to distinguish the science and the art of political economy, it is Marshall who develops the distinction between economics as a positive science that develops and tests hypotheses and political economy as the development of principles of economic policy.

Many Type II economists are interested in both macro and micro issues of national economic policy, and the term "political economy" is increasingly used in studies of international economic relationships and the problems of less developed and underdeveloped countries. Most of these studies emphasize the interaction of state and market. They suggest that the ideal worlds of the economists (particularly the concept of self-regulating markets) and also of certain political scientists provide an inadequate account of the real world. A more integrated approach is required, within which the latest techniques and understandings generated by positive economics can be used and even developed further in their various applications. For this type of economist, economics appears useful chiefly for its contribution to the solution of social problems. Type II economists do not denigrate positive economics (in fact they often contribute to its development), but they seem not to accept such a complete demarcation between positive and normative economics as Type I economists do. The Type II attitudes are captured, for example, in a recent article on political economy by Peacock, in which he states: "By making reference to welfare and policy questions as well as to analytical issues this paper is best described as an exercise in political economy."[21]

If Type I economists may be roughly characterized as interested in pushing back the frontiers of knowledge in certain technical areas, Type II economists may be characterized, equally roughly, as interested in applying such knowledge to address a wide variety of societal problems. Some economists fall into both classifications in different aspects of their work.

Most economists practicing today probably fall into either the Type I or Type II classification. Those of Type II would be more comfortable with the use of the term "political economy" to describe their work, although in fact not many actively use the term. The most frequent users of the term "political economy" are found in the two other categories. These categories are difficult to separate, and one could argue, with some merit, that they are simply variants of a single classification; but I prefer to treat them as two separate groups. An important aspect of both (and a factor that argues for considering them a single group) is their critical stance toward the methodology, technical achievements, and content of much Type I economics. What separates these two groups is their ideological presuppositions. For Type III I take as representative the founders of the Union for Radical Political Economy and for Type IV those associated with public choice economics. Each group frequently uses the term "political economy" to describe its work.

Type III economists consider themselves to be outside the mainstream of economics. In addition to denigrating the technical virtuosity and the technical advances claimed by Type I economists, they suggest that the positive-normative dichotomy is false or counterproductive and that value-free economic analysis is not possible. They think that, despite claims to deal only with positive issues, the work of Type I economists is suffused with normative assumptions and political premises.[22] Type III economists tend to view much modern economic analysis and many policy recommendations as reflecting the values or interests of the economically and politically dominant segments of society. Although such notions might be held by scholars across the entire political spectrum from left to right, in fact the dominant ideology in this group seems to occupy the fringes of the ideological distribution.

The very title of the Union for Radical Political Economy (URPE) suggests that its founders consider political economy to include more than a body of knowledge and a set of techniques—more than the technical economics with which Type I economists concern themselves. Political economy is thought to include a point of view, a set of explicitly stated and invoked values, an ideology. These economists come together at URPE for mutual support and to advance their cause under the banner of a political economy that they choose to call radical. URPE was founded in the 1960s, when some economists thought their profession was unwilling and its tools inadequate to address what they considered to be the important economic issues of the day. In their journal, the *Review of Radical Political Economics* (*RRPE*), the following advice is offered to anyone wishing to submit a paper:

> *RRPE* encourages articles from all perspectives within a broad definition of radical political economics. A non-exclusive list in this tradition includes: Marxism, Institutionalism, the Cambridge approach, Patriarchy, Social Democracy, Anarchy, Feminism, and Trotskyism. If any article is written in this general framework, the editors of *RRPE* are committed to *judging it on its merits and scholarship, not in terms of the political point-of-view of the author(s). Information and procedures for appeals regarding evaluations of articles are available from the Managing Editor.*[23]

This statement reflects the view among URPE economists that articles submitted to other journals are often rejected, not because they are technically incompetent (that is, not on their technical merits), but because of the political point of view represented. That these articles probably do reflect political views at variance with those held by many Type I and II economists is suggested by the list of perspectives that are explicitly encouraged, and by the following excerpt from the instructions to authors submitting articles to *RRPE:* "The *Review of Radical Political Economics* publishes original articles and book reviews that contribute to the development of a radical political economic analysis of society and *assist individuals and groups working for a radical change in American society.*"[24] It is reasonable to conclude from these two quotations that URPE and *RRPE* work within a self-imposed set of political points of view. Within this set, articles submitted for publication are to be judged on their technical and scientific merits. This policy provides a publishing outlet for individuals who hold normative views at variance with those espoused by the dominant professional journals, and discriminated against by the economists who control those journals. The members of URPE did not attempt to establish a publishing outlet for all types of political economy, but only for what they call "radical political economy." They see themselves as providing a counterweight to what they think is presented elsewhere. They suggest that political economy should combine positive and normative analysis, as theirs surely does, but they oppose what they consider to be discrimination against the values they hold.

A strong Marxian or neo-Marxian influence runs through the URPE literature. One can gain some additional understanding of Type III economics by examining several entries in *A Dictionary of Marxist Thought*. The entry for "political economy," for example, contains the following:

> A term often used synonymously with economics. . . . Its more specific meaning in a Marxist context relates to the corpus of work . . . of Adam Smith, Ricardo, James and J. S. Mill, and McCulloch, Senior. Marx himself drew a sharp distinction between scientific political economy (Adam Smith and Ricardo, but mainly the latter . . .), and vulgar economics which developed after 1830 (see VULGAR ECONOMICS).[25]

Turning to the entry for "vulgar economics" we find:

> An epithet chosen by Marx to characterize post-Ricardian economics. The word has since been used as a portmanteau expression by Marxist writers to cover post-Ricardian classical economics and neo-classical economics. Vulgar economics refers in particular to writings which concentrate on an analysis of *surface phenomena*, e.g., demand and supply, to the neglect of structural *value* relations, and also analysis which is *reluctant to inquire into economic relationships in a disinterested scientific manner*, and especially afraid to probe into the class relations underlying commodity transactions.[26]

The entry for "economics" simply says "see POLITICAL ECONOMY."

The final category of economics and economists, Type IV, can be considered more or less as a subgroup of those economists who emphasize the economic approach to human behavior rather than the scope of economics. Although the range of topics examined by such economists as a group is wide, our interest is in those who use the economic approach to examine political things.

Among the several representatives of this group whose work we could sample to define the characteristics of Type IV, probably the best known are Buchanan and Tullock. They have conveniently provided a capsule summary of their work in the preface to their book *The Calculus of Consent:*

> This is a book about the *political* organization of a society of free men. Its methodology, its conceptual approaches, and its analytics are derived essentially from the discipline that has as its subject the *economic* organization of such a society. Students and scholars in *politics* will share with us an interest in the central problems under consideration.

Their colleagues in *economics* will share with us an interest in the construction of the argument. This work lies squarely along that mythical and mystical borderline between the two prodigal offsprings of political economy.[27]

The authors clearly intend to apply the economic approach to political topics, specifically to the issue of political organization. Although they speak of a borderline between politics and economics, a better metaphor might be an area rather than a line: the topical intersection of economics and politics.

Buchanan and Tullock developed a field within economics called "public choice" which, as with URPE, has its own journal, the *Journal of Non-Market Decision Making*. Mueller defines public choice as the "economic study of non-market decisionmaking, or simply the application of economics to political science." He goes on to assert that the subject matter of public choice is the same as that of political science, namely,

> the theory of the state, voting rules, voter behavior, party politics, the bureaucracy, and so on. The methodology of public choice is that of economics . . . the basic behavior postulates . . . [being] that man is an egoistic, rational, utility maximizer. This places public choice within the stream of political philosophy extending at least from Thomas Hobbes and Benedict Spinoza, and within political science from James Madison and Alexis de Tocqueville.[28]

In Mueller's view, public choice evolved from two separate forces: an interest in the possibility of developing social welfare or choice functions; and an interest in market failures, particularly in problems associated with collective goods and externalities. Much of the historic content of these two interests is related to the perceived failure of self-regulating competitive markets to generate a desirable solution to both the production and the distribution of goods and services. Of course, to specify what is desirable in both production and distribution (but especially the latter) involves value judgments and leads to normative economics. The movement from the old to the new welfare economics, influenced by positivism, attempted to minimize the extent of this normative exercise and thus eventually invoked what are now called the Pareto criteria. Nevertheless, it should be emphasized, the exercise was undertaken.[29] Similar criteria were invoked for other issues like pollution and so-called market failure. Many such failures were attributed to the absence of clearly defined or assigned property rights—a political omission; once this omission was remedied, regardless of to whom property rights were given, a Pareto optimum could be reached (as is illustrated by the now famous Coase Theorem). A frequent topic, then, in the public choice literature is how changes in political institutions might remedy or ameliorate market failures. Such analysis is often conducted by applying techniques associated with the economic approach to questions of how the structure of political institutions may be changed to obtain different results from those encouraged by existing institutions.

One aspect of how the economic approach to human behavior was applied in the public choice literature might be told as follows. Once upon a time two separate disciplines existed, economics and political science. Economics concerned itself with one set of topics (those captured by the definitions of Marshall and Robbins) and political science with another. As the economic approach to human behavior became more fully developed, this barrier or topical demarcation became increasingly artificial and began to fall. In this narrative, economists like Buchanan and Tullock are contentious—disciplinary imperialists, invading others' territory for their own discipline's gain. However one views these transdisciplinary issues, one must recognize that the nature of political economy, as reflected in the public choice literature and as influenced by the economic approach to human behavior, contains an integrating element, implicit in public choice's premise that economic man and political man are not different persons, and are not portions of the same person responsible for achieving different kinds of objectives. Rather, they are the same person concerned with achieving what that person considers to be the good. This good contains elements that have of late been considered separable into two sets, political and economic; but, even if not often inextricably linked together, they can nonetheless be analyzed with a common approach.

Political Philosophy, Economics, and Political Economy

So far I have presented a brief history of how the name of a discipline changed from political economy to economics, but I have noted several ways in which the term "political economy" continues to be used. This final section examines some commonalities in current usage and develops a characterization of political economy that, though grounded in current usage, admittedly includes some of my own idiosyncratic views.

Our search for commonalities is centered on Types II, III, and IV, whose representatives actively use the term and display a common interest in exploring the interplay between political and economic factors. For Type II economists this interest expresses itself primarily in the study of national and international economic policy, with attention given to institutional factors in general and political factors in particular. Type III economists extend this interest to the study of how economic forces affect social order, political governance, and the distribution of power and economic well-being, often with the critical assertion that most modern economics is little more than apologetics for the current political structure. Type IV economists seek to apply what we have called the economic approach to a wide range of topics; of particular interest for this chapter is the application to topics traditionally considered to be within the purview of politics.

All three groups recognize that, although politics and economics provide alternative means of solving what is often called the economic problem (after Robbins' definition of economics as the study of the resolution of conflicts over scarce resources), even so-called efficient solutions require their joint efforts. Finally, a greater proportion of economists in these three groups than in Type I consider the positivist separation of fact and value an open question; consequently they remain more open in their ways of addressing this alleged separation. They are less concerned with trying to eliminate all evaluative discourse from their work and thus trying to separate descriptive and prescriptive analysis. This stand is not surprising, given their strong interest in economic policy, much of which aims at the improvement of the general welfare (somehow defined), and in the role that political and other institutions do (and should?) play in the development and execution of such policy.

Until the past two decades, the predominant view of political economy could be most easily understood from the perspective of definitions of economics like Marshall's and Robbins'—which emphasize the scope of economics as compared to the economic approach. From this perspective, economics is a science that studies the production and distribution of goods and services and answers the questions of what, how, and for whom things are produced. The mechanisms for accomplishing these functions are markets, ideally based upon voluntary exchange, but often found in less than ideal condition. Politics in this view treats such topics as the origin of states, the nature of government, the development of law, and distributions based upon authority and power. These two topical areas can be visualized as a Venn diagram that depicts economics as one set of topics and politics as another. In so far as the two sets contain common elements, they intersect in an area named political economy.

This visualization of political economy's topical domain rests on too simple an assumption: a degree of topical independence that excludes the mutual influence of politics and economics. This mutual influence may be visualized as creating an independent set of topics, or it may be depicted by flow charts and feedback diagrams rather than sets in a Venn diagram. However depicted, political economy studies how voluntary exchange systems interact with, influence, and are influenced by political systems that require the exercise of authority and power. Some may think the intersection and interaction small, others large. If large, then political economy may be important; if small, then it might more easily be ignored (or at least not given a separate classification in the publications of official journals).

These observations encourage me to extend this characterization of political economy along lines suggested by a specific view of its origins, by reflection on an appropriate methodology, and by awareness of continuing problems with its positive and normative content. The specific view regarding the origins of political economy is succinctly expressed in Cropsey's observation that "for twenty centuries there was but one social science, namely, political philosophy" and that the birth of political economy was an act of separation from the hegemony of political philosophy.[30] It follows from our preceding characterization of political economy that many think this separation has gone too far, at least for certain topics, and that some topics would benefit from a more integrated approach. This integration could be facilitated by using the methodology of the economic approach to study human behavior. This approach rejects the view that one methodology is suitable for studying one aspect of human behavior and another methodology is suitable for studying another. Rather, it claims to be robust enough to apply a single methodology to several aspects of human behavior. It is reluctant to separate economic man from political man and hence to view economics and politics as representing two separate sets of knowledge with at most some common elements. It considers problematic the ability to draw disciplinary lines, or to set one domain of knowledge against another. The economic approach is an integrating force, a force that might almost return us to the pre-Smithian situation of one economic-social-political discipline.

Embodied within some of what is called political economy today is a return to a more integrated stance toward issues that combine political and economic matters. Political economy thus characterized, it seems, has closer ties to political philosophy. But this connection involves difficulties of the sort that led before to the relative demise of political economy—the issue of positive versus normative economics or, more broadly, the fact/value problem. The division between positive and normative, description and prescription, was far from neat in Smith's time, not only because such distinctions had not yet been so well developed, but also, and perhaps more importantly, because the tradition of political philosophy out of which political economy came was openly and chiefly concerned with the values that define a good society. The conflation of positive and normative in the early period of political economy can be partially explained, therefore, by characterizing political philosophy's objective as the "attempt truly to know both the nature of political things and the right, or the good, political order."[31] If this description of political philosophy is correct, then the tradition out of which political economy arose was seeking to discover the nature of the good society and made no distinction between facts and values.

This tradition in the background of political economy raises the difficult issue of what political economy should encompass. Clearly, some who use the term "political economy" do not accept a complete separation of positive and normative; hence they conjoin fact and value in their work. This is true certainly for Type III economists, but also, admittedly to a significantly lesser degree, for many other economists. Take, for example, a problem much discussed a few years ago on the question of how market capitalism is to be evaluated when the criteria are equality and efficiency.[32] Most of the best-selling microeconomic textbooks make the case for market capitalism on grounds of efficiency. Such expositions, however, often leave unstated their adherence to the principle of individualism (that is, that only individual values or utility functions matter); to private property; to a negative, as opposed to a positive, concept of (economic) freedom; and to a value-added (ethical) theory of distribution. These four items reflect or embody certain values, albeit (as many practicing economists would emphasize) widely shared ones. Such values are suffused throughout much Type I economics, but they come more readily and openly to the surface in the various forms of political economy.

To indicate that many textbooks omit explicit discussions of assumed values is not to prove that they should include such analysis, although intellectual honesty requires that all assumptions be clearly stated somewhere in the analysis. Furthermore, insofar as particular economic behavior occurs within a society where the unstated values prevail, the analysis of that behavior might be presented within an if-then framework—if we assume these values, then we shall obtain this result. Although this is not "science," from which all so-called philosophical topics have been removed, it is scientific analysis established on a particular foundation. What political economists tend to engage in is examinations of these and alternative foundations. Such examinations do not often emphasize the question of how economic things are produced—the question of efficiency—although this is important to them; more often they dwell upon the distribution of such things—the question of distributive justice. We are again led back to the interaction between political and economic things, between state and market, between power and voluntary exchange.

And so our extension of the initial characterization of political economy, as dealing with the interaction of political and economic things when the questions are asked of what, how, and for whom economic things exist, arrives at the assertion that political economy is also that area within economics that overtly addresses normative issues. This does not imply that political economy is a medium for advocacy of certain economic institutions or policies, but rather that it is a medium where the political, ethical, and economic aspects of problems are examined. It is that part of economics that maintains its connection with its roots in political philosophy while using the analytical and empirical advances that its past separation from its roots enabled it to accomplish. Political economy straddles two domains— firmly, we hope, but with an awareness of the problems that straddling these domains might pose for its balance.

Five   Steven E. Rhoads

Economists on Tastes and Preferences

Mainstream economists usually assume that tastes and preferences are "given"—that they are primary and stable—and that individuals in their actions seek to further their ends. Furthermore, they assume that all this is as it should be.[1] Societal welfare is seen as dependent on individuals' subjective sense of satisfaction, and that satisfaction is thought to be best achieved by letting individuals' preferences determine the use of societal resources. As E. J. Mishan has said, "All . . . the economic data used in a cost-benefit analysis, or any other allocative study, . . . is based on this principle of accepting as final only the individual's estimate of what a thing is worth to him at the time the decision is to be made."[2] Moreover, consumers not only know what they want, they should get what they want. In William Baumol's words, "It is essential . . . that the pattern of public intervention be designed very explicitly in terms of the desires of the public."[3]

If one wants a world in which consumers are sovereign, two general goals follow. The first is economic efficiency, which allocates society's scarce resources according to the willingness of consumers to pay. The second is equity: some societal decisions must be made about whose preferences should count the most or, alternatively, about the initial distribution of dollar votes.

This chapter seeks to raise doubts about the treatment of tastes and preferences that underlies this consumer-determined approach to public policy. The first sections raise general questions about economists' approaches to consumer information, to taste changes, to revealed preferences, and to individual preferences that affect many others in a society. The next sections discuss two policy areas, poverty and higher education, where economists' assumptions about tastes and preferences make systematic, balanced policy analysis impossible. I have elsewhere argued,[4] and still believe, that despite their proclaimed neutrality about tastes and preferences, in practice many economists give unbalanced emphasis to the importance of money as both a controlling motive and a route to happiness. This chapter sets that issue aside and examines issues that arise even if economists are neutral in their treatment of particular tastes and preferences.

Informed Consumers?

Economists tend to emphasize the many ways that markets provide information to consumers—not just through advertising but also through brand names or the presence of items in "quality" stores. They acknowledge, however, that information is a public, collective-consumption good and thus markets will not handle it optimally. If consumer groups develop a price index that rates supermarkets on their overall prices, they cannot sell this information at its full value. Many who value the information will not pay for it because they can obtain it free from others. Similarly, many who consult *Consumer Reports* when making a major purchase have never subscribed to the magazine. This helps explain why, for almost all product lines, *Consumer Reports* can test only some of the models available. Because information is a public good, a case can be made for government testing agencies, for government provision of information, and for required disclosure of certain product characteristics.

Despite a growing theoretical literature on the economics of information, economists have provided little useful advice on the host of controversies over government information policy in recent years (such as sodium labeling on food, or advisory inserts in prescription drugs).[5] I believe that economists are reticent on such controversies because advice is often impossible without abandoning neutrality and making judgments about tastes and preferences. Whether one thinks consumers are adequately informed about some aspects of their lives depends on what one thinks should be important to a thoughtful consumer. How important is the free-rider problem, which makes it hard to make a profit on the sale of lists comparing grocery store prices on a whole range of items? Much depends on how important money is to human happiness. If money is crucial to happiness, then perhaps government should provide comparative price information for consumers. If money is not so important, and if the real cause of the information problem is the market's overemphasis on money and goods, then such a price list might only encourage consumers to place still more emphasis on purchased goods as the source of happiness.

What should one conclude about the unwillingness of consumers to wear seat belts? By now most drivers should know that they are safer in a seat belt, so perhaps government's information role can be abandoned. But perhaps people do not really know how much safer they are with seat belts and how high the costs of accidents are; perhaps they will not really understand until they are forced to see films that show the blood and broken bones, and the grief-stricken families. Alternatively, if people fail to wear seatbelts because the desire for convenience overwhelms their better judgment, one might favor mandatory air bags in all cars. In the final analysis, an issue like seat belts versus air bags forces a judgment about how important a fear of violent death in an automobile should be to a thoughtful individual.

Most economists want no part of such questions. They point out that it costs time and money to produce and consume information, and thus the "optimally" informed consumer will never be perfectly informed. They tend to assume complacently that consumers are for the most part informed adequately—well enough to be able to decide rationally for themselves what decisions are likely to increase their welfare.

Kenneth Arrow points out that considerable evidence from psychology and other fields calls into question his discipline's assumptions about consumer rationality. For example, even though the monetary stakes were large, very few citizens took the government up on its 1969 offer of flood insurance at rates well below their actuarial value. A careful study found no reason for the lack of interest that would be consistent with the usual explanations of economic rationality.[6]

Most economists would probably be surprised by these findings. They are not likely to be surprised, however, by the extent of citizens' ignorance about public affairs. For example, in April 1986, only 38 percent of Americans knew that the U.S. government was supporting the Contras and not the Sandinista government in Nicaragua.[7] In 1980, 52 percent said that a nuclear power plant could explode and cause a mushroom-shaped cloud; another 16 percent were not sure.[8] Economists argue, in fact, that a typical voter has little interest in studying how he would be affected by a policy proposal. More information on that issue will probably not lead the voter to change his mind about which candidate to vote for if they differ on many other issues as well. Moreover, his single vote and campaigning almost certainly will not decide the election, nor will his representative's vote often be decisive in the legislature.

Pessimism about consumers' and citizens' knowledge of public issues does not, however, lead most economists to abandon the consumer sovereignty standard for public affairs. Both benefit-cost and public choice economists seem to believe that citizens' views on public policy should be decisive, and thus that a democratic representative should be a clerklike aggregator of consumers' preferences. Such a public philosophy dramatically compounds the risks posed by the political ignorance of ordinary citizens. Why not, instead, have representatives' judgment be decisive where citizen knowledge and interest is low? If consumers are asked how much they would pay for more frequent trash collection, they can easily visualize what is at issue, and their preferences should carry great weight with representatives. Their preferences about a new missile system are likely to be less informed and more dependent on arbitrary changes in media coverage. Representatives should consequently be less bound by estimates of benefits that rely on such preferences.

The classic controversy in the literature on representation pits those who see representatives as delegates, mere agents, against those who see them as independent trustees.[9] Economists writing on representation often give no sign that they know of the controversy. For James Miller the "ideal of representation" demands instant recall;[10] for Amacher and Boyes "less responsive" equals "less representative."[11] Economists writing in the benefit-cost literature seem to agree. For example, Thomas Schelling has said that consumer sovereignty in public policy is derivable from the principle "No taxation without representation."[12] Economists claim to speak for the people; but the people themselves are not sure that they want to govern directly. When asked if members of Congress should follow their own best judgment or the feeling and opinions of their district, the public is very closely divided. Sometimes the trustee view commands a majority; sometimes the delegate view predominates.[13]

Changing Tastes

A small mainstream economic literature treats the problem of changing tastes. An early article by Sidney Schoeffler acknowledges that when tastes change, economics can say nothing about whether consumer sovereignty achieves a higher level of well-being with the first set of tastes or with the second. Schoeffler also acknowledges that tastes change all the time since "any given governmental action or policy tends to remold the preference maps of the individuals in society." He asks biologists for help. An "absolute ordering would very likely have to be derived from *physiological* measurements of some sort, possibly, for example, from the 'size' of chemical disequilibrium within the body of the person. We have no choice but to await the future findings of biological science on this point."[14]

With regard to changing tastes, the approach that has gained the most recent support among economists solves the problem by defining it away. Kelvin Lancaster argues that utility is derived from the characteristics of goods, not from the goods themselves:

> In this model, the whole process is extraordinarily simple. A new product simply means addition of one or more activities to the consumption technology. Given the technology (or the relevant portion of it) and given the intrinsic characteristic of the activity associated with the new good, we simply insert it in the technology, *and we can predict* the consequences.

Lancaster goes on to state that when a consumer replaces an old good with a new one, a welfare improvement occurs because the consumer can now more efficiently "reach his preferred combination of characteristics."[15]

Lancaster provides no illustrations of how his model might be used to make predictions, and if one tries to make such predictions, it is easy to see why. Where does a personal computer fit into the "consumption technology?" What is the "intrinsic characteristic" of the activity associated with it? Many consumers might buy a computer primarily for the video games. Some of these consumers might see it as preferable to Monopoly, others to a stereo, still others to the movies. A different set of consumers might see the computer as an educational device for their children, whereas a third set might see the computer as an improved filing cabinet. All of these consumers would define differently the characteristic that the computer adds.

Lancaster deals with the inconveniences of changing tastes by defining them away; George Stigler and Gary Becker go one step further. They believe that both assumptions about changes in tastes within individuals and assumptions about differences in tastes between individuals "have been a convenient crutch to lean on when the analysis has bogged down. They give the appearance of considered judgment, yet really have only been ad hoc arguments that disguise analytical failures."[16] Stigler and Becker recommend that economists assume not only stable tastes within people but similar tastes between people, regardless of their cultures. Becker explains:

> In the standard theory all consumers behave similarly in the sense that they all maximize the same thing—utility or satisfaction. It is only a further extension then to argue that they all derive that utility from the same "basic pleasures" or preference function, and differ only in their ability to produce these "pleasures." From this point of view, the Latin expression *de gustibus non est disputandum* suggests not so much that it is impossible to resolve disputes arising from differences in tastes but rather that in fact no such disputes arise![17]

The Becker approach is a little more plausible than it sounds. For example, it may be helpful to see that the young in developing countries may be more willing than older people to "invest in capital attuned to the new environment"[18] because, even if their preferences and motives are identical to those of older people in their country, they have more to gain and they have less investment in capital attuned to the old environment. But in the same week that I read Becker, my *Washington Post* spoke of men and boys surrounding a corpse in a suffocatingly hot little room in Tehran: "'There is only one God,' they intoned beating their chests loudly with the flat of the hand. 'You will now go to heaven. For every one who falls, 10 more martyrs will rise up to go to the war.'"[19] Not much of this goes on in Charlottesville, Virginia. Becker would no doubt argue that more of it now goes on in Tehran than before because the costs of not participating have risen dramatically. Fair enough, but have not many preferences changed also? Would not much of the new religious fervor remain even if the Shah's family returned to power? What cost changes could explain why some people exchange the bottle for the Bible in the United States? And if we all have similar tastes, why do some people make this exchange whereas others similarly situated do not? After passage of the fair accommodations law in the 1960s many whites in the South ate in restaurants with blacks because the costs of not doing so had changed, not because their preferences had. But many have seen their preferences gradually change, too. Many whites would now say that they used to have a strong aversion to eating with blacks, but they no longer do.

Ronald Reagan's conversion from liberal Democrat to conservative Republican is just one of the latest of the changes in tastes and preference that have altered human history. Becker believes his approach yields more falsifiable predictions about human behavior; and it may. But when he states that tastes do not change and that when they seem to change, the "global" goods of "envy, prestige, physical and psychological health . . . and so on"[20] remain the same, he is putting forward a proposition that no empirical work is ever likely to verify. In any case, the demands of scientific method should not determine the conclusions we are allowed to reach about the way the world works, since good politics often requires action on the basis of evidence that does not meet such demands.

The mainstream economic literature today interprets all events in the world in a way that does not threaten the fundamental assumptions of economics. Thus the typical economist is quick to say that what appears to be a change in a person's tastes may just be a shift toward the purchase of a new product that better suits his unchanged, fundamental preferences. If a person frequently purchasing product A suddenly stops and begins frequently purchasing old product B instead (religious literature instead of liquor, for example), economists argue that he now has more information and experience and thus can more "accurately" order his purchases "in accordance with unchanged underlying propensities."[21]

Schoeffler seems complacent when he disposes of the thorny issues by expecting the biologists to find a chemical panacea. Becker seems even more complacent when he suggests that if genetic natural selection and rational behavior reinforce each other, "in the very long run, perhaps those preferences survive which are most suited to satisfaction given the broad technological constraints of human society (e.g., physical size, mental ability, etcetera)."[22] No need to wait to discover our chemical nirvana. It is here. What is, is best.

Which Preferences?

Socrates saw powerful bodily desires at war with reason in the souls of most humans. In the well-ordered soul, the spirited part, the home of anger and shame, helped reason gain control over animal passions so that man could know the higher, uniquely human pleasures.[23]

Social scientists today are likely to find this view quaint and archaic. But if you substitute mind for soul, some elements of it become perfectly compatible with the latest scientific research. Robert Jastrow puts it this way:

> It is as if two mentalities resided in the same body. One mentality is ruled by emotional states that have evolved as a part of age-old programs for survival, and the seat of this mentality is in the old-mammal centers of the brain, beneath the cerebral cortex. The other mentality is ruled by reason, and resides in the cerebral cortex. . . .
>
> In man, the cerebral cortex, or new brain, is usually master over the old brain; its instructions can override the strongest instincts toward eating, procreation or flight from danger. But the reptile and the old mammal still lie within us; sometimes they work with the highest centers of the brain, and sometimes against them; and now and then, when there is competition between the two mentalities, and the discipline of reason momentarily weakens, they spring out and take command.[24]

Applied economists usually assume that we have a single, integrated set of preferences about private and public goods and that it is found most accurately by examining decisions made in the marketplace. But brain research aside, we often do seem to be at war with ourselves; and when we reflect on the conflict, we usually decide that reasoned resolution is our better half and the temptations of appetite or animal passion the worse. Our better half may sometimes side with the higher passions: it may tell us to act out of love or compassion rather than selfish calculation. But since our reflective selves approve of many such acts, they merely show that reason may be more than narrow calculation.

Many who regularly indulge themselves with food, alcohol, cigarettes, drugs, gambling, incest, prostitution, or pornography hate themselves for doing so and would love to be able to stop. For these people there is no reason to think that some kinds of outside intervention would violate consumer sovereignty if the relevant consumer is the reflective, higher side. One father who carried on an incestuous relationship with his daughter for two years said, "I knew it was wrong. When I was finished, I hated myself. I said I would never do it again, but I had no will power."[25] Cigarette smoking is a less dramatic vice, but most of its practitioners clearly see it as a vice. Surveys in England and the United States show that a majority of smokers have tried to stop.[26] An informal survey I conducted as a graduate student showed that most would not mind some financial penalty to encourage them to stop. I asked fifty smokers (in Ithaca and Philadelphia) the following question:

> If it were determined that the Federal Government had to raise a certain amount of revenue, and the choice was between raising the income tax or raising the cigarette tax, and either increase would bring in the same amount of total revenue from the population as a whole, which tax would you prefer to be raised?

Thirty of the smokers preferred to raise the cigarette tax, eleven the income tax, and nine had no preference. Among the twenty-two heavy smokers (those smoking more than ten packs per week), eleven chose the cigarette tax, eight the income tax, and three had no preference. Ten of the cigarette-tax supporters volunteered some reasons, and they are revealing. Four said that if cigarettes are taxed, "then I'll quit" or "people will quit." The other six made comments like the following: "It's a habit I can do without. It won't hurt to cut down." "You don't have to pay." "You always contemplate that you will stop." "It's my fault; I might stop."[27]

We also seem to regret our susceptibility to the allure of material goods. Eighty-four percent of Americans believe that most people "buy a lot more than they need," and 49 percent believe that they themselves do. By 76 to 17 percent, a sizable majority would stress "learning to get our pleasure out of nonmaterial experiences" rather than "satisfying our needs for more goods and services."[28]

The term "self-satisfied" is one of reproach. Many people, and most of those we admire, are not entirely happy with the preferences they reveal through their behavior. They aspire to be better friends, better parents, better teachers. They want to improve themselves in various ways, from losing weight to spending more time reading or traveling instead of watching television. The average American spends almost ninety minutes a day watching television. But surveys of viewers show that many are bored. The author of one of the surveys calls a large minority of viewers "compulsive." Viewers were asked, "When you're watching T.V. do you ever feel you'd rather do something else but just can't tear yourself away?" and "About how often do you feel that way?" Twenty-four percent answered "Occasionally"; another 12.5 percent answered "Almost always."[29]

Many of us wish that we had different tastes. We make remarks such as "I wish I could appreciate classical music," or "I wish I could learn to like Shakespeare." The word "learn" is significant. When we make such statements, we usually think that we could come to appreciate the activity if we knew more about it. We may have a friend who likes classical music. We readily acknowledge that she knows more about music than we do and that this is at least part of the reason she likes it more. She as quickly acknowledges that someone else knows more than she. This sort of agreement comes about because when two people listen to music or discuss a book, it is sometimes clear to one of them that the other sees or hears things that he misses. It is commonly assumed that greater knowledge makes possible greater appreciation and pleasure.

This section has argued that a person's behavior does not necessarily indicate his preferences if "preferences" means what he thinks is best for himself or what he thinks will maximize his well-being. Behavior seen in the market may be even further removed from what the person believes is best for the community. Many voters vote against their financial self-interest. There are also reported cases such as that of a union member who did not like to go to dances with blacks but thought nonetheless that all union members, including blacks, should be invited to the union's dances.[30] There no doubt are people who purchase liquor, pornography, or the services of prostitutes, but who think that the community, if not they themselves, would be better off if those products and services were not available. They may vote against their local availability. Though a strong proponent of markets, James Buchanan has nonetheless acknowledged that

> the sense of participation in social choice may exert important effects on the behavior of the individual. It seems probable that the representative individual will act in accordance with a different preference scale when he realizes that he is choosing for the group rather than merely for himself. . . . His identification will tend to be broadened, and his "values" will be more likely to influence his ordering of alternatives, whereas in market choice his "tastes" may determine his decision.[31]

If we want to learn about people's views on public policy, we may have to look to voting or to polls rather than deduce values from market analogues of public goods. Economists, however, have a strong preference for the market analogue. Though in theoretical discussions one sometimes finds an acknowledgment such as Buchanan's,[32] Amartya Sen is correct when he says that "much of the empirical work on preference patterns seems to be based on the conviction that behavior is the only source of information on a person's preferences."[33] Indeed, this bias is so great that when Freeman discusses polling approaches to environmental improvement benefits, he defines an "accurate response to a question about willingness to pay" as one that is "consistent with the underlying preference ordering or utility function and with the behavior that would be revealed if the public good could be ordered in a market where exclusion was possible."[34]

This bias can lead to serious mistakes in the treatment of preferences for goods where appetite fights reason. For example, economists' discussions of the cigarette tax often acknowledge that the tax is justified by the external financial costs, such as higher publicly subsidized medical costs and health insurance premiums, that result from cigarette smoking; but a tax as high as the present one may not be justified on externality grounds alone.[35] Thus the standard economic mode of analysis might see the present high tax as both discriminatory against smokers (many of whom are poor) and inefficient because of the high tax wedge driven between the costs of production and the market price. This wedge induces some consumers who would like to consume more cigarettes to shift instead some or all of their purchases to other, less pleasurable goods and services. However, polls showing that most smokers want to quit reveal that smokers tend to see their liking for cigarettes as coming from a part of them that they wish to tame. Moreover, my informal poll shows that by a margin of almost three to one, smokers like to be "discriminated" against with respect to their habit. Smokers do not mind higher cigarette taxes because they think they and others might be led to give up their compulsive habit.

Meddlesome, Illegitimate, and Publicly Beneficial Tastes

In their work, mainstream economists almost always take tastes and preferences as given and normatively compelling. A handful of economists have, however, worried about this practice. In his cost-benefit analysis text, E. J. Mishan argues in a note that envy and other interdependent psychic externalities (unpriced effects on third parties) that decrease a person's welfare should, on ethical grounds, be excluded from the calculus of social welfare.[36] In addition, Kenneth Arrow, Amartya Sen, and Leland Yeager all argue that we may want to preserve some sphere of personal liberty where the preferences of others are irrelevant.[37]

Two economists suggest focusing on externality cases where there has been an "absolute deterioration" in position "such as reduced incomes."[38] This is similar to Mishan's proposal that we look for a "palpable impact" on an individual's circumstances.[39] Both would agree with Friedrich Hayek's view that no account should be taken of psychic pain caused by "the mere dislike of what is being done by others."[40]

Some of the economists concerned about illegitimate tastes are quite prominent, but their views have had little effect on the work of their colleagues.[41] Most of the extensive commentary on Sen's argument has been critical. James Duesenberry and others consider that the existence of envy, or the psychic pain felt by the poor when the well-off consume more, argues in favor of the redistribution of income.[42] Even Mishan relegates his concerns about illegitimate tastes to a long note at the back of his text. In the text itself he presents a detailed methodology for valuing life that requires the analyst to take account of the preferences of those who might be financially or psychically worse off as more lives are saved.[43] For example, an analysis of a health program especially effective in reducing the risk of death for the elderly would add together the willingness to pay of the elderly themselves and that of their friends, their family, and kind-hearted members of the public at large—but would then subtract from this total the amount necessary to compensate any greedy heirs despondent over measures that lengthen the lives of their eventual benefactors. Similarly, Mishan's formula would ask analysts to take account of the costs to white racists of a program to combat sickle-cell anemia.

Presumably, the reason why Mishan ignores in the body of his text the views he expresses in his note at the end is that he believes his colleagues will not sit still for a cost-benefit text that rules out individuals' preferences on the basis of ethical criteria. Most economists hope to avoid the deepest, thorniest normative problems by preserving their neutrality toward tastes. They take tastes as they find them. The underlying belief seems to be that one can avoid controversial value judgments if one simply refuses to make value judgments. But one is hardly avoiding controversial value judgments if one states that lifesaving programs that are in the public interest from the point of view of all but certain heirs and racists cease to be in the public interest if those heirs and racists are sufficiently greedy or prejudiced. Perhaps some of the heirs and racists themselves would acknowledge that their gains from others' deaths should not influence a public policy that might lead to those deaths. For example, some people might believe that their material circumstances would improve if their rich uncles died, and yet not wish for them to die. And some who do wish that their rich uncles would die might quite consistently think that such wishes should not be entitled to public recognition.

Criminal justice programs provide another case in which the refusal to make value judgments is far more controversial than the value judgments that people typically make. A recent benefit-cost analysis of the Job Corps program considered the reduction in stolen property which resulted from the program as

> a benefit to those other than Corpsmembers, but part of its value should be viewed as a cost to Corpsmembers, who no longer receive the income from stealing. The social benefit of a reduction in stolen property (the difference between the Corpsmember's cost and everybody else's benefit) is the decrease in property value associated with the operations of fences, the damage to stolen property, and the loss of legal titles.[44]

In other words, it is only because stolen goods are "hot" or damaged and thus not worth as much to criminals as to victims that there are any societal costs at all from stolen property.[45]

The authors of the Job Corps study are not members of the Mafia. Other applied studies have treated this issue in the same way, and their methodology enjoys the support of some of the best economic theorists.[46] The applied methodologies are presented in a matter-of-fact manner without the slightest hint that they might be controversial. These economists are doing what they were taught to do: treat preferences in an "evenhanded," nonjudgmental manner. But most of the rest of the world will think that someone who tries to adopt a nonjudgmental, amoral perspective when looking at an immoral act necessarily becomes an accomplice to the crime. Jeffrey Sedgwick has noted the older term for a criminal: an outlaw; one who breaks the law puts himself outside the law and, for so long as he does so, outside society.[47] The gains to outlaws from their illicit activities can thus be safely ignored when judging society's welfare.

As noted above, some economists have suggested that the ethical dilemmas might be avoided if the profession focused only on "palpable impacts" such as reduced income. But note that the effects on the greedy heirs and the thieves deprived of their loot are quite palpable and income reducing, yet to count these effects would be quite controversial. Not to count some unpalpable, "merely" psychic external effects could be equally controversial.

If only a tangible cost to other humans can justify outlawing an activity, there can be no justification for the laws against cock and dog fights. A few states permit such fights, and in many more they are conducted illegally. For followers of dog fights there is even an underground newsletter, *Pit Dogs*. It keeps devotees up to date, with pictures and reports like the following:

> One hour and a half. Scout working a down dog for 15 minutes, occasionally stopping to lick, then going back to chewing Buck. Mike starts encouraging the dog to kill Buck. . . . Queenie's front legs gone now and her time to go, but she goes across like a dog should. . . . She reminds me of a seal walking, her front legs just flapping.[48]

The animal fights appeal to brutal passions, and one could argued that if these passions are encouraged, they may lead to brutality toward humans as well. But we should not have to show such an effect in order to ban these fights. It should be enough that we do not want our children raised in a society where one of the legal forms of entertainment is watching animals die painfully and unnecessarily. Even the psychic pain felt by adults from the knowledge that animals are being cruelly destroyed should be justification enough. Some of the least "palpable" externalities are felt by those possessing public-spirited, praiseworthy sentiments. They should be entitled to public recognition.

An earlier section argued that consumer information problems inevitably lead to the largest questions about human nature and the conditions for achieving happiness. Judgments about many externalities do so as well. If some people want to do what shocks others, one must decide if the latter are narrow-minded, meddlesome pests or farseeing defenders of civilization alert to the "slippery slope" of human degradation. A difficult balancing process is inevitable. We will want to preserve the right of individuals to a sphere of private action worthy of a freedom-loving nation, but we should not sanction tastes that threaten our humanity. As Joseph Cropsey has argued, consumer sovereignty, individualism, or the importance of each of us as a unique phenomenon cannot be the bulwark of human dignity. What dignifies human beings "proceeds from their common relation to nonhuman things. . . . Their dignity is the attribute of their common nature, of what they possess jointly, not severally, and it inheres in what elevates them above nonhumanity rather than in what merely distinguishes them from each other."[49]

American economists, like the rest of us, are democrats, and thus it is perhaps not surprising that they would be slow to condemn even the revolting tastes of any of the equal citizens among us. But why have they shown so little interest in finding ways to enhance and promote tastes that clearly yield beneficial externalities for the rest of us—higher ethical standards and law abidingness, greater goodwill and civility? There is evidence that good character is a far more effective cause of moral and law-abiding behavior than are financial or other types of legal incentives. Other evidence suggests that both good and bad behavior, volunteerism and vandalism, can mushroom and can become pervasive once they take hold in a community.[50] For example, at my son's public elementary school an initially small parent-teacher assistance program has mushroomed to the point where more than ten parents volunteer every week for each class of less than fifty students. One suburban mother of small children explains her volunteer work for my community's "Meals on Wheels" program as follows: "You get so attached to the people on your route. As soon as I started it, I got hooked. Now I really look forward to it." Another volunteer, seventy-four years old herself, says, "I have eighteen stops to make and everybody wants to talk. Often I'm the only person who stops by. If you could see how grateful they are, you'd know why I've been doing this for two years."[51]

More volunteers mean more public benefits can be secured without the inefficiency of bureaucracy and taxes. And if people get their pleasure from giving others pleasure, society obviously gains. If someone decides that he would rather volunteer than go to the movies, the economist must see both him and those assisted as better off—a clear Pareto improvement. The externality concept should in general make economists eager to support policies that seem likely to increase volunteerism—such as tax breaks, public-service television announcements, civic education in the schools, and government starter money for programs like "Meals on Wheels." Few people know of all the volunteer organizations in their community. Imaginative publicity about the accomplishments and pleasures of volunteerism might thus increase participation significantly.

Many of the older economists, such as J. S. Mill, Jeremy Bentham, and Alfred Marshall, were alert to the benefits of encouraging more public-regarding tastes. For example, though Bentham thought people always sought to maximize their personal satisfaction, he also thought they could be trained and educated to get the maximum satisfaction from helping others.[52] Marshall discussed the possibility of using awards such as knighthood and the Queen's Award to Industry to encourage the development of public-regarding behavior. He said, "No doubt men are capable of much more unselfish service than they generally render; and the supreme aim of the economist is to discover how this latent social asset can be developed more quickly and turned to account more wisely."[53]

One contemporary economist, Burton Weisbrod, argues that some utility (preference) functions may be superior to others on grounds of economic efficiency because they generate fewer external costs for others. Weisbrod notes that educational and religious efforts to shape preferences can thus be assessed within a conventional allocative efficiency framework.[54] Weisbrod's views are clearly atypical of the economics profession, and they have been largely ignored.

The nineteenth-century mainstream economists were not as wedded to models that assume people have fixed preferences and are motivated by narrow self-interest. I suspect that helps explain their greater willingness to consider such matters as less tangible externalities that in principle are important to the achievement of societal welfare, even as economists themselves envision it.

Tastes, Preferences, and Poverty

As mentioned at the start, economists see two general goals for government: first, to ensure that society's scarce resources are allocated in accordance with the consumers' willingness to pay; second, to ensure that all individuals have a fair share of income. Noneconomists who defined the poverty problem in the 1960s had many different things in mind; but economists, because of their belief in this normative framework, almost always had only one: the poor have too little income. James Tobin explains as follows:

> While concerned laymen who observe people with shabby housing or too little to eat instinctively want to provide them with decent housing and adequate food, economists instinctively want to provide them with more cash income. Then they can buy the housing and food if they want to, and if they choose not to, the presumption is that they have a better use for the money. To those who complain about the unequal distribution of shelter or of food, our first response . . . is that they should look at the distribution of wealth and income. If the social critics approve that distribution, then they should accept its implications, including the unequal distribution of specific commodities. If

they don't like it, then they should attack the generalized inequality rather than the specific inequality.[55]

In the 1960s economists lifted this outlook on poverty from their texts and used it as a guide to reform the antipoverty apparatus in Washington. They argued that there were too many discrete antipoverty programs, resulting in too much money going to white-collar professionals and too little to the poor. They argued further that the poor should be able to be sovereign too. Instead of building housing for the poor, why not let competitive market forces word for efficiency and allow some freedom of choice to consumers by providing housing vouchers instead? Better yet, why not allow for still more consumer choice by doing away with all in-kind programs such as housing and food, and just give the poor money?

Two decades ago the economist's outlook on poverty was quite influential. Prominent social scientists who were not economists, such as Daniel Patrick Moynihan and James Q. Wilson, joined the chorus of economists calling for a cash-based negative income tax. The housing programs were gradually transformed in the direction economists supported, and several experiments to test the negative income tax idea were launched.

Time has not been kind to the economists' prescriptions for the poverty problem. The negative income experiments showed that the guaranteed incomes led to greater reductions in work effort than many proponents had expected.[56] More surprising still, the economists, preparing to determine just how much guaranteed incomes for all would strengthen marital stability, found instead that they weakened marital stability. While these results were coming in, the poverty problem as noneconomists saw it—not just low income but crime, drugs, unwed motherhood, and dependency—got worse and worse.

Much current thinking about poverty directly contradicts core elements of the economic worldview by in effect asserting that tastes do change, and that the tastes of many in poverty should change because their current tastes and choices will not make them happy. This new element in thinking about poverty is perhaps seen most dramatically by looking at black thought on the subject. Jesse Jackson realizes that many of the young blacks he addresses see unwed parenthood as a source of pride and affection. He asks that they instead see "babies making babies" as both morally wrong and self-destructive. He asks further that they choose "hope not dope." Other leading black figures are trying to cultivate a taste for superior academic performance, which too many poor blacks now associate with "acting white" and therefore reject. Similarly, in late 1985 an ad hoc group of black educators, politicians, and civic leaders promoted an experimental public school curriculum that had as its fundamental aim the creation of "a new self-image" among young blacks.[57] The school principals who have had some success in making inner-city black youth "feel good about themselves" usually argue that the first step is some restrictions on student sovereignty, such as a dress code and strict discipline.[58]

All this could not seem more foreign to most economists. Some of them go out of their way to point out that requiring the poor to consume nutritious food when they might prefer drugs or alcohol makes the poor "worse off."[59] Whereas noneconomists frequently see dependency as degrading, humiliating, and dehumanizing, many economists see it as a rational choice. When the welfare economist is concerned about work effort, he is not concerned about what dependency does to the poor. If a high benefit reduction rate keeps a poor person who would otherwise like to work from doing so, that is cause for concern. But if high welfare benefits induce a poor person to quit his job or not to want one in the first place, whatever the tax rate, then he is better off on welfare without the job. The work effort problem exists because the nonpoor are unhappy that they must pay to support those who choose not to work.[60]

It would be both unfair and incorrect to suggest that recent work by economists on poverty takes no account of the new thinking on poverty described above. One now sees some economists praising the multiple antipoverty programs that make it possible to have cash assistance for the disabled and to have different, in-kind approaches for young adults in poverty, for whom the work disincentives of cash payments are large.[61] And black economists such as Glen Loury have been in the forefront of those emphasizing the fundamental importance of moral leadership, personal values, and social norms.[62]

Loury did not get this prescription from normative economics, however. That discipline's rigid framework and categories continue to hinder an evenhanded look at all approaches. Thus, for example, two of the economists who have come to praise a complex system and in-kind aid do so on the grounds that in-kind programs are so much less attractive than cash to recipients that the non-needy will be less likely to sneak in and grab some goodies for themselves.[63] Such praise, based on the programs' targeting efficiency, is still a long way from praise based on an understanding that only in-kind programs can have much effect on drug use, teenage parenthood, or dependency.

Still, some economists have clearly begun to consider the relevance of noneconomic variables. Thus, one recent study has shown that those young blacks who have been sexually active longer are much more likely to become absent fathers.[64] Another very interesting study, by Freeman and Holzer, finds that black youth who have strong long-term career desires and those who go to church are more likely to avoid crime and to find jobs when they look for them. The Freeman and Holzer study also finds that the employment deterioration of black youth in recent decades cannot be explained by an absence of jobs in the cities, by the minimum wage, by sluggish growth, or by other common economic variables. When drawing conclusions, however, the authors seemed to go on automatic pilot, emphasizing the need to change economic incentives rather than the need to change the attitudes that seemed to have explained so much more than economic incentives in the body of the paper.[65] The authors' training in a discipline which assumes that tastes are given and fixed may explain the puzzling way the article ends.

Even those economists doing action-oriented research are much more likely to focus on poverty as a low-income problem than are their peers from other disciplines (who often emphasize dependency, dysfunction, and the like). What the economists have learned in school leaves them uncomfortable with the new approaches, for in academic economics the canon on poverty has hardly changed at all. The 1987 edition of the Brownings' popular public finance text continues to devote most of its attention to the negative income tax. It notes the wide support for this approach in the economics profession and argues that "most welfare reform proposals build on certain features of the NIT."[66] Similarly, the new text by Joseph Stiglitz assumes that the welfare system's purpose is to decrease income inequality. In a half-page discussion, Stiglitz seems to associate the new noneconomic thinking with a concern for "the outward manifestations of poverty, the slums, malnutrition, etc., that result from it" as opposed to "the welfare of the [antipoverty programs'] recipients" themselves.[67] Once again we see the assumption that a simple concern with the recipients' "welfare" would lead to advocacy of cash transfers. After a discussion of the inefficiencies of in-kind redistributions, Stiglitz's text again brings the negative income tax to center stage.

Though economics has progressed in many ways through the years, it has forgotten as much as it has learned about the problem of poverty. Adam Smith could see that the problem was not fundamentally one of inadequate income. The poor had the "necessities of nature" and a little more besides. But they were ashamed of how others saw them.[68] More cash payments will not make that shame go away.[69]

Tastes, Preferences, and Higher Education

The most widely read and discussed book with philosophic content in at least a generation was published in 1987, Allan Bloom's *The Closing of the American Mind*. This book brings before a large audience powerful, decades-old arguments that Bloom has been making against student sovereignty in the university. Bloom sees the best students at the best universities as extraordinarily ignorant. They know next to nothing about our political or intellectual heritage. They have never made friends with serious books. They have no heroes. They mouth words like "creativity" and "commitment" without having a clue about the thought that made the use of such words necessary or about the reasons why the newer thought has called into question older words like virtue, industry, rationality, and character.

Bloom believes that what the students need is a liberal education at the heart of which is the freedom-enhancing introduction to classic texts, which they may never have heard of but which speak to their "love of truth and passion to live a good life."[70] "True liberal education requires that the student's whole life be radically changed by it, that what he learns may affect his action, his tastes, his choices, that no previous attachment be immune to examination and hence reevaluation."[71] What the students do not need is encouragement to construct their own curriculum, for that will mean that "the most vulgar and philistine things which proliferate in society at large will dominate the university, for the university cannot, as it should, counterpoise them. If the university does not provide alternatives to the prevalent, where else could the student find them?"[72]

In recent decades universities have dropped requirements and student sovereignty has taken hold; and many others besides Bloom have resisted these trends. Jacques Barzun complains that students have been "indoctrinated with the error that their 'needs' are the same as their wants, which means of course that later needs not yet felt, later relevance gradually disclosed do not exist."[73] The Stanford psychologist Neville Sanford has argued that higher education should seek to create "developed personalities" and that this requires a conscious resistance to the "prematurity" that makes students "feel they already know what they want to be and how they want to live."[74] The journalist Henry Fairlie has described a young woman who came from a middle-American, nearly bookless, home whose "whole concept of the world" changed while attending a state university. Her education had been an education in how to enjoy life, for "one cannot be alone or fecklessly idle if one has been properly educated. One can never be bored if one can read a book."[75]

My purpose here is not to defend the critics of student sovereignty in the university or to explore differences among them, but rather to argue that mainstream economic assumptions make it nearly impossible for economists to take these critics seriously. Economists typically assume that tastes do not change and are normatively compelling. The professional stake in these assumptions is great. If consumers' tastes cannot be trusted, the very meaning of economic efficiency becomes ambiguous, and the foundation for applied evaluative work collapses.[76] Since so much rests on these assumptions, those who find them implausible are likely to end up in other professions.

Two decades ago I read extensively in the literature of the economics of higher education, and I interviewed Washington economists whose work was politically influential at a time when public and congressional interest in this area was high. A Department of Health, Education and Welfare *Report to the President*, quite influential on later legislation, was written for an advisory committee by a staff consisting entirely of economists. The economist who headed the staff, the assistant secretary for planning and evaluation, was proud that her support had helped steer the new federal aid for education toward students rather than toward institutions, where, without the report, it might well have gone. The principal purpose of the student aid approach was to help those students with low incomes to attend college (the equity objective). The report also argued, however, that the recommended approach of student aid plus a cost-of-education allowance to those institutions able to attract the low-income students might also encourage a more effective and efficient use of resources, because educational institutions "will presumably be more responsive to student needs (and thereby more effective) if they must compete for students who have the financial flexibility to choose among a greater number of institutions."[77] The report cheers on student sovereignty and equates student needs and wants in the way Bloom and Barzun warn against.

When I wandered over to the Office of Education to see if things looked different from there, I again found the analytical staff headed by an economist. He ridiculed the notion that a university man should think differently from a nonuniversity man and assured me that "our colleges are machines which impart skills and facts, rather than institutions designed to produce leaders or the elite."

In all that I have read by economists on higher education in the last two decades, I have yet to find a nonradical economist treat sympathetically the idea that a liberal education should be a transforming experience. Very few even consider the possibility. Typical of those few is Roger Bolton, who in his exhaustive study of the economics and financing of higher education says only the following:

> Another non-earning benefit which some might claim is that the educated person "enjoys life more." What this really means is that the educated person enjoys the life of the typical educated person more than a non-educated person would. The statement that being educated permits one to enjoy life more is empty of empirically verifiable content, since we cannot measure enjoyment very well. Casual empiricism suggests that the educated person certainly lives differently, and allocates his consumption expenditures differently, but that he may not really enjoy life any more.[78]

Economists of the past thought it was part of their task to remind their readers that there are high and low pleasures (Mill and Marshall), that many of the high ones require reason and the sometimes painful acquisition of knowledge (Wicksteed), and that we aspire to tastes better than our current ones (Knight).[79] Today's economists are more likely to feel a professional obligation to combat such sentiments than to support them. Thus, when quarreling with Alfred Marshall's view that alteration of character or of tastes over time explains the fact that the taste for good music increases as one hears more of it, Stigler and Becker put the word "good" in quotation marks. Not content simply to question the idea that there is such a thing as good music, they later go on to define "good" music as "music that educated people like."[80]

The condescending attitude of today's economists toward their intellectual ancestors can perhaps best be seen by briefly examining Martin Bronfenbrenner's attempt to arbitrate the Bentham/Mill quarrel about pushpin and poetry by using "circa 1970 model" utility analysis. Using the same tools, Bronfenbrenner also seeks to examine "the claims of my humanist colleagues that Mill rather than Bentham was right, that poetry is indeed superior to pushpin, and that this superiority should be recognized by a return to heavy weighting of educational curricula with *litterae humaniores.*"[81]

Bronfenbrenner begins by heaping scorn on Mill's arguments. He complains that Mill provides no evidence for one of his statements that Bronfenbrenner sees as an "exquisite and labored amalgam of priggish condescension, intellectual snobbery, and what Bentham would call *ipse-dixitism.*"[82] Providing no evidence of his own, Bronfenbrenner associates himself with this rebuttal: most proponents of adult equivalents of pushpin have sufficient education to make as rational a choice as the representative poetry partisan makes. All in all, the Mill arguments seem to Bronfenbrenner so weak that he thinks their only real content is "middle-brow prejudice" in support of "comfortable conventionality"—all perhaps part of a "public relations" exercise aimed at improving the reputation of utilitarianism among genteel Victorians.[83]

The central part of the article, however, is in the long, technical, middle section. After making some Herculean assumptions, Bronfenbrenner offers the requisite indifference curves and algebra. What does he conclude from his analysis? Toward the end he says:

> If now, after completing this exercise, I were personally requested to advise an acquaintance on the advisability of subjecting his preferences to some once-and-for-all wrenching and massaging process at the hands of instructors in the humanities, what advice could I offer him on individualistic utility-theory grounds?
> On a simple yes-or-no basis, little or none.[84]

But as Bronfenbrenner sees it, the technical exercise has not been completely barren. He says instruction in the humanities is more likely to be a good thing if it emphasizes the positive, especially "propaganda and public enlightenment for the lower-cost culture activities." Similarly, such instruction will be better the more it serves as a complement to the student's future income and wealth and the more it safeguards him against becoming "an unemployable intellectual."[85] So an introduction to high culture might be all right, provided you emphasize low-cost high culture and remember mom and dad's admonition about the primary importance of earning a good living.

Bronfenbrenner would replace what he sees as Victorian prejudice with contemporary middle-class prejudice—a form of complacency from which we have more to fear. His examination of Mill's

Utilitarianism bypasses a chance to reflect on the modern ways of his discipline, for Mill offers interesting arguments for the view that a lack of mental cultivation is the second most important "cause which makes life unsatisfactory." For Mill, only selfishness is a more important cause of unhappiness.[86] Contemporary economists are often cheerleaders for selfishness,[87] and contemptuous of the notion of high mental cultivation. So let the debate be joined. But it never really is. Today's economist retires to his study with his indifference curves and with general, abstract discussions of "utility," often unaware that contemporary utilitarian philosophers are more likely to side with Mill and praise the "incomparably more fecund"[88] higher pleasures than to side with Bentham in his unwillingness to distinguish high from low.

Conclusion

The treatment of tastes and preferences in modern mainstream economics is glaringly inadequate. Deficiencies in consumer information are never really confronted, and the techniques intended to avoid acknowledging the phenomena of changing tastes are quite unpersuasive. The unwillingness to focus on changing tastes leaves unexplored those policies that seek to encourage meritorious tastes and discourage bad ones. Indeed, nothing in modern economics reminds practitioners that some tastes may be illegitimate and not entitled to public recognition, and that even some people holding questionable tastes regret them and aspire to others.

In his book *The Tragedy of Political Science*, David Ricci argues that my discipline, despite its defects, is unlikely to abandon a "scientific" approach to politics when scientific pretensions count for so much in the modern university.[89] If political science will not do so, it is not likely that its more prestigious sister, economics, will either. Scientific pretension clearly rules the journals at present; much thoughtful reflection by economists on their discipline is published in obscure journals or not at all.

Nevertheless, it is encouraging that some of this ruminating is going on. Donald McCloskey's attacks on modernism, and his call for openness to nonscientific evidence and argument, should help give the ruminators new confidence;[90] and so should the fact that luminaries such as Arrow, Sen, and Yeager find something to quarrel with in the typical economic *modus operandi*. Perhaps the discipline may yet become tolerant enough to allow the real Mishan—the Mishan of *The Costs of Economic Growth*—to find a comfortable home in Mishan's *Cost-Benefit Analysis*.

The most effective force for change may be external to the discipline. Economists, the guardians of benefit-cost analysis and of the opportunity cost concept, pride themselves on their ability to see the big picture—their ability to get all the way around policy problems like poverty and education. Once certain techniques and assumptions are clearly seen to make that claim preposterous, change may come.

Six   David Gauthier

Economic Man and the Rational Reasoner

Economic man bids fair to join the list of endangered species.
Amartya Sen shakes his head sadly and murmurs "Rational fool!"
Herbert Simon nods sagely and commands "Satisfice!"[1] And these
are the views of his friends. Economic man recalls David Winch's
statement that "we assume that individuals behave rationally and
endeavor to maximize utility."[2] Memories arise of the good old days,
in which maximization was an article of faith, part of the conceptual
grid on which behavior was analyzed. Economic man did not even
have to put his mind (if he had one) to it; whatever choice he made
was read as maximizing the value of a function defined in terms of
preferences ascribed to him on the basis of his choice. As Winch also
noted, "We assume that individuals attempt to maximize utility, and
define utility as that which the individual attempts to maximize."[3]
But economic man should be uncomfortably aware that Winch's
study was itself intended as an exposé.

As long ago as 1951, in *Social Choice and Individual Values* Kenneth
Arrow noted: "Many writers have felt that the assumption of rationality, in the sense of a one-dimensional ordering of all possible alternatives, is absolutely necessary for economic theorizing. . . . There
seems to be no logical necessity for this viewpoint; we could just as
well build up our economic theory on other assumptions as to the
structure of choice functions if the facts seemed to call for it."[4] Do
they? Is economic man a character in a useful story? If we are interested

in the explanation of some significant part of human behavior, can we fruitfully appeal to a model of which one component is maximizing choice? Another component, if the model is to be fruitful, must be some independent account of what the choice maximizes. We can always interpret choice as *maximizing,* defining preferences to fit; but then we can always interpret the motions of the heavenly bodies geocentrically. Here the question we are asking is: How good are our maximizing theories of, for example, households and firms? And if our theories are not very good, are they nevertheless better than any available alternatives, and promising enough to offer a worthwhile research program? Geocentric theories of heavenly movement have long been outclassed by their competitors.

Instrumental Rationality

Maximizing theories, however, have a kind of appeal that geocentric theories lack, an appeal that lies in the word "rationality." Our forebears may have thought it fitting that the heavenly bodies should circle about their abode, testifying to the central importance of human beings in the order of creation; but other accounts of celestial motion, less flattering to our egos, are neither more nor less rational. Indeed, one of the conceptual shifts that constituted the emergence of modern science was the elimination of such normative standards as rationality from the substantive evaluation of explanations. (To be sure, some aspects of rationality, such as consistency, remain relevant in assessing the structure of theories. But we do not suppose that rationality enters into substantive matters that affect, say, the choice between geocentricity and heliocentricity.)

When it comes to our own behavior, things are different. We interpret ourselves as rational animals, by which we mean that we have an instrumental capacity to direct means toward the attainment of ends. We have a capacity to envisage and evaluate alternative courses of action in relation to their outcomes, and then to act in the light of our evaluation. We understand not only the behavior of others, but also our own behavior in this way—indeed, in accounting for our own behavior, we often *rationalize* it by imposing an instrumental pattern of choices adapted to ends, where the observer finds either no pattern or a very different one. I may understand my choice of an apple from the fruit bowl as a free expression of my preference for apples over pears and peaches; an observer might think that I am instead manifesting my compulsive need to exhibit my abject unworthiness by repeating humankind's primal sin. There seems no ground, however, for supposing that our self-understanding in terms of instrumental rationality is generally misplaced.

This "instrumental rationality" mode of interpretation is not strictly discontinuous with our accounts of the behavior of other living things; but until we reach the higher mammals and birds (and just possibly the higher cephalopods), the adaptations we observe are programmed or learned responses, lacking the complexity implied by the vocabulary of belief, preference, and choice. A fly passes through a frog's field of vision; the frog's sticky tongue flips out and the fly is caught. The frog no more believes that there is a fly passing by than a mechanism such as my thermostat believes that the house is cold when it responds to a fall in temperature by activating the furnace. The frog no more chooses to catch the fly than my thermostat chooses to heat the house.

Our interpretation of human behavior in terms of instrumental rationality requires that we have, and attribute to our fellows, a capacity for intentional states—belief, desire, and emotion—which we share with the higher mammals, birds, and cephalopods. If further requires that we have a capacity to represent these states semantically, which, if not unique to our species, seems to be found only nascently in the higher apes. A dog believes that its master is at the door but is not aware of its belief; it cannot make the belief an object of consideration, question, doubt, or commitment, or relate it to other beliefs that are not part of its present experience. These feats require the representation of beliefs.

When we interpret behavior instrumentally, we need not suppose that the actions are best or maximally adapted to their ends. And, more relevant to our present concerns, we need not suppose that even maximally adapted behavior need be maximizing behavior. For example, consider a hypothetical animal that feeds by scanning its environment until it detects a food source satisfying certain threshold requirements, and then capturing, or trying to capture, the detected source. Suppose that once a source is detected, the animal no longer engages in detection behavior: if a superior source should now present itself in a way that the animal in its scanning mode would detect and select, it will be ignored. The animal's food-selection procedure meets satisficing requirements, and violates maximizing standards. Nevertheless, the procedure may be maximally effective for the animal. Once it detects a satisfactory food source, it does bettter to invest all its energies in the attempt to capture it, rather than keeping energy available for the possible detection of a superior source.

However, an animal with a capacity for semantic representation, such as a human being, is a natural maximizer. She recognizes inconsistencies and incompatibilities among her beliefs, desires, and feelings, and is forced by this recognition to endeavor to unify her beliefs, desires, and feelings into a consistent and coherent whole. In this unifying process, which we may think of as a naturalized version of Kant's transcendental unity of apperception, rationality makes its evolutionary debut.[5] As part of this process we naturally find maximization. Aware of various desires, and various actions each of which would satisfy these desires to greater or lesser degrees, the human being must choose; and the evident basis for her conscious choosing is a maximizing one, selecting the action that best or most fulfills her several desires. Such a basis is naturally related to the motivating force exercised by the desires, in a way that some other supposed bases are not. Compare the basis that underlies "Choose what the members of the tribe always choose." Indeed, we may say that full awareness that one faces choices turns on being aware that alternatives are capable of evaluation in relation to one's desires.

To be sure, it would not always be cost-effective to make each particular choice on a maximizing basis. A rational individual will assess her choice procedure in maximizing terms, and adopt sensible shortcuts. Thus in some situations she may appear to act as a satisficer, selecting by appeal to a threshold device and then investing no further energies in selection. When she reflects on such a procedure, however, she will be concerned with its underlying maximizing rationale. She will satisfice in order to maximize; and this "in order to" will be part of her self-understanding, not merely an evolutionary adaptation. She will agree with Michael Laver when he says, in criticism of one possible interpretation of Simon's view of satisficing, that he "will consider the conscious adoption of a course of action, which is known to be less cost-effective than another, to be irrational."[6]

I take rationality to have a nonarbitrary, substantive content. This content is captured, or is intended to be captured, by the theory of rational choice—itself fundamentally a justificatory, rather than an explanatory, theory. In giving an account of human behavior, our theory construction begins from our self-understanding. It is true that we could build on foundations other than those of rational choice if the facts seemed to call for it—that is, if we could not plausibly impute preference maximization to much of human behavior.

Such foundations, however, would raise a core problem absent from the rational-choice foundation. We should have to explain how beings who apparently possess a capacity for rational evaluation nevertheless fail to act in a way consonant with it, not just on particular occasions through weakness of will, but generally, so that their capacity is motivationally impotent. We should have to treat the interpretations that we offer, both of others' behavior and of our own, as mere smoke screens covering events that in reality exhibited no substantive rationality. There are those who accept this view, believing that the real story of human behavior is a tale told by an idiot, signifying nothing. I shall not follow them.

I shall assume that we can and should continue to endorse the endeavor to offer explanations of human actions and choices by appealing to a maximizing conception of practical rationality. To be sure, I want to insist that these explanations must be fitted into a plausible account of preference formation and belief formation. We must not be content with purported explanations that simply impose a maximizing structure on behavior and then define an individual's preferences and beliefs so that they fit the structure. Rationality should not be treated, in the manner of some economists, as merely tautological, but should be given a content based on its justificatory role. Will this serve to rehabilitate economic man as a respectable member of our explanatory club?

The real problem facing the survival of economic man is a different one. His mid-life crisis arises, not from the threat of explanatory impotence, but from the prospect of normative inadequacy. We may ascribe only a limited rationality to his behavior, for even if he is not a rational fool, his self-understanding is sadly defective. And since economic man is the creation of economic theorists, we must conclude that their understanding of rationality is similarly defective. The critique I want to present does not turn on the purely instrumental dimension of economic man's rationality. For the explanatory purposes to which he is typically put, economic man need not concern himself with his ends; yet I believe that he is right, and his critics wrong, if he insists, with Hume, that it is not contrary to reason to prefer the destruction of the world to scratching one's finger.[7] To be sure, such a preference is unlikely to commend itself to the reflective consideration of many, but it is a mistake to suppose that reason is the final arbiter of whether objects of preference are appropriate or inappropriate. It is not contrary to *reason* for the celestial bodies to rotate about the earth. We should not assign to reason tasks that are inappropriate to its station, such as deciding the truth of factual statements or choosing between preferences.

I accept an instrumental conception of rationality, and suppose, as I have indicated, that rationality is manifest in the unifying tasks set us by our capacity to represent our beliefs, desires, and feelings in semantic space. I agree that, in the realm of choice, this conception is appropriately understood in a maximizing way. What I want to question is the peculiarly simple-minded character of the orthodox maximizing conception of practical rationality. I want to question whether economic man is the rational reasoner.

Our awareness of our future selves, and our capacity to represent relationships between actual and possible states of affairs, lead to our facing sequential decision problems. I shall restrict myself to very simple sequential problems, in which chance, risk, and uncertainty may largely be ignored. I shall assume a fixed and determinate horizon, so that after a finite number of choices the agent reaches a terminal outcome. And I shall suppose that the agent or agents can order all possible terminal outcomes. The first problem is familiar in the literature; it is the problem of Ulysses.[8]

Ulysses and the Sirens

Ulysses is about to embark on a voyage past the island of the Sirens. He prefers, of course, to sail past the island rather than to land and dally with its inhabitants. When he hears their song, however, he will prefer to land and dally. He thus faces a choice: to sail past or to land. His preference is different at different times: before he hears the Sirens' song he prefers to sail past; once he hears it he prefers to land (Figure 1). Suppose now that he has a second choice: he can decide at the outset whether to leave himself in free control of his vessel or to bind himself to the mast so that he cannot alter his course as the voyage proceeds. When he reaches the island of the Sirens they will sing to him, and only if he is unbound will he face the choice between sailing on or landing on their island. The terminal outcomes, as Ulysses now considers them, are three: sailing freely to his destination, which results if he neither binds himself to the mast nor succumbs to the Sirens' song; sailing bound to his destination; and landing on the Sirens' island, which results if he does not bind himself and succumbs to the Sirens' song. Before the voyage, Ulysses prefers sailing freely to his destination to sailing

Figure 1   **Ulysses' First Choice**

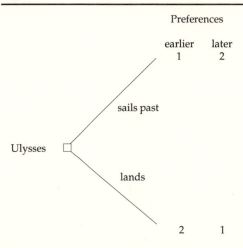

bound, and sailing bound to landing on the Sirens' island (Figure 2). If he considers only these present preferences, he will choose not to bind himself to the mast.

Ulysses knows, however, that when he hears the Sirens his preferences will change, so that he will then prefer landing on their island to continuing freely to his destination, and continuing freely to his destination to being bound to the mast. For this change in preference to occur, neither we nor Ulysses need ascribe to the Sirens any magical power to render their hearers incapable of resistance to their song. For our purposes, we want to depart from the myth and treat Ulysses throughout as a rational chooser. He faces a problem whose structure is familiar. On his way home, Jones can stop by the pub. Before he reaches the pub, Jones prefers stopping by for one pint rather than not stopping, and not stopping rather than stopping and spending the whole evening in the pub. Once in the pub, his companions at hand, Jones prefers to spend the evening there rather than leave after a single pint. There is no magic involved.

Knowing that his preferences will change, Ulysses reconsiders his initial choice. His best plan from his present standpoint is not to bind himself to the mast, and to ignore the Sirens' song. But given his preferences when he hears the Sirens, he will then succumb if he can. Reasoning backward, he concludes that since he will choose to

Figure 2   **Ulysses' Second Choice**

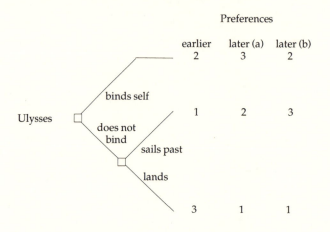

Preferences

	earlier	later (a)	later (b)
binds self	2	3	2
sails past	1	2	3
lands	3	1	1

succumb if he can, it is better that he not have the opportunity, and so he chooses to bind himself to the mast (Figure 2, "later [a]"). Jones, if he reasons similarly, will choose to pass by the pub.

My analysis of this familiar example is not original. The distinction I have drawn—between choosing to sail by without binding oneself (but then succumbing and landing), and choosing to bind oneself so that one does not succumb and land—is the familiar distinction between myopic and sophisticated choice.[9] Myopic Ulysses ignores any possible future change in his preferences; sophisticated Ulysses accommodates his present choices to the anticipated effects of such changes. Note that sophisticated Ulysses does not choose on the basis of his future, *ex post* preferences: if he did, he would plan to land on the Sirens' island. He takes the effects of his future preferences into account, but he does so from the standpoint of his present, *ex ante* preferences. Sophisticated Ulysses settles for the second best: he resigns himself to being bound to the mast. The later self, who prefers dallying with the Sirens, ends up with his least preferred outcome—no dalliance, and bound to boot. On the orthodox view of rational choice, sophisticated Ulysses is an exemplar of rationality. But is he?

Figure 3 **The Farmer's Problem**

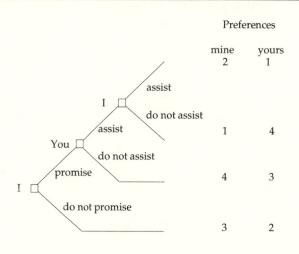

Preferences

	mine	yours
assist	2	1
do not assist	1	4
do not assist	4	3
do not promise	3	2

The Farmer's Problem

Consider another situation. You and I are farmers. Next week, my crops will be ready for harvesting; the following week, yours will be. Then, the harvest season over, I am selling my farm and retiring, far away from where we now live. Each of us can bring in the harvest unaided; or we can help each other. Each of us would prefer to help and be helped, rather than work alone. But giving assistance to the other is in itself a cost. I therefore face a problem. My best course of action would seem to be to promise you my assistance in return for yours. A fortnight hence, however, whether or not you have helped me get in the harvest, I will do best not to help you. Helping you is a cost, and I can expect no benefit in return. If you have assisted me with my crops, I already have received the benefit; if not, there is no benefit. So it is common knowledge that it would not benefit me to help you, even if you have helped me and I have promised you my help in return for yours. If I am rational I will not be able to promise sincerely to assist you if you first assist me; and if you are rational you would not accept any so-called promise that I might offer (Figure 3).

Figure 4 **The Bond Solution**

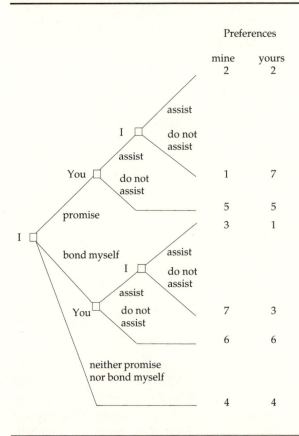

Fortunately, for a small fee I can bond myself to aid you on condition you assist me. If you fail, my bond is returned to me. If you aid me and I do not reciprocate, my bond is forfeit; it is paid to you, less commission (Figure 4). I would, of course, do better if I could arrange an exchange of services without taking out a bond. But I must settle for second best. Rationality can do no better.

The farmer's problem is a sequential adaptation of the familiar prisoner's dilemma. In the dilemma, cooperation is mutually profitable but individually disadvantageous. In the sequential version, you are unable to take advantage of me, since I have the last move; but if you cooperate you risk my taking advantage of you. I have no fear of being disadvantaged, but, should you cooperate, I can take advantage of you. Here the two components of the classic dilemma are distinguished and isolated. You must decide whether to trust. I need not decide whether to be trustworthy unless you decide to trust, but in adopting an initial plan I face the question of my trustworthiness. And trustworthiness is irrational, or so it seems.

Ulysses' Internal Constraints

In each of the situations we are considering, there is a plan which, if its adoption ensured that it would be carried out, and if this were common knowledge, would be judged best by the agent *ex ante*. I shall call this the best prior plan. Ulysses' best prior plan is not to bind himself to the mast and to sail past the Sirens' island. In the farmer's problem, my best prior plan is to aid you if and only if you aid me. Each of these plans seems to be infeasible, however, because it would require the agent to be at least conditionally willing to perform an act which, were the conditions satisfied, would be dispreferred. Each of these plans requires the agent to accept an internal constraint on directly maximizing choices. Ulysses would be required to sail past the Sirens' island; I should be required to aid you should you assist me.

These constrained choices are deemed infeasible. A rational agent, it is maintained, cannot carry out a plan, however advantageous it may be, that requires him to perform an act that would be dispreferred at the time of performance. Some take this to be tautological; the choice of an action shows that it is preferred to its alternatives. I have indicated my rejection of this view, insisting that we must have a plausible account of preference formation that gives us at least partially choice-independent access to a person's preferences. I want to say, then, that it is conceivable that a person should choose a dispreferred action; maximization is not necessary for reasoned choice. In general, however, the choice of a dispreferred action will be evidence of irrationality, at least to the extent of weakness of will. If we assume rationality, then it may seem that a plan requiring the choice of a dispreferred action is infeasible, even though such a choice is itself conceivable.

On this orthodox view, a plan is feasible if and only if, at each choice point, it requires the agent to choose an action that, given her preferences at that point, is not dispreferred to some alternative. This view rules out the plans that I have identified as best prior plans in our two situations. Although this consequence has been recognized as troubling, it has generally been accepted. This is not surprising. One does not generally reject a theory because of anomalies, unless a better theory is at hand. Rational choice has been no exception. No plausible alternative theory has been advanced that would accommodate plans that the orthodoxy has deemed infeasible. The inaccessibility of best prior plans to rational agents in certain situations has therefore remained a mere anomaly.

This seems to me an unsatisfactory state of affairs. In the remainder of this chapter I want to explore a revised account of rational choice, one that will accommodate constraints on maximizing behavior in order to accept as feasible some (although not all) of the best prior plans that the orthodox view rejects. More generally, let a plan be termed "prior superior" if it is better, *ex ante*, than any plan considered feasible on the orthodox view, that is, any plan not requiring an agent to make a dispreferred choice at any choice point she can reach given adoption of the plan. Then I want to develop a theory that constrains choice to allow some prior superior plans to be feasible. I do not yet have a comprehensive theory to present, but I do want to suggest what seems to me a promising direction for developing such a theory.

Let us begin again with Ulysses. He has three logically possible plans: bind himself to the mast; do not bind and sail past the Sirens; do not bind and land on the Sirens' island. On the orthodox view the second plan is infeasible. Given the choice between the first and the third, sophisticated Ulysses naturally chooses the first. However, the second, allegedly infeasible, plan is superior to the first, not just as a prior superior plan from the standpoint of Ulysses' *ex ante* preferences, but also from the standpoint of his *ex post* preferences. To be sure, it is not Ulysses' best plan given his *ex post* preferences; that would be not to bind himself and to succumb to the Sirens' song. This "plan" is what myopic Ulysses would actually carry out, although not what he would intend *ex ante*. It is, of course, not a plan that would be adopted by Ulysses *ex ante*, for it is inferior to an alternative that he can enforce from that perspective, namely to bind himself to the mast. From Ulysses' *ex post* perspective, the plan of sailing freely past the Sirens' island has this merit: it leaves him better off than any alternative he could enforce *ex ante*, even though it requires him to perform a dispreferred act. *Ex post* he prefers sailing freely past rather than sailing past bound to the mast. It will be convenient to distinguish two "selves" here, each characterized by a set of preferences; let us call them prior Ulysses and posterior Ulysses. We may then say that the second plan (do not bind, and sail past the Sirens) is a Pareto improvement on the first (binding himself to the mast).

Having distinguished prior from posterior Ulysses, we may now consider the prospect for an agreement between them. Prior Ulysses notes that he can obtain his second preference by binding himself to the mast; from his standpoint, binding is a "minimax" strategy. He reminds posterior Ulysses that posterior Ulysses cannot ensure anything better than his worst outcome—which he will get if prior Ulysses follows his minimax strategy. Being bound to the mast thus can be thought of as the status quo in a potential bargain; each can act to achieve it without the cooperation of the other. But not being bound to the mast and sailing past the Sirens is Pareto-superior to the status quo and Pareto-optimal; it belongs to the bargaining negotiation set, and is indeed the sole member of the set. (Not being bound and succumbing to the Sirens is of course Pareto-optimal, but not Pareto-superior to the status quo.) Hence there is a unique bargain available to prior and posterior Ulysses. Is it not rational for them to make it?

The problem, it will immediately be insisted, is that prior Ulysses cannot enforce adherence to the bargain, and risks doing worse than had he not agreed. Posterior Ulysses cannot lose; if prior Ulysses ignores the bargain, posterior Ulysses ends up no worse than if no bargain had been made. If prior Ulysses adheres to the bargain, posterior Ulysses inevitably gains. Posterior Ulysses therefore has no problem with the deal. What can we say about prior Ulysses' problem? At least this: It would be downright foolish of prior Ulysses to make and adhere to a bargain unless he could count on posterior Ulysses to do his part. If he were reasonably sure that posterior Ulysses was the sort of person who complied with his agreements, then prior Ulysses would have good reason to adhere to the bargain and not bind himself to the mast. Through posterior Ulysses' compliance—even risking some very slight chance of noncompliance—prior Ulysses would expect to do better by not binding himself to the mast than by binding himself to it.

What of posterior Ulysses? He recognizes that prior Ulysses will not make and keep a bargain with him unless prior Ulysses believes him to be the sort of person who himself complies with agreements. Posterior Ulysses therefore wants to convince prior Ulysses that he is indeed this sort of person. The best way of convincing prior Ulysses, especially given the rather intimate relation between the two, may well be actually to be the sort of person who complies with his agreements. Despite the opposed preferences that divide him, therefore, it is rational for Ulysses, prior or posterior, to choose to be that sort of person—the sort I have called elsewhere a constrained maximizer.[10]

Posterior Ulysses is not departing from sound maximizing reasoning in choosing to be a constrained maximizer. He expects to do better as a result of his choice. He reasons that unless he so chooses, he cannot expect to benefit from an agreement with prior Ulysses. He does better by the agreement, even though keeping it means choosing his dispreferred action, than he would do without the agreement. The outcome of his dispreferred, agreement-keeping action is better than the outcome he could expect were he not the sort of person who kept his agreements. Better to sail freely by the Sirens' island than to be bound to the mast.

From the standpoint of prior Ulysses, the result of his bargaining with his posterior self is that he is able to choose his best plan—what I have called the best prior plan for Ulysses undivided. Prior Ulysses does not consider this plan infeasible, given that his posterior self is rationally constrained to choose that which at the time of choice he disprefers, but which yields posterior Ulysses a more advantageous outcome than he would expect were he not constrained to choose it.

We might be tempted to think that we have provided a general defense for best prior plans against the charge of infeasibility. But we have not, as reflection on an alternative version of Ulysses' situation will show. This version is represented by "later (b)" in Figure 2. Suppose that the effect of the Sirens' song is such that it inverts his prior preference order, so that on hearing their song, he prefers going to their island to sailing past bound, but sailing past bound to sailing freely past. Here, the best prior plan requires Ulysses to perform an action that, at the time of performance, would yield his least preferred outcome, leaving him worse off, in terms of his then present preferences, than had he instead initially bound himself to the mast.

Now consider the situation facing Ulysses' divided selves. As before, prior Ulysses can enforce his second preference by choosing to be bound. Now, however, posterior Ulysses can also ensure at least his second preference. If prior Ulysses chooses to be bound, then this yields his second choice; if prior Ulysses chooses to be unbound, then posterior Ulysses is free to bring about his preferred outcome of dallying with the Sirens. As before, being bound to the mast can be taken as the status quo outcome; but given posterior Ulysses' different preferences, it is now Pareto-optimal. Being unbound and sailing past is no longer preferred to it by both of Ulysses' selves. The negotiation set is empty; there is no mutually advantageous agreement to be made. However willing posterior Ulysses may be to constrain himself to bring about an advantageous opportunity, here no such opportunity is to be had.

We do not want to say, therefore, that a best prior plan must be feasible. In the case just described, the best prior plan—of not being bound and sailing freely past the Sirens' island—is clearly infeasible. Nor do we want to say that if a plan requires a dispreferred action, then it is feasible only if it is best from every perspective. In the original version of the situation, the plan of not being bound and sailing freely past is, I have claimed, feasible, but it is not best from the *ex post* perspective. Rather, it seems that we should begin by identifying that plan (or those plans), from among those feasible on the orthodox view—that is, those not requiring the performance of any dispreferred action—which is best from the *ex ante* perspective, the point of view of prior Ulysses. We should then consider whether there are any other plans Pareto-superior to such a plan or plans. Such plans will of course be prior superior, though not necessarily best prior. If there are such plans, then these will meet our revised conception of feasibility, as possible outcomes of a bargain that each party can find it rational to be disposed to uphold. We may then suppose that choice among them would be treated as a bargaining problem.

The Farmer's Internal Constraints

Ulysses in hand, we may move from preference change to interaction. Indeed, we have in effect already done so, by treating preference change as if it involved interaction between two persons, each characterized by one of the sets of preferences. Let us now consider literal interaction in the situation of our two farmers. Leaving aside bonding myself for the present, I have two choices to make, whether to promise you assistance or not, and whether actually to assist you or not. Coming between these choices is your decision whether to assist me. We may simplify our analysis by supposing that assistance will be promised or given only on the condition of receiving the other's assistance. There are then four possible plans: (1) promise to assist if and only if assisted, and do; (2) promise to assist if and only if assisted, but do not assist; (3) make no promise, but assist if assisted; and (4) make no promise, and do not assist. On the orthodox view, since actually assisting you is dispreferred, no plan requiring it is feasible. There are then only two plans to consider, the second (promise but no aid: the myopic approach) and the fourth (no promise and no aid). Promising to assist you is then pointless; you will know that, since my plan must be feasible—that is, since I will not choose a dispreferred action—I will not assist you. From the sophisticated standpoint, therefore, my only remaining plan is not to promise to assist you and not to do so. You, of course, will not assist me, and so I will end up worse off than if we had each assisted the other. Call this the no promise, no aid plan.

Now reconsider the first plan: promise to assist if and only if assisted, and do. Call this the conditional assistance plan. If I were able to adopt this plan, and you were to believe that I had, then you might consider it worthwhile to assist me (depending on how firm your belief was). In adopting the plan, I should then expect to do better than under the no promise, no aid plan, since I should expect some probability of mutual assistance. Note that I could not do worse, since if you do not assist me, I am no worse off than under the no promise, no aid plan. It is therefore in my interest to be able to adopt this plan. It is in my interest to dispose myself to be a promise keeper, just as it was in posterior Ulysses' interest to dispose himself to be an agreement keeper. If I am so disposed, then I can adopt the plan, and you can have reason to believe that I have adopted the plan, to our mutual advantage.

There is a catch, however. If I can adopt the conditional assistance plan, then we must reconsider the promise but no aid plan. Previously, we dismissed it because the promise would be pointless. Now, however, if I may be disposed to promise keeping, you may believe that, if I make a promise, I will be disposed to keep it, even if in fact I am not so disposed. The promise but no aid plan therefore offers the advantage of increasing my chance of getting your assistance (in relation to the no promise, no aid plan) without requiring me to perform a dispreferred action. I will be better off, if I do get assistance, than with the conditional assistance plan. If conditional assistance is better than no promise and no aid, then it seems that a promise but no aid is better still.

Since you presumably are aware of this, then even if you believe it possible for me to be disposed to promise keeping, you will not believe me actually so disposed. In effect my capacity to be a promise keeper is pointless; I have no reason so to dispose myself. To draw this conclusion would, however, be mistaken. It is possible for you to have a reason to believe that I am disposed to promise keeping that is based on my actually being so disposed. If you take yourself to have such a reason, you may not discount my promise. It is therefore possible that, by actually disposing myself to promise keeping, I make it more likely that you will believe my promise and will aid me, than were I to promise insincerely. My *ex ante* expectation may thus be greater if I adopt the conditional aid plan than if I adopt the promise but no aid plan.

Consider now the situation from the *ex post* standpoint. If you did not assist me, then of course on any feasible plan I will choose not to assist you; this is unproblematic. Suppose that you did assist me; how do I regard the conditional assistance plan? It is clear that I would do better not to assist you. I may not, however, infer that I should now be doing better had I adopted some other plan from the admitted fact that I should now do better to make a choice different from that required by my actual plan. I must realize that, were I not intending to assist you, as the conditional assistance plan requires, then I should likely not have received your assistance. Indeed, had I adopted any alternative plan, I should rationally have expected you not to aid me. It is probable then that I have received your assistance only because I have adopted conditional assistance (after all, in adopting it, I judged that it increased my prospect of receiving your assistance enough to make it better than the insincere promise but no aid plan). Thus I have good reason, even *ex post*, to suppose that I should now be doing worse were I following a different plan. I have good reason to suppose that were I following a different plan you would not have aided me and I should be worse off than I now am when, following my actual plan, I make the dispreferred choice to aid you. Thus I regard the conditional assistance plan as best, not only *ex ante*, but also *ex post*.

I do not want to claim that it is rational for me to adopt and carry out the conditional assistance plan no matter what the circumstances. Perhaps you are gullible, and I can trick you by adopting the promise but no aid plan. Perhaps you are so committed to the orthodox view of feasibility that you will not believe any promise I make; so that the no promise, no aid plan is best. I do want to claim, however, that the situation can be such that it is rational for me to adopt the conditional assistance plan, and therefore rational for me to dispose myself to keeping my promise, as that plan requires. Indeed, it may be rational for me to dispose myself to promise keeping in general. If I have such a disposition, others may be more likely to enter into arrangements advantageous to me but requiring that I be trusted, than if I decide whether to promise sincerely or not on a case-by-case basis. The benefit I gain from others' increased trust may be greater than the costs I bear because my sincerity prevents me from taking advantage of them when the opportunity arises. I shall not pursue this line of thought here, however, since it is more appropriate to my concerns with moral issues. My point here is that some plans requiring the performance of dispreferred actions may be best (or at least better than any alternative not requiring the performance of a dispreferred action) not only from a person's expectation in an *ex ante* perspective, but also *ex post*, in relation to his expectation of what his situation would have been given any relevant alternative plan. I claim that such plans are feasible for rational persons.

On the orthodox view of feasibility, the best one can do, in a situation in which an otherwise better plan would require the performance of a dispreferred action, is to impose some external constraint on one's behavior that alters one's preference ordering. Thus, as I noted earlier, I might bond myself to performance, forfeiting a sum, should I fail to aid you, large enough to ensure that giving assistance is worth my while. But a bonding procedure, indeed any imposition of an external constraint, involves some cost. Recognizing this; a rational agent must prefer to impose an internal constraint on herself, insofar as such a constraint is less costly. To suppose, as the orthodox position does, that the imposition of such a constraint is impossible, is to view rationality as in some ways a hindrance to, and not an instrument for, maximizing one's utility. The orthodox position treats rationality as self-undermining in situations with prisoner's dilemma–type structures. My alternative account of rational feasibility removes this incoherence.

The Nature of Internal Constraints

I have argued that a person can be disposed to perform certain dispreferred actions in order to follow a plan, or to comply with an agreement, or to fulfill a promise, or indeed in other ways. What is essential to such a disposition is the possibility of internal constraints on maximizing behavior, not merely external constraints that alter certain outcomes or eliminate options. I now want to consider what we should take to be involved in being so constrained.

A first interpretation is suggested by such discussions of rational irrationality as those of Thomas Schelling and Derek Parfit.[11] There are circumstances in which a person will rationally choose to be irrational, if he can. My best defense against someone who has me in his power, who is willing to threaten me with dire consequences—perhaps the torture and murder of my children—if I do not do his nefarious bidding, and who would not hesitate to carry out his threats, may be insanity. If my behavior is sufficiently abnormal and unpredictable, he may realize that he cannot control my behavior by threats, since I am as likely to welcome them and urge him to carry them out as I am to acquiesce in them. It may then be fully rational— it may maximize my expected utility—for me to become temporarily insane, if I can. But no one would suppose that my insane behavior was itself rational. No one would suppose that my responses to his threats, whatever they might be, were themselves rationally chosen. Rationality is the norm of reason; rational behavior is correctly reasoned behavior. In becoming insane, I depart from reason. Even were it possible to interpret my behavior, however erratic, as if I were maximizing the value of some function defined in terms of the possible outcomes, such an interpretation would only show how unreasoned behavior could simulate reason's norm of rationality.

One might then propose the following model for internal constraint. In disposing myself to follow plans or to comply with agreements, I make myself, if not insane, yet beyond reason. I rationally put reason and its norms of rationality to one side, because maximizing behavior will not serve me well in the circumstances. But the model as it stands is evidently inappropriate. In putting myself beyond reason I remove the possibility of my offering an account of my behavior as reasoned. The model requires that I put my actions quite literally out of my control. But the person who rationally internalizes constraints has available a perfectly cogent, reasoned account of her behavior. She can give reasons for her choices that are not mere rationalizations. Ulysses (in the original situation) sails past the Sirens' island because that is what his best plan prescribes; Ulysses can offer this as both an explanation of and justification for his action.

If we wish to compare internally constrained choice to behavior in response to threats, we need a different model. We need to consider the person who, faced with a threat, does not become aberrant and unpredictable in his behavior, acting out of control, but instead makes clear the pointlessness of threatening him because he finds it advantageous to be a committed threat resister. His reaction to a threat is like rational Ulysses' reaction to the Sirens—he ignores them because this is what his best plan prescribes. Is his reaction then to be dismissed as rational irrationality? Surely he exhibits another aspect of internal constraint, and it would beg the question to suppose that we can assume he is irrational and then infer that all constraint is similarly irrational.

I do not deny that irrationality can be rational. But such irrationality is, I suggest, to be understood in the individual's inability to control her behavior, or to offer a cogent, reasoned account of it. It provides no reasonable parallel to the deliberate adoption of plans or dispositions that require dispreferred choices.

At the opposite extreme from purely erratic, unpredictable behavior is rigidly programmed behavior. It may be suggested that disposing oneself to perform dispreferred actions in the contexts of following plans and keeping agreements and promises, should be understood as eliminating rather than constraining choice by closing off all options but one. If Ulysses disposes himself to be a plan follower, then in adopting his best plan he eliminates the option of landing on the Sirens' island; all he can do as a plan follower is to sail past. To be sure, Ulysses can provide a reasoned account of his behavior. But so, it may be urged, does the subject of a posthypnotic suggestion. Just as the person instructed under hypnosis to recite Keats's "Ode to a Nightingale" when the telephone rings exhibits only the illusion of choice when she then decides to do so, so Ulysses exhibits only the illusion of choice when he decides to ignore the Sirens and sail on. Indeed, it may be claimed that the Ulysses of our story, who ignores the Sirens' song, is no more free to choose than was the Ulysses of the original myth, who could not resist its appeal.

A person acting in accordance with a posthypnotic suggestion provides an account of her action that, we believe, has nothing to do with its real basis. Her account is a mere rationalization, constructed in accordance with the tendency, to which I referred earlier, of human beings to represent their actions to themselves by imposing an instrumental pattern of choices adapted to ends where the observer finds either no pattern, or a very different one. Ulysses' account, on the other hand, is not a rationalization; he is aware of his plan, his reason for adopting it, and the conformity of his action to it. If we think of him as nevertheless rigidly programmed so that he has only the illusion of choice, then it would seem that we should think of the orthodox maximizer as equally rigidly programmed with only the illusion of choice. The difference between Ulysses and the maximizer would then be only that they are programmed differently.

If we think of Ulysses as having no alternatives open to him in virtue of his disposition, then of course we shall deny that he chooses a dispreferred action. We shall say either that he did not really choose, or that he chose the only action available to him—which is then necessarily the most preferred action. We may in this way seek to deny that a disposition to plan following or agreement keeping requires nonmaximizing actions. If we argue in this way, however, we make vacuous the claim that one chooses one's most preferred action. For we shall say of anyone who is disposed to act in whatever way, that she has no alternatives open to her in virtue of her disposition, and so either does not really choose, or chooses the only available, and so necessarily the most preferred, action. This characterization would obscure the real difference between maximizing and nonmaximizing dispositions.

The plan follower evaluates the various actions open to him in terms of his plan. The maximizer evaluates the various actions open to her in terms of her utility, the measure of her preferences. Each is able to consider alternatives and select one that meets his or her criterion. This is to be able to choose. Neither is in the position of the subject of posthypnotic suggestion, who in effect must adjust her criterion so that she selects an action already determined for her in a quite different way, a way of which she is now unaware. I want therefore to insist that the person disposed to follow a plan has alternative actions, not conforming to his plan, available to him in just the way that the maximizer has alternative actions, not maximizing her utility-expectation, available to her. Neither will select one of these alternatives, but that does not make them unavailable. Each can give a reasoned account of why he chooses as he does, and this account is not a rationalization, but reveals his actual criterion for choice.

In drawing this parallel, I am of course assuming that we must have some account of the maximizer's preferences that is not entirely dependent on her actual choices. Were this not so, we could simply assume that choice reveals preference, and we could interpret all behavior, including plan following and agreement keeping, as maximizing. In regarding someone as choosing only preferred actions, we should not be concerned with her ability to offer a reasoned account of her choices in maximizing terms. Nor should we consider that because someone offers a reasoned account of his choice in terms of following a plan, he is therefore disposed to perform dispreferred actions should his plan call for them. We should identify his preferences in terms of his actual choices, whatever story he may tell. We could say of every person in normal circumstances that she has a number of alternative actions available to her, and determines one as utility maximizing by choosing it. We could not similarly say of the plan follower that he has a number of actions available to him, and determines one as plan following by choosing it. The parallels that I have endeavored to develop by treating straightforward maximizing and plan following as alternative ways of choosing among possible actions, would not hold on a purely behavioral account of maximization. As I have insisted, however, that is not my approach.

Actions and Outcomes

So far, my argument has been negative, resisting various attempts to assimilate constrained maximization to forms of behavior that do not involve the rational choice of dispreferred actions. I want now to turn to a proposed interpretation of disposing oneself to follow plans, keep agreements, and so forth, that requires no constraint on maximization, and so no choices of dispreferred actions, but that nevertheless recognizes what appear to be such choices as normal instances of rational behavior.

On this interpretation, advanced by McClennen, preferences with respect to possible actions are sensitive to context.[12] The preferences a person would have, were she to confront two options *de novo*, need not be the preferences she has if she confronts them in the context of a plan. This contextual sensitivity is not arbitrary, at least not insofar as the person is rational. Rather, McClennen says, "context dependent preferences for actions can be understood as rooted in the disposition to maximize."[13] On the orthodox view, a person "maximizes with respect to his preferences for outcomes in an incremental fashion"; on McClennen's model of resolute choice, he "maximizes his preferences for outcomes in a more holistic fashion."[14]

Consider Ulysses. He recognizes that his best plan requires him to sail freely past the Sirens' island. He realizes that, were he to hear the Sirens' song and then face the alternatives of sailing past or landing on their island, he would, outside the context of a plan, prefer, and choose, the latter. But "his *ex post* preferences among available actions are disciplined or shaped by what he judges, from the perspective of plans taken as wholes, to be the best plan to pursue."[15] Thus Ulysses forms the contextually dependent preference for sailing past the Sirens' island rather than landing on it.

In McClennen's view, a rational agent can, at every choice point, be said to choose his most preferred action. His preferences are not exogenously given, however, but in the context of plans, are endogenously determined to ensure adherence to the best plan. McClennen's persons are not internally constrained from maximizing, but they are constrained in preferring; they engage in direct psychological manipulation of their preferences, rather than their choices. One might ask why an agent such as posterior Ulysses allows his preferences over actions to be manipulated. The answer, of course, is that from the perspective of his preferences over outcomes, he can expect to do better by coming to prefer to sail by the Sirens' island rather than to land, than if he bases his preferences for actions directly on his preferences over outcomes. McClennen does not suppose that posterior Ulysses' preferences for actions are to be determined simply by appealing to a best prior plan—one that is best *ex ante,* given the preferences for outcomes held by prior Ulysses, but that ignores his own preferences for outcomes. Thus McClennen would not suppose that in the alternative situation, posterior Ulysses would come to prefer sailing by the Sirens' island to landing on it, even though such a preference would enable him to follow the plan that would best satisfy prior Ulysses. McClennen must, I think, agree that in the alternative situation, the plan of not binding himself to the mast and then freely sailing past the Sirens' island is infeasible. For he insists that "if one thinks of the self as separable into discrete time slices, then . . . a commitment to chosen plans recommends itself on the grounds that each of the relevant time slices can judge himself to be better off if the plan is adopted and followed than if no such plan is put into effect."[16] Prior and posterior Ulysses can both judge themselves better off with the plan of sailing freely by the Sirens' island if posterior Ulysses prefers the outcome of sailing freely by to the outcome of being bound to the mast, but not if, as in the alternative situation, he prefers the outcome of being bound to that of sailing by.

My objections to McClennen's account may be primarily terminological—objections to speaking of and distinguishing preferences with regard to outcomes from preferences with regard to actions that yield the outcomes. I believe, however, that more than mere terminology is at stake. Consider, yet again, posterior Ulysses choosing to sail past the Sirens' island. How shall we understand Ulysses' choice? How will Ulysses himself understand it? Need we postulate a preference for the action of sailing past the island, rather than landing on it? I think not. We understand Ulysses' choice, surely, by beginning with the underlying preferences regarding outcomes— preferences that characterize, and distinguish, his prior and posterior selves. We suppose that each self has a maximizing concern: to fulfill his preferences to the fullest extent possible. We then consider the various ways in which prior and posterior Ulysses can act in relation to their maximizing concerns. We show that one plan of action is best, not just from the *ex ante* perspective of prior Ulysses, but, in relation to alternative feasible plans or to no plan, from both *ex ante* and *ex post* perspectives. We now understand why Ulysses would adopt and follow this plan. And we now understand Ulysses' choice by relating it to this plan. We need not postulate any further preference, beyond Ulysses' *ex ante* and *ex post* preferences over outcomes, to give this explanation, which is equally a rational justification, of Ulysses' behavior.

What point, then, can there be in introducing preferences regarding actions that in a clear sense run counter to Ulysses' preferences regarding the outcomes that the actions bring about? Note that we must not suppose that these alleged preferences regarding actions replace Ulysses' preferences regarding outcomes. We must not think that posterior Ulysses does not prefer the outcome of landing on the island to the outcome of sailing freely past—for we must appeal to this preference in explaining and justifying the plan that Ulysses adopts and follows. We must appeal to his preference regarding the outcome to understand the point, if there is one, of attributing to him a preference for the action of sailing past.

It seems to me that there can be only one rationale for attributing to posterior Ulysses a preference for the action of sailing past the Sirens' island. If we attribute such a preference to him, then we can represent his choice in maximizing terms. But why should we want to represent his choice in this way? The answer may seem obvious: because we take Ulysses to be rational, and rationality involves maximization. But reflect. Ulysses is rational, that is, he seeks to maximize the fulfillment of his preferences over outcomes. Utility is the measure of such preferences; so Ulysses, being rational, seeks to maximize his expectation of utility. In many cases, the best way for Ulysses to do this is to choose an action whose outcome has an expected utility that is greater, or at least as great, as that of the outcome of any possible alternative action. It will then be plausible to represent Ulysses as a maximizer at the level of individual choices among alternative actions. But this maximizing behavior on Ulysses' part is rational insofar as, and only insofar as, it contributes best to his maximizing objective, his expected utility. There is no reason to attribute to Ulysses a concern with maximizing choices that is apart from, or independent of, his concern with maximizing his expectation of utility. As in his encounter with the Sirens, if choosing an action whose outcome has greater utility than that of any alternative possible action is not part of the plan most conducive to his maximizing objective, there is no reason to suppose that Ulysses will be rationally concerned with a maximizing choice. To represent his particular choice here as maximizing, by attributing to him context-dependent preferences concerning actions, is to obscure the real, deep role that maximization plays in our understanding of Ulysses' behavior.

We may expect that Ulysses will be tempted to land on the Sirens' island. To be sure, were he the sort of person who gave way to temptation, then if he were aware of his weakness, he would have bound himself to the mast. We may therefore expect a rational and self-aware Ulysses not to give way. The temptation will be there, however, and there is no problem in accounting for it, given posterior Ulysses' real preferences with respect to outcomes. It seems to me that this temptation, which after all is to choose to land on the Sirens' island—to choose an action different from that prescribed by his plan—is less easily understood if we suppose that Ulysses has disciplined his preferences regarding actions so that he actually prefers sailing on.

My appeal to temptation is secondary, however. My main criticism is that McClennen's context-sensitive preferences with respect to actions constitute an explanatory (and justificatory) fifth wheel, doing no useful work. To think that their presence is needed to understand Ulysses' behavior in maximizing terms is simply a mistake. The role required of maximization in a rational explication of Ulysses' behavior is not related to his particular choices among actions, but rather to his objective.

Conclusion

We are now finally in a position to return to, and modify, our idea that an animal who represents its intentional states to itself and reasons about them, such as a human being, is a natural maximizer. I said earlier that a human being, aware of various desires, and various actions each of which would satisfy these desires to greater or lesser degrees, must choose, and the evident basis for conscious choosing is a maximizing one, selecting the action that best or most fulfills her several desires, since it is naturally related to the motivating force exercised by the desires. We have learned from Ulysses, however, that the person who maximizes only at the level of choice may fail to maximize at a deeper and more important level. The endeavor to unify her beliefs, desires, and feelings into a consistent and coherent whole leads her beyond particular maximizing choices, to a consideration of her choices, not one by one, but more holistically, in the context of plans.

I propose that we think of the rational reasoner as beginning her practical deliberations by evaluating, in terms of the beliefs, desires, and feelings that form the contents of her conscious awareness, the various outcomes that might result from her possible actions. In characterizing this evaluation we introduce the conception of preference, and its measure, utility; and we attribute to the rational reasoner a concern to maximize her expectation of utility. This leads to the next stage of her deliberations, in which she evaluates actions in relation to utility. It is natural to link actions directly to their outcomes, and to suppose that an agent's reasons for choosing a particular action are determined directly by her preferences for its outcome, so that choice follows straightforwardly from preference. Our argument shows, however, that this linkage can be too direct, so that the rational reasoner will not always proceed to evaluate actions one by one, but rather will appreciate the importance of sequences of actions, of plans, in her endeavor to maximize utility. Her reasons for choosing an action may then be determined by her preferences for the outcome or possible outcomes of the plan into which it fits. These preferences may not be simple; she must take into account her preferences as they will be throughout the time period encompassed by the plan.

The rational reasoner, like any other animal, is moved by her desires. But her capacity for semantic representation enables her to distance herself from the directly motivating force of unconceptualized desires. This distancing is the form her psychological self-manipulation takes. She can harness the motivating force of desire to her representations of desires, and, in unifying them, to their fulfillment. Only from this maximizing objective is the motivating force directed to particular actions. How it is directed is determined by the objective, but need not itself involve a maximizing procedure.

In this account, preferences are conceptually distinct from practical reasons, or reasons for acting, and enter at a different point into the agent's practical deliberations. The account of deliberation is admittedly more complex than that offered by the orthodox view, but this complexity is clearly needed to accommodate situations involving preference change or interpersonal interaction. Maximization is situated at the center of the account, and explicates its own constraint, as it were, in the formation of reasons for making particular choices.

In the traditional account of economic man, his basis for choice is fully given by his preferences and the probabilities for the respective outcomes of his possible actions. I have sought to show the inadequacy of this basis for rational choice, to illustrate some of the features of an alternative account, and to sketch some of the conceptual underpinnings of such an account. Even if I have been successful in these endeavors, I have only pointed in the direction of a theory of the rational reasoner.

Seven   Nathan Rosenberg

Economic Experiments

This chapter offers a historical examination of a certain kind of freedom and its economic consequences. It focuses on the freedom to
perform economic experiments, including experimentation with
new forms of economic organization as well as the better-known experiments that have been responsible for new products and new
manufacturing technologies. It is taken as axiomatic that long-term
economic growth, which historically has centered upon the process
of industrialization, has involved the adoption of radically new technologies. Much less well understood, although intimately inter-
twined with experimentation at the technological level, has been an
associated process of organizational experimentation of profound
economic significance. Indeed, this chapter argues that the freedom
to undertake economic experiments has been the essential element of
the industrialization that uniquely has been a historical product of
capitalist countries.

The perspective suggested here is not, of course, entirely novel.
Marx understood very well that the new technology that was transforming Great Britain in the century before the publication of *The
Communist Manifesto* was inseparably linked to capitalist institutions.
Marx grasped a part of this story so firmly that his treatment must,
necessarily, be the starting point for this chapter. We now have the
advantage of more than a century of further capitalist performance
and seventy years of a socialist economy that has, at least until now,

adopted a distinctly different posture toward organizational experiments. I therefore start with Marx and the big issues connected with the economic growth experience of the West. I then proceed to a discussion of organizational aspects of capitalism and socialism that will take us far from this starting point, including an analysis of some of the central difficulties of contemporary socialist economies.

It is, of course, easy to caricature and ridicule the "freedom" of capitalist societies. For example, it has been said that the law, in its infinite wisdom and impartiality, forbids the rich as well as the poor to sleep under bridges. Some of the least attractive features of contemporary capitalism derive from the extreme inequalities of income that the system generates. It should be pointed out, however, that twentieth-century socialist societies, especially the Soviet Union and China, continue to tolerate, if not to encourage, large income differentials. In addition to those that are built into the structure of wages and salaries, there are those that are built into an elaborate system of differential access to stores, health care, and vacation and educational facilities. Perhaps most important has been the persistence of immense regional differentials.

The central argument of this paper is a simple one: the freedom to conduct experiments is essential to any society that has a commitment to technological innovation or to improved productive efficiency. The starting point is that there are many things that cannot be known in advance or deduced from a set of axioms or first principles. Only the opportunity to try out alternatives, with respect both to technology and to the form and size of organizations, can produce socially useful answers to the bewildering array of questions that are continually occurring in industrial (and in industrializing) societies.

The Emergence of Capitalism

How does Marx (and Engels) account for the intimate historical association of capitalism and industrialism? How are these connected with the decline of feudalism? Is the independent variable technological or economic?

Although Marx is sometimes portrayed as a technological determinist, he surely did not believe that it was technological changes that initiated social changes. He was, rather, an economic determinist who visualized economic forces as shaping the forces of technology. Even with respect to improvements in navigation and transportation, where one might argue that it was technological changes that initiated subsequent economic changes, Marx and Engels state clearly (twice) that it was the prior opportunities of expanding trade that provided the stimulus and the incentive to improvements in transportation. Technological changes, historically, need to be understood as a response to market forces. The rise of capitalism itself, was not directly associated with any major changes in the methods of production. Indeed, in Marx's view, capitalism arose in the sixteenth century, but the dramatic changes in technology that are associated with the industrial revolution came more than two hundred years later, in the second half of the eighteenth century.[1]

In the opening pages of *The Communist Manifesto*, Marx and Engels emphasize that it was the economic opportunities associated with the expansion of trade and overseas markets that provided the initiating impulses to the growth of capitalism and the unique technologies that capitalism brought with it:

> From the serf of the Middle Ages sprang the chartered burghers of the earliest towns. From these burgesses the first elements of the bourgeoisie were developed.
>
> The discovery of America, the rounding of the Cape, opened up fresh ground for the rising bourgeoisie. The East Indian and Chinese market, the colonization of America, trade with the colonies, the increase in the means of exchange and in commodities generally, gave to commerce, to navigation, to industry, an impulse never before known, and thereby, to the revolutionary element in the tottering feudal society, a rapid development.
>
> The feudal system of industry, under which industrial production was monopolized by closed guilds, now no longer sufficed for the growing wants of the new markets. The manufacturing system took its place. The guild-masters were pushed on one side by the manufacturing middle class; division of labor between the different corporate guilds vanished in the face of division of labor in each single workshop.
>
> Meantime, the markets kept ever growing, the demand ever rising. Even manufacture no longer sufficed. Thereupon, steam and machinery revolutionized industrial production. The place of manufacture was taken by the giant, Modern Industry, the place of the industrial middle class, by industrial millionaires, the leaders of whole industrial armies, the modern bourgeois.
>
> Modern industry has established the world-market, for which the discovery of America paved the way. This market has given an immense development to commerce, to navigation, to communication by land. This development has, in its turn, reacted on the extension of industry; and in proportion as industry, commerce, navigation, railways extended, in the same proportion the bourgeoisie developed,

increased its capital, and pushed into the background every class handed down from the Middle Ages.[2]

Marx's account emphasizes the growth in profit opportunities that were associated with the growth of overseas markets (it is noteworthy that Marx and Engels pay no attention to the internal growth taking place in European markets). The feudal economy lacked the capability to respond to these market opportunities. The organization of its industry was fundamentally restrictive and conservative. The craft guilds that controlled handicraft industry severely restricted entry into specific trades, dictated the quality of the product, and controlled the relationship between buyer and seller—including the price at which a product could be sold. The feudal system was overthrown by an emerging class of capitalists who swept away feudal institutions and replaced them with institutions of their own making. Above all, these institutions accorded a more prominent role to market forces than would have been possible in the Middle Ages.

Perhaps the most striking aspects of *The Communist Manifesto* are the passages calling attention to the unique role of capitalism in bringing about a historic growth in human productivity:

> The bourgeoisie has . . . been the first to show what man's activity can bring about. It has accomplished wonders far surpassing Egyptian pyramids, Roman aqueducts, and Gothic cathedrals. . . .
>
> The bourgeoisie cannot exist without constantly revolutionizing the instruments of production, and thereby the relations of production, and with them the whole relations of society. Conservation of the old modes of production in unaltered form, was, on the contrary, the first condition of existence for all earlier industrial classes. . . .
>
> The bourgeoisie, by the rapid improvement of all instruments of production, by the immensely facilitated means of communication, draws all, even the most barbarian, nations into civilization. . . .
>
> The bourgeoisie, during its rule of scarce one hundred years, has created more massive and more colossal productive forces than have all preceding generations together. Subjection of Nature's forces to man, machinery, application of chemistry to industry and agriculture, steam-navigation, railways, electric telegraphs, clearing of whole continents for cultivation, canalization of rivers, whole populations conjured out of the ground—what earlier century had even a presentiment that such productive forces slumbered in the lap of social labor?[3]

Note that, in the paean of praise in the last paragraph quoted, the great accomplishments are referred to specifically as creations of the bourgeoisie, not of science, the Protestant ethic, or some other force exogenous to a particular form of economic organization. Why, according to Marx, is capitalism such an immensely productive system?

Marx's answer is that the bourgeoisie is a unique ruling class on the stage of world history. It is the first ruling class whose economic interests are inseparably tied to change and not to the maintenance of the status quo. The bourgeoisie "cannot exist without constantly revolutionizing the instruments of production." In essence, capitalism has created a very powerful set of incentives that drives the system in the direction of continuous technical change and capital accumulation. The market pressures of competitive capitalism force the capitalist to maximize the output from his labor force. These pressures compel the capitalist to plow back the profits that he has earned by adopting new, economically superior, labor-saving technologies as rapidly as possible. Capitalism is historically unique in two distinct ways. Its institutions and internal pressures bring about the rapid generation of new and more productive technologies, and then the rapid adoption of these new technologies once they have been developed.

Marx did not view capitalism as a highly productive system from the beginning (although some passages in his writings seem to suggest such a view). According to Marx's historical analysis, capitalism in its earliest stages still made use of an essentially handicraft technology. This system—the manufacturing system— was more productive than the handicraft system that it displaced, but not enormously so. Although it involved a much more extensive division of labor, it did not yet utilize any drastically new technology. Capitalism did provide the necessary incentives to raise productivity, but productivity was greatly improved only when capitalism's more powerful incentive structure led to the emergence of modern industry. That emergence took over two hundred years, in Marx's view.

Marx's argument here has an important component that was foreshadowed in the above quotation from *The Communist Manifesto*. The great increases in productivity are attained only when capitalism leads to a mode of production to which science can be directly applied. This is perhaps the most distinctive feature of what Marx refers to as Modern Industry. For Marx, then, the application of science to industry is the essential step leading to the rapid productivity growth of modern industrial societies; it was capitalism that made that application possible. In fact, Marx's view is that modern science itself developed primarily in response to the problems that first expressed themselves historically in the sphere of production. Far from being an exogenous force, science arose out of the incentive structure and culture of capitalism.[4]

Thus, the Marxian view is that capitalism has served as a vehicle for the increase of human productivity because it provided powerful incentives to generate new technologies, it generated high rates of investment that led to the rapid diffusion and exploitation of new technologies, and it generated incentives for the development of science as well as for the application of science to the problems of industry.

Of course it was also central to Marx's thinking that advanced capitalism would finally give way to socialism after it became caught up in its own internal contradictions—but also after it had brought about the vast increases in human productivity that it was uniquely capable of bringing about. It is perfectly obvious, from the vantage point of 1990, that this prediction was wrong. The fact is that socialism has not been introduced into any country at an advanced stage of capitalism—at least not without the assistance of the Soviet army. On the contrary, twentieth-century socialist revolutions have occurred only in societies—such as Russia, China, and Cuba—that had not yet passed through the stage of advanced capitalism, with all of its attendant expansion of productive capacity.

One of the ironies of the present world situation is that socialism has been embraced as an anticapitalist ideology, and many Marxists in positions of political power today look to Karl Marx and his writings for guidance on how to organize a socialist society for rapid economic growth. Marx himself did not believe it was possible thus to bypass the capitalist stage on the road to socialism. He thought a socialist revolution had to be preceded by a capitalist stage of the kind that occurred centuries ago in Western Europe, because only capitalism could bring about the improvements in productivity to the point where socialist societies could be indifferent to further productivity growth. Socialist societies would not have to be concerned with raising productivity to high levels, because it was the historic role of capitalism to accomplish precisely that. Marx was obviously wrong in believing that sequence to be inevitable. Nevertheless, many of the economic difficulties in socialist societies today derive from trying to find guidance in Marx for the achievement of rapid industrialization and economic growth. Recent events strongly suggest that many parts of the socialist world are belatedly accepting Marx's belief that societies with socialist objectives cannot so easily bypass the capitalist stage.

Technological Innovation

Marx's account of the reasons why industrialization first occurred within a framework of capitalist institutions is incomplete, or at least incompletely specified. He is much more explicit about the importance of the special incentive mechanisms of capitalism than about the specific forms that economic organizations have taken and why they have taken those particular forms. Capitalism's historic success in generating new technologies depended heavily upon its ability to fulfill certain other conditions. What were the additional features of capitalism that have rendered it such a powerful instrument for technological innovation? The general answer that has already been advanced is that capitalism has offered the freedom to engage in experiments of all sorts. But to see why that freedom has been so critical, it is first necessary to examine with greater care the nature of the process of technological innovation.

The essential feature of technological innovation is that it is an activity fraught with uncertainty. This uncertainty, by which I mean an inability to predict the outcome of the search process or to predetermine the most efficient path to a particular goal, has a very important implication: the activity cannot be planned. No person, or group of persons, is clever enough to plan the outcome of the search process, in the sense of identifying a particular innovation target and moving in a predetermined way to its realization—as one might read a road map and plan the route to a historical monument.

If we wanted to push an analogy, we might say that achieving a technological innovation is more like winning a military engagement. A battle cannot be completely planned in advance because the commanding officer doesn't know how the enemy will respond, or what the outcome of that initial response will be.

Without pushing the analogy too far (because, after all, a battle has a more simple, foreseeable goal than does the search for a technological improvement), what innovation and military combat have in common is that decisions need to be made in a sequential way. That is to say, at some future time vital information will become available that cannot, in the nature of the case, be made available now. It would be folly to lock oneself into a predetermined pattern of behavior that deprived one of the benefit of additional information that may be decisive to success or failure, but which can only become available in the future.

It is inherent in the research process that information accumulates, even if it is only the information that certain alternatives are unproductive and should be discarded. There is no way of knowing, in advance of research (that is, of experiments), which alternatives are worth pursuing further and which are not. This is one reason why taking out a patent discloses valuable information to a firm's competitors, even though the award of the patent provides the owner with certain legal protections, and even though the contents of the patent document may not disclose sufficiently detailed information to permit imitation. The mere knowledge that something is possible (say, in pharmaceuticals), or that a particular procedure can achieve a particular end result, is likely to be extremely valuable. It is important evidence that research in certain specific directions, or employing certain specific methods, is likely to prove fruitful. The appropriate analogy here is to the information provided when someone has struck oil. Competitors will want to locate their drilling equipment as closely as possible to the successful well.

Thus it is in the nature of the research process that it is more likely to prove successful, and far more likely to proceed efficiently, if decision making is sequential in nature. The failure to take this aspect of research fully into account has been responsible for many of the most spectacular failures of government-sponsored research and development projects in the postwar period. A fundamental reason why government agencies have had such a poor record at picking technological winners has been that large commitments were made long in advance, without the built-in flexibility (or incentive) for changing course as more information became available.

Historically, government programs have been most effective when they have been directed at improving the infrastructure of support, by providing the educational facilities, as in agriculture, or by supporting research at the most fundamental level where market incentives have been weakest, as in medical research. Government support has been much less effective with respect to later stages of the product design process, where commercial judgments have to be made.

At this later stage, cost considerations tend to be increasingly significant. The preferences of buyers with respect to trade-offs between higher cost and improved product performance often make the decisive difference between success and failure. The generalization may be hazarded that the more closely one moves to the final stages of new product development, the less effective are the judgments and decisions of government officials, and the more effective are those of businessmen who are investing and risking private funds. Public officials have little incentive to limit costs, and they do not have enough specialized information to make intelligent judgments about the needs of particular markets.

The classic examples here are from the aircraft industry. The supersonic transport was finally terminated in the United States after large initial libations of federal government support. It is extremely unlikely that Boeing would have gone as far as it did with its preferred design if it had been risking its own funds and not the taxpayers'. The Concorde was built by a consortium of European governments. It is fair to describe that aircraft (only sixteen of which were manufactured) as a brilliant technological success but a commercial disaster. The dismal experience of the British commercial aircraft industry in the years after World War II, when the development costs of new aircraft were overwhelmingly financed by the British treasury, is another case in point. The more recent experience of Airbus Industrie suggests that some useful lessons have indeed been learned, but it is too early to say whether this international consortium will prove to be commercially viable.

A closely related issue is the matter of timing. Timing is a crucial consideration, because the critical decision is often not *whether* a particular project ought to be supported, but when and on what scale. When Richard Nixon was president, the idea of conducting a war on cancer commanded widespread support in principle. The problem was that no one really knew, at that time, how to spend large sums of research money on such a program. Although some good scientific research was supported in microbiology, much money was, inevitably, wasted. There is another trade-off here, between time and cost: proceeding more rapidly, on a large scale, is very costly. When one is allowed to proceed slowly and sequentially, one can keep numerous options alive. As new information becomes available from the ongoing research enterprise, options can be reevaluated and more informed allocative decisions can be made. Unpromising avenues can be abandoned. By committing larger amounts of money only at a later and better-informed stage, research resources are utilized more efficiently.

The trouble with a war on cancer, as with a supersonic transport plane, is that large amounts of money are committed to a particular project, or to a particular design, long before sufficient information is available to permit an intelligent evaluation of the research options. Where government funds are involved, the problem is compounded by the failure to terminate a project or a design, even after compelling evidence has accumulated that the thrust of research and development (R&D) expenditures is in a direction unlikely to yield acceptable results. The postwar American experience is littered with such instances in nuclear energy, synthetic fuels, and the procurement of new military hardware of all sorts.[5] Although there may on occasion be a compelling case for rapid development, as in the Manhattan Project of World War II, the evidence is overwhelming that there is an inherent pathology of wastefulness in such an approach, as compared with a slower pace of development that permits frequent revision and redirection as new information becomes available.

Capitalist Institutions Favorable to Innovation

The relevance of this discussion to the historical efficiency of capitalist institutions in encouraging innovation is clear. For activities that involve a high degree of uncertainty, capitalism provides multiple sources of decision making and initiative, as well as strong incentives for proceeding one step at a time. Planning and centralization of decision making do not lead to efficiency when there is a high degree of uncertainty and when goals and objectives cannot be clearly defined.

One of the less heralded, but considerable, virtues of competitive capitalism has been the speed with which firms have unsentimentally cut their losses as it became apparent that a particular direction of research was unlikely to prove fruitful. Where funds come from the public sector, by contrast, spending is likely to continue much longer on unpromising avenues. Inertia and the reluctance to admit failure publicly play an important role here, but so does the fact that the decision makers in government are not personally concerned in the financial losses that result.

The historical creativity of capitalism as an institutional mechanism for encouraging technological and organizational innovation has to be examined against the background of pervasive uncertainty. The uncertainty inherent in the search for new technologies has meant that the risks associated with this search could best be approached in certain specific ways. Capitalism historically developed a cluster of novel organizational forms that had the result of reducing certain intolerable risks to more tolerable levels. These were the risks associated with the decision to commit financial resources to the search for technological improvements. A high level of risk was inseparable from technological innovation because, as we have seen, the search for new technologies was uncertain in the extreme. Moreover, even if one did succeed in developing a new technology that was a clear improvement over anything that already existed, the prospect of making any money out of it was still highly uncertain.

It is of particular interest to note that Marx himself recognized this uncertainty, although his rather begrudging recognition only made its appearance in the third volume of *Capital*, published after his death and many years after the publication of the immensely influential first volume. In the third volume Marx called attention to "the far greater cost of operating an establishment based on a new invention as compared to later establishments arising *ex suis ossibus*. This is so very true that the trailblazers generally go bankrupt, and only those who later buy the buildings, machinery, etc., at a cheaper price make money out of it."[6] This is an extremely interesting passage, since it constitutes explicit recognition by Marx of the extreme vulnerability of the capitalist in his social role as a carrier of technological innovation. Had Marx given more attention to this vulnerability in volume 1 of *Capital*, it would have been necessary to portray the capitalist in a distinctly different light. It would also have been necessary to face up more candidly to the painful trade-offs all societies must confront between greater equity and greater efficiency.[7] But such an examination would have highlighted the weakness of capitalists, whereas Marx was intent on portraying their social power and their capacity for exploiting others.

The history of capitalism involved the progressive introduction of a large number of institutional devices that facilitated the commitment of resources to the innovation process by reducing or placing limitations upon risk. Among the most critical were new institutions and laws that limited the liability of an investor in any particular enterprise, provided for the easy marketability of ownership shares, established stock markets which were obviously essential to the achievement of ready marketability, reduced risk by the fundamental technique of insurance, and defined the obligations between principals and agents.[8]

The emergence of business firms with limited liability for their owners, and of ownership shares that were easily marketable, was central in facilitating investment in risky undertakings. From the point of view of the individual investor, a limited liability corporation made it possible to convert a long-term risk involving large amounts of capital into a short-term risk that was limited to small amounts of capital. Marketability of assets and the existence of efficient markets for the sale of these assets meant that owners were not undertaking commitments equal in duration to the life of long-lived capital assets. On the contrary, they could realize their financial gains or cut their financial losses whenever doing so appeared to be expedient. In this way a capitalist proprietor's long-term risk was converted into an investor's short-term risk. At the same time, the ownership of the firm's assets was effectively divided into two levels: first, those of the corporation as an ongoing entity; second, those of the shareholders who supplied the firm with its capital. The first-level risks remained as great as they always had been, but the second level risks were of a different order and were much more readily acceptable. This division of risk obviously bears a close resemblance to the redistribution of risk that takes place between a property owner and his insurance company.

Looking back on Marx, it is apparent that, although he had a profound appreciation of the technological dynamism of capitalism, he did not appreciate how far this dynamism was due to institutional measures that reduced risk and, by so doing, encouraged the experimentation that made innovation so commonplace under capitalism. There is obviously a close connection between reducing risk and encouraging experimentation. The willingness to undertake experiments in both the social and the technological sphere depends upon some sort of limitation upon the negative consequences for the owners if the enterprise should fail, as it frequently does. The great technological achievements of capitalism are inseparable from the system's success in reducing risk to more tolerable levels while at the same time offering the prospect of huge financial rewards if the risky enterprise should succeed.

These technological achievements were thus based upon capitalist legal institutions and property rights that legitimated experimentation with new organizational forms as well as with new technologies. The final arbiter of whether something new was socially desirable was not a government authority, or the religious clergy, or the guild members or merchants whose personal interest might be threatened by some innovation. Rather, the final arbiter was the marketplace. Capitalism did indeed legitimate innovation, but only if it could pass the market test. It was, as Marx recognized, the first form of social organization in which economic life was dominated by groups whose economic interests caused them to challenge the status quo.

Decentralization of Economic Authority

The freedom to conduct experiments required several other conditions. One of these conditions was that the economic sphere had to attain a greater degree of autonomy from external forces, especially freedom from arbitrary and unpredictable interventions by government authorities.

A critical aspect of this increasing autonomy was the emergence of new political institutions that reduced the risk of arbitrary exactions and appropriations (or even expropriations) by a powerful ruler. The rise in western Europe of parliaments in control of government purse strings was an essential part of this story. So was the emergence of new legal concepts, precedents, and institutions for the enforcement of contracts and property rights generally. In this respect, the bourgeois political revolutions of the seventeenth and eighteenth centuries were central to the economic achievements of capitalism.

The swiftness and the extent to which business organizations were freed from government control in the early years of capitalism should not be exaggerated. Government approval, in the form of a charter or franchise, long remained the normal practice—at least for specific forms of organization, such as limited liability companies; or for companies that wished to trade in certain regions, such as the Hudson Bay Company, the East India Company, and the Muscovy Company; or for organizations providing certain kinds of services, such as canal building and road building.[9] It was only in the course of the nineteenth century that business firms attained a reasonable degree of freedom in selecting new activities or new product lines. Nevertheless, the trend in Western Europe and North America in the eighteenth and nineteenth centuries was in the direction of increased freedom of action of the enterprise.

The freedom to conduct experiments not only required a high degree of autonomy; it also required, as mentioned earlier, a large number of decision makers, as opposed to a hierarchical, centralized system of decision making. In effect this meant not only decentralization but also the inability of the experimenters to influence the outcome of the market evaluation of the new product. In fact, some of the most decisive failures of twentieth century socialism flow from the failure to allow experimentation, and from the resulting loss of opportunities to observe the outcome of such experiments.

The need to expose investment decisions to the risk of being proved wrong implies the decentralization of decision-making authority, since any central authority will have a strong motivation for withholding financial support from those who are bent on proving that the central authority made a mistake, or on imposing on the central authority the cost of scrapping splendid-looking facilities whose only fault is that some interloper has devised more productive facilities or discovered that the work done in the facilities can be accomplished more cheaply in some other country—or perhaps need not be done at all. The social costs and risks associated with such moves might be well worth financing, but the costs and risks to centralized decision makers might well be prohibitive.

Historically, one of the most distinctive features of capitalist economies has been the practice of decentralizing authority over investments and spreading it among a substantial number of individuals who stand to make large personal gains if their decisions are right, who stand to lose heavily if their decisions are wrong, and who lack the economic or political power to prevent at least some others from proving them wrong. Indeed, this feature can be considered as providing the definition of capitalism. Its importance for Western economic growth lies in the fact that the choice of capital investments includes the choice of which proposals for innovation are to be funded. The diffusion of authority to select programs for capital expenditure and the diffusion of authority to select projects for innovation thus cover much the same ground.[10]

Organizational Diversity

The long-term freedom to conduct experiments, as I have argued, has been the central feature of Western capitalism. The historical outcome of this freedom has been an economy characterized by a truly extraordinary pattern of organizational diversity. This diversity may usefully be thought of as the end result of a process of social evolution in which a wide range of organizational forms have been introduced, and in which firms have been allowed to grow to sizes that were influenced by the underlying conditions of technology, location, market size, range of products, and so on. The particular outcomes achieved with respect to firm size, pattern of ownership, product mix, and so on, have essentially been determined by a market process in which the underlying conditions of different industries have generated patterns of survival reflecting their own special conditions and not some *a priori* notion of a single best model to which they were expected to adhere.

It is very common to stress the importance, indeed the dominance, of large firms in Western capitalist economies. This perspective has been particularly common among Marxists (although by no means confined to them), who have seen the trend toward bigness and greater industrial concentration as part of the "inner logic" of capitalism. According to this view, the emergence of monopoly capitalism not only reflects the pervasive advantages of bigness, but also conveniently facilitates the transition to socialism through the mechanism of nationalizing the giant firms. Unfortunately, the commitment to this view has absolved several generations of critics from the much more serious task of examining, and accounting for, the remarkable institutional complexity of contemporary capitalist societies. Such an examination would have shown, for example, that although large firms are the predominant users of capital, smaller firms are the predominant employers of labor. It would also have shown not only that organizational structures differ immensely among the agricultural, manufacturing, public utilities, and service sectors, but also that immense differences exist within each of these sectors. Giant corporations do indeed play a most important role, but so do millions of self-employed individuals. Any perspective that sees only giant corporations misses the most impressive feature of Western economies: the great subtlety with which organizational modes have been adapted to, and modified by, the particularities of products and markets.

Consider those sectors of the manufacturing economy that are regarded as quintessentially big. The very largest American manufacturing corporations, as measured by assets, size, and sales, are in the petroleum and automobile manufacturing industries. Yet according to the Bureau of the Census, in 1972 there were 152 companies in petroleum refining, 165 companies in motor vehicles and car bodies, 1,748 in motor vehicle parts and accessories, and 788 in automotive stampings. In fact, in almost all of the industries where the very largest firms are found, there are also a large number of smaller firms. Thus the aircraft industry in 1972 contained 141 firms, the electronic computing industry 518 firms, and photographic equipment and supplies 555 firms.[11]

Problems of Socialist Organization

The discussion of organizational diversity as the outcome of a process of prolonged experimentation forms an appropriate bridge to a consideration of some of the economic problems of contemporary socialist societies. The failure of these societies to permit experimentation has been compounded by an undiscriminating ideological commitment to the economic advantages of bigness—a commitment that has its origins in the writings of Marx. The reluctance to allow organizational size and structure to be tailored to the specific needs of different economic activities has been combined with an incentive system that is pervasively hostile to risk taking. This combination goes a long way toward explaining one of the most fundamental, and perhaps surprising, difficulties of contemporary socialist societies: their failure to take full advantage of superior technologies.

It is, on first consideration, not so obvious why hostility toward experimentation and risk taking should have created such serious obstacles to the exploitation of better technologies. After all, in a world where technologically advanced capitalist economies already exist, a socialist economy has the invaluable option of acquiring such technologies from abroad. There are no compelling reasons why foreign capitalist economies cannot serve as sources for the more sophisticated technologies that socialist economies are unable to develop.

Of course, to a considerable extent that is precisely what has happened. The Soviet Union has been a large-scale importer of Western technologies since the 1920s. Her inability to generate the incentives, or to provide the social space and opportunity for experimentation, has been at least partially offset by the ability to import technologies developed by the technologically dynamic, capitalist West. Thus, although Marx was wrong in arguing that socialism would arrive only in societies that had already passed through the state of mature capitalism, one might argue that this mistake has not carried so severe a penalty as might be expected, because advanced capitalism in the West has made its technologies universally available. This is, indeed, an important truth, and it should be further acknowledged that all industrializing countries except for Britain (the first one) have managed to grow more rapidly by borrowing foreign technologies. This was true of Japan in the twentieth century, as is widely acknowledged, but it was also a central element of America's rapid industrialization in the nineteenth century—an industrialization that built upon the already existing technologies of metallurgy, power generation, railroads, and textiles in Great Britain.

Even though twentieth-century socialist societies did not have to develop their own technologies, however, the mode of organization of their economies imposed rather sharp limits on the economic benefits they could derive from foreign technologies. First of all, technology transfer is never simply a matter of shipping hardware from one location on the earth's surface to another.[12] Rather, such borrowing presupposes a sizable cadre of engineers, technicians, and managers to modify, adapt, maintain, and repair the hardware. Such skilled persons require an efficient infrastructure of training, organization, and facilities. Unless these preconditions are reasonably fulfilled, the prospects for successful technology transfer are poor.

But there are more fundamental and systemic considerations at issue here. Central planning, and the negligible freedom of action accorded to plant managers under the Soviet system, are deeply hostile to the introduction of new technologies. Such technologies are, by their nature, disruptive of established routines. Although they hold out the considerable promise of long-term improvements in productivity, they exact the short-term costs of installing new equipment, teaching different skills, establishing new work routines, working out the inevitable bugs with respect to product design and process technologies, developing new arrangements with suppliers of doubtful reliability, and so on. However, the entire central planning apparatus is geared to short-term goals. The success of a plant manager is based relentlessly upon his ability to fulfill the annual output quota given to his firm by the central planners. Although there have been innumerable attempts to introduce greater flexibility into this system, there has been little evidence of success. In its present form, it inflicts severe penalties upon the plant manager who fails to fulfill his annual output goal, whereas the managerial reward for fulfillment or overfulfillment is small—probably a modest, once-and-for-all annual bonus. Thus, aversion to the risks of new technology is endemic to the incentive system.

Indeed, the situation is often even worse than this. Since the setting of annual targets is based upon the central planners' estimate of a plant's productive capabilities, it is distinctly dangerous for the plant manager to reveal a capability considerably in excess of recent annual targets. The plant manager has a strong incentive to under-represent his capabilities in order to keep his future targets low and therefore easily attainable.

This managerial risk aversion and dissimulation is, of course, powerfully reinforced by a huge and well-entrenched Soviet bureau-cracy. The recent attempts at reform in the direction of greater mana-gerial discretion and flexibility threaten both the power and the perquisites of that bureaucracy. Decentralization would carry with it a devolution of power to the regions and to the plant managers. For these reasons, a greater reliance upon the associated apparatus of markets and market-determined prices is likely to remain anathema to the bureaucrats.

The systematic neglect of the consumer or, at best, the attach-ment of a low priority to consumer needs, has weakened even fur-ther the incentive at the plant level to introduce improved products.[13] It is notorious that, within the perpetual seller's market that the Soviet system has created, selling the product is never a problem. As a result, the effort involved in improving a product, or the disruption involved in changing the productive apparatus in order to introduce an entirely new, more attractive product, has a zero payoff for the plant manager. His continual preoccupation is, not with the marketing of his product, but with the unreliability of his suppliers in providing him with the inputs that are essential for meeting his annual goals.[14] Here again the system provides no incen-tive to innovation.

> The problem is the lack of institutions and organizations which despite all obstacles can effect the introduction of revolutionary new technical innovations, accepting all the risk concomitant with this work, includ-ing that of failure, the struggle against conservatism and deep-rooted habit. Why should an enterprise director accept this risk and take up a struggle when . . . he is able without such effort to sell the products of his firm easily? With the buyers lining up for the firm's old product, why take upon oneself all the trouble involved in the introduction of a new product?[15]

The failure of socialist societies to conduct and learn from exper-iments has been most conspicuous, of course, in the uncritical accep-tance of the desirability of large size, or what is sometimes referred to as "giantism" in Soviet central planning. Giantism may be defined as an uncritical commitment to a belief in the existence of indefinitely continuing economies of large-scale production.[16] Its intellectual antecedents undoubtedly lie in Marx's admiration for the large-scale technologies of the British industrial revolution and his forceful articulation of the view that, in the competitive process, the larger-scale capitalist always wins against the smaller one. In Marx's words: "The battle of competition is fought by cheapening of commodities. The cheapness of commodities depends, *caeteris paribus*, on the productiveness of labor, and this again on the scale of production. Therefore, the larger capitals beat the smaller."[17]

Marx was certainly one of the first economists (together with J. S. Mill) to call attention to the economic significance of large-scale production. He appreciated the importance of indivisibilities[18] and pointed to numerous cases (especially in the capital goods sector) where economic advantages were derived from doing certain things on what he called a "cyclopean scale."[19] Marx also pointed to the possibilities in certain industries, when the scale of production was sufficiently large, of utilizing wastes or by-product materials.[20]

It is far from clear, however, that Marx, a very careful and perceptive observer of the industrial scene, would have advocated indiscriminate giantism as it has been pursued in Soviet Russia. There is evidence, moreover, that the thrust toward giantism was fed, during the Stalinist years, by a determination to emulate certain of the largest American establishments, which were believed to be highly efficient—for example, in the steel industry.[21] (It is tempting to say that, in its pursuit of the economies of large-scale production, the Soviet Union has provided the world with much evidence on the diseconomies of large-scale production.) Also, as a matter of administrative convenience, central planners undoubtedly found it much simpler to deal with a small number of large plants rather than a large number of small ones. Bigness clearly served the interests of the central bureaucracy. This was most apparent in the disastrous experience in agriculture, the sector where bigness was least appropriate. However inefficient the large collective farm may have been in transforming agricultural inputs into outputs, it served as a powerful organizational device for collecting an agricultural surplus that could then be made to serve the interest of rapid industrialization.[22]

Ironically, whereas Marx predicted that bigness would emerge out of the competitive process under mature capitalism, there is a far greater concentration of employment in large firms in the Soviet Union than in the United States or Japan. Data from the 1960s suggest that 24 percent of Soviet enterprises had more than five hundred employees. The corresponding figure for the United States was only 1.4 percent and for Japan a mere 0.3 percent. At the other extreme, only 15 percent of Soviet enterprises had fewer than fifty employees, whereas 85 percent of American firms and 95 percent of Japanese firms had fewer than fifty workers.[23] Obviously, the larger size of Soviet firms has been imposed by deliberate government policy and is not the outcome of historical experience—either that of an earlier, mature capitalism or that of socialist experimentation.

The purpose of experimentation, of course, is to provide useful information for answering certain kinds of questions; but Marxism, at least in some of its most influential twentieth-century forms, has been unwilling to admit that the answers to some questions were in doubt. This unwillingness has often taken the form of simply asserting the priority of ideological purity over technical expertise. In China, both the Great Leap Forward and the later Cultural Revolution involved a denial of the role of technical expertise in the attainment of an efficient industrial society. Mao further claimed that a new socialist man would pursue economic efficiency and embrace an ideal of hard work merely out of a sense of commitment to socialism, and without any strong material rewards. His followers made important technical and economic decisions without consulting technical specialists. The only test of suitability for important managerial and technical positions was ideological. It is fair to say that these episodes set back the industrialization of China by at least a generation. (Curiously, the Great Leap Forward may be said to have involved experimentation of a very perverse sort: the attempt to set up backyard blast furnaces and chemical plants involved a test of the nonexistence of economies of large-scale production in precisely those sectors of the economy where they are of critical importance!)

The socialist preoccupation with bigness in industry is hostile to technological innovation in another fundamental way. Some of the disadvantages of bigness are minimal in an environment characterized by a high degree of stability and routine; but where the technology is changing rapidly, or might be made to change rapidly, bigness is much more likely to be a serious handicap. Many experiments are easier and less costly to conduct on a small scale. It is inherently difficult to introduce numerous small changes, and to do so frequently, in a large, hierarchical organization where permissions and approvals are required from a remote central authority.

The history of industries that have recently undergone rapid technological change—such as electronics and biotechnology—suggests that the flexibility offered by small firms is highly advantageous to experimentation and exploration. Large firms, operating through layers of management and with rigid rules, are not well suited to rapid changes and frequent on-the-spot decisions. Where technological uncertainties are high, it is far more efficient to conduct experiments in small firms on a small scale.[24]

The Soviet thrust toward larger scale and centralization has even pervaded the organization of research and development activities within each of the ministries that has planning responsibilities for major sectors of the economy. Among other consequences, this has resulted in the isolation of research and development from managerial decisions relating to production planning, and has thus intensified the difficulties, discussed earlier, of introducing new technologies.[25] It also further isolates the findings of Soviet science from possible industrial applications. This is a consideration of great significance. Improving the links among the separate components of the R&D process is crucial to successful innovation in all industrial economies.[26] In the case of the Soviet Union, the costs of poor linkages are undoubtedly very great, since much Soviet research at the basic end of the R&D spectrum is at the highest international standards.

Conclusion

This chapter asserts the strategic role played by the freedom to experiment in the long-term process of economic growth and industrialization. I have argued that a peculiar strength of capitalism, historically, has been its manner of accommodating the special needs of the innovation process. I have also argued that the failure to provide for such accommodation, in terms of organization and incentives, has been responsible for the persistent failure of socialism to generate new technologies or even to adopt technologies that already exist. It should be obvious that this discussion does not exhaust all the significant things that one might say about capitalism and socialism as alternative ways of organizing economic activity. It should also be obvious, however, as recent developments in Eastern Europe and China are emphasizing, that it is extremely difficult to make socialist societies more amenable to technological change without, at the same time, making them more capitalistic.

Eight

Donald N. McCloskey
and John S. Nelson

The Rhetoric of Political Economy

The phrase "political economy" is contested because it is worth own-
ing. The winner gains the prestige of an earlier economics, ante-
dating the metaphor of mathematics, and gains too the prestige of
realism—for who would deny the politics in the economy and the
economics in the polity?

Political economy can of course be attached to the politics in economic policy, those "political constraints" so irritating to economists.
"Why can't we have a rational farm policy?" Well, take note of the
senators from Vermont and Iowa. It is no accident that economics
became detached from the label "political economy" in the middle of
the last century, at the nadir of interference in the economy. Defining
"political economy" as the politics in economic policy makes it a
branch of political science. It is the low-status economics of practical
policy, scorned by deep thinkers, who nonetheless watch it closely.
The slow-motion wrestling between the octopus of corporate capitalism and the giant squid of government makes good viewing.

Such a political economy is plainly rhetorical, in the agora, in the
World Bank, in Senate hearings. It fits with the definition of "rhetoric" in the newspapers, as the speaking that politicians use when
they have nothing much to say. "Ask not what your country can do
for you . . . " But political speaking has more to it than "rhetoric" in
the popular and ornamental sense. If politicians gave only inaugural

addresses, not much could be learned about politics from their words. But they talk much more than that.

Ornaments are not without meaning, of course, and even inaugural addresses repeat the sustaining myths of democracy. But speech also moves people to action by "deliberative" rhetoric (as opposed to "epideictic" rhetoric, to use the old categories). Contrary to the assertions of a vulgar Marxism that reduces words always to material interests (as does for instance George Stigler, America's leading vulgar Marxist), argument counts. The political scientist G. R. Boynton has recently given the example of agricultural hearings in the Senate. He examined every exchange over twenty years, and found that stories of "our experience" dominated the proceedings, restricting the range of policies that were considered seriously. The senators practically never asked the opinion of economists. "We tried that in 1955," a senator would say, and the advocate would fall silent.[1]

Two other definitions of political economy are parallel to each other. They either reduce politics to economics (thus Stigler, Anthony Downs, and Mancur Olson) or reduce economics to politics (thus J. K. Galbraith, Albert Hirschman, and Brian Barry). The rhetoric comes from the professors' mouths. The reductive moves are metaphors. The professors say, "Power, you see, is money." Or they say, "Money, after all, is power." Political parties are "just like" business firms and cartels, or business firms and cartels are "just like" political parties. Such metaphors, as the philosopher Max Black put it, have "the power to bring two separate domains into cognitive and emotional relation by using language directly appropriate to the one as a lens for seeing the other."[2] Note the political metaphor of power and domain.

The study of rhetoric, then, allows one to watch what is at stake in an argument about politics, whether among senators or among professors. The division of the economic from the political sphere is itself a rhetorical move, as when economic experts take certain politics as their own or when political economy brings vote trading in Congress under an economic and therefore a Scientific model. The arguments can be serious and scientific, or mere puffery and guile; but they will always be rhetorical. Rhetoric is not confined to phony persuasion or to "soft" evidence. Taking note of the available means of persuasion is not necessarily a condemnation of the means. It may be just fine that senators use stories, and economists use metaphors, to argue about politics. In fact, it is hard to imagine what else they would do.

The study of what they all do is called the "rhetoric of inquiry"— much exercised recently in economics, history, political theory, and other subjects.[3] The name says merely that inquiry is rhetorical. It notes that an academic subject, such as the study of political constitutions or of partial differential equations, will consist of argument. The argument will of course be a matter of proofs and facts, but what counts as a proof or a fact will vary from time to time and from field to field. In the exordium of his book *Political Argument,* Brian Barry quotes the economist Jacob Viner: "There is a third kind of rhetoric ... whose task is ... to discover for particular values their appropriate place in the process of persuasion. To me this last kind of rhetoric seems a most appropriate one for the academic scholar."[4] That's about right.

The neglected arguments surface in the details of polities and economies. Rhetoric, like God, is in the details. Noticing how scholarship itself consists of such devices is the rhetoric of inquiry. Paying attention to rhetoric of inquiry is a way of becoming self-conscious about scholarly arguments. You may, if you wish, sneer at self-consciousness as something only Californians would desire, but you are likely to end up sneering out of the other side of your mouth. Awareness of rhetoric redeems an economist from enslavement to some defunct philosopher.

Philosophies of inquiry, as distinct from rhetorics, are influential in the social sciences, mainly because they are narrowing and therefore simplifying. Mainly they say, "You can't do that,"—in other words, "You needn't bother with that." George Stigler and Gary Becker, for instance, tell economists to stick to budget constraints and other "objective" matters, because about tastes one should not dispute.[5] But a few economists such as Albert Hirschman argue persuasively against such specialization, and a sociologist like Pierre Bourdieu has of course gone further.[6] Similarly, a long-standing rule in economics, said by its advocates to derive from positivism and other good ways of narrowing the conversation, forbids economists to use questionnaires. (Statistical questionnaires are all right, such as income tax forms and census returns, in which the respondents are of course candid. It's those devilish verbal questionnaires—about investment plans, price expectations, or even presidential preferences—that are epistemologically suspect. Why? Well, people, you know, *have been known to lie.*) The political economist who stops worrying about self-consciousness will end up a zombie to some Method.

Talking about "rhetoric" is a rich way of talking about self-consciousness in argument. It allows one to adopt narrowing philosophical rules if one wishes, but provides a way to watch the adoption. As a method of observing academic behavior, it tends to-ward wider arguments and freer societies.

Economics and Law: An Example

Consider a straightforward example, from the political and legal economy of Judge Richard Posner:

> Our survey of the major common law fields suggests that the common law exhibits a deep unity that is economic in character. . . . The com-mon law method is to allocate responsibilities between people en-gaged in interacting activities in such a way as to maximize the joint value . . . of the activities. . . . The judge can hardly fail to consider whether the loss was the product of wasteful, uneconomical resource use. In a culture of scarcity, this is an urgent, an inescapable question.[7]

The argument is attractive, at least to McCloskey, who is fond of its author (among other reasons, for learning ancient Greek as an adult); we did not pick the passage because we think it wrong or think Richard Posner the embodiment of evil. Unhappily there is a rhetoric of rhetoric, at least as it is understood these days, which we wish to oppose. Attention to rhetoric need not be debunking. We picked the Posner passage because it typifies one branch of political economy, the one that looks at the political (and in this case, the legal) world economistically. Economics, we are suggesting, is not immune to lit-erary scrutiny. Accordingly, look at the words as scholarly poetry. Go back to freshman English, and read them for their effect.

Posner's argument is carried in part by the equivocal use of the vocabulary of economics. *Allocate, maximize, value,* and *scarcity* are technical words in economics, with precise definitions; here Posner uses them also in wider senses, evoking scientific power to claim pre-cision without necessarily attaining it. The sweetest turn is the use of *uneconomical,* not in fact a technical word in economics. It encapsu-lates Posner's argument that judges act as though they followed eco-nomic models, because to do otherwise would be "wasteful." The economical/uneconomical figure of speech supports the claim that economic arguments (arguments about scarcity) are pervasive in the law. Triple repetition (technically, *commoratio*) hammers it home: first in the word *uneconomical;* then in the reference to a "culture of scar-city" (a nice echo of "a culture of poverty," from the other side of the tracks); and finally in the repetition, "urgent, inescapable."

People involved with one another in auto accidents or breaches of contract are said to be "engaged in interacting activities." Posner does not, however, acknowledge that they interact also in political and moral systems. A farmer and a railroad "interact" when a spark from the engine burns the wheat, but a judge does not "interact" with citizens who believe that big enterprises like railroads are blameworthy merely because they are big. The Latinate vocabulary of "engaging in interacting activities" makes an appeal to the character of the observer or, better, the scientist. Technically speaking, the argument is an "ethical" one, making use of the *ethos* (the character) of the speaker. The scientific vocabulary partakes of the clinical—but carries with it, unspoken, a philosophy of community. The words matter. The style is the substance.

Again, the passage uses the metaphor of "deepness" in unity to support its metaphors, as do similar attempts to change minds. The University of Chicago legal economist will claim, with Posner, that the deep structure of American law celebrates capitalism. A critical legal theorist, similarly, will claim that the deep structure of law apologizes for capitalism.

And so forth: one can in this way examine the texts of political economy rhetorically. One can ask what genres it uses, what figures it deploys, who are its implied readers, whether there is a text in this class.

Public Choice: Another Example

The approach is applicable to any passage whatever. Consider for instance five sentences from another seminal book in political economy, from which we quote the third complete sentence on each of five pages chosen by random number:

1. *"Moreover, a significant factor in the popular support for socialism through the centuries has been the underlying faith that the shift of an activity from the realm of private to that of social choice involves the replacement of the motive of private gain by that of social good."*[8] Read the sentence twice, as students of poetry are advised to do, noting the force of the words. Even a sentence chosen at random produces nuggets of close reasoning. Yet notice that the main clause is routine to the point of cliché and redundancy: "significant factor" (why would one bother if it were not significant?); "through the centuries" (again, why bother otherwise? A historian would be embarrassed to

use such a tinkling phrase); "underlying faith" (come now: isn't all faith "underlying"?). The clause lulls with conventionality, and with a little "rhetoric" in the street sense. We are about to be treated to a Political Opinion. But the counterrhetoric of Science works here, too. If the phrases "through the centuries" and "underlying faith" would fit an inaugural address, "popular support" would not, and "significant factor" most assuredly not. In fact, the dual rhetorics of political passion and scientific observation pervade the book. No one can doubt that the authors are passionately committed to freedom, and freedom by an individualistic definition (despite what the authors say on p. vii). Yet it is undoubtedly true, as the blurb to the paperback edition announces, that the book is also "a *scientific* study of the political and economic *factors* influencing democratic *decision-making,* based largely on the *methods* of *modern* economics and *game theory*" (emphasis supplied).

The second, dependent clause (following "that") is where the sentence and the ideas come to life. The clause has an eighteenth-century air, as though plucked from Smith or Hume. Note the Ciceronian parallels, reinforced by parallel syntax: "the realm of private to that of social" corresponds with "the motive of private . . . by that of social." Common opinion would say that private choice leads to private gain, social choice to public good, and even the alliteration of "gain" and "good" drives the point home. The phrasing is ornamental, but an ornament with substance: here we have, it says, a mistaken symmetry in human thinking, persisting "throughout the ages" (as the next sentence reiterates, while the historian squirms with embarrassment).

2. *"All externalities, negative and positive, will be eliminated as a result of purely voluntary arrangements that will be readily negotiated among private people."*[9] We are here taken away from the elegance of the eighteenth-century philosophers. If the word "externalities" has become too familiar to convey the message that this is twentieth-century Science, the reader will catch the message nonetheless in the mathematical talk of "negative and positive." Scientific prose, Newton's invention, favors two passive verbs in one sentence—"will be eliminated . . . will be . . . negotiated." The passive suggests, as the sentence avers, that the result is unstoppable, the result of no named human agency (even as the sentence names the agency as "private people"). The removal of agency is part of the rhetoric of mathematical proof, giving a strange double message to a social science

approaching society scientifically. There is no contradiction here, merely countercurrents of suggestion.

3. *"In order to be able to do so, [the modern welfare economist] falls back on the criterion designed by Pareto."*[10] The "modern welfare economist" is of course personified, a figure extended over two pages, the better to quarrel with him. If the criterion were not named, and not fallen back on by a namable person, it would be one of those undiscussable parts of the furniture that the passive voice announces. It would have to be, "Another criterion must be fallen back on" ("must," to retain the force of "in order to be able to do so"). But the superiority of the veil of ignorance over the Pareto criterion is the thing to be discussed. So it had better *not* be part of the furniture. The mention of Pareto, by the way, looks in isolation like an appeal to authority, that commonest of academic figures, but in context is not. It is merely a name to conjure with.

4. *"If less than a simple majority should be required for carrying a decision, the expected external costs would be greater, but the costs of reaching the necessary agreement among members of the effective coalition would be lower than under the operation of simple majority rules."*[11] The sentence repeats one of the main analytic results of the book: that with larger majorities required, the rising costs of reaching an agreement to vote for x works against the falling levels of "external costs" (namely, the hurt to the outvoted if something less than unanimity is required). The involved and lawlike formulation would be unintelligible without preparation. It occurs as recapitulation at the beginning of a chapter late in the book; the recapitulation says, this is the ground we have already covered. As the preceding sentence puts it, "the results . . . will be apparent to those who have understood . . . the preceding chapters." It does not invite doubt, and is cast in wholly "positive" terms. No passion fuels it. The vocabulary is academic, as befits the statement of a scientific finding. As usual in economics, however, the finding is a blackboard finding, not "empirical" on a narrow definition. The repetition is made necessary by the nonstatistical character of the finding. If the result had been 3.14159, there would have been no need to keep reminding the reader of the logic that sustains it. The logic, not the numbers, will justify the authors' claim.

The authors do not use positivistic standards of proof, though they bow to them occasionally (on this page: "Given the behavioral assumptions of our models"; but as in most economics, their observable implications are commonplaces). Note the conditional, "would be," continued in the next and concluding sentence of the paragraph. The conditional is the mood of frankest theorizing (as it sees itself), announcing itself to be conditional on certain assumptions being met. Here it changes to the future of prediction—the apodosis of a general condition, to be exact—sustained throughout the next two paragraphs, after the absolving phrase, "Given the behavioral assumptions." Thus, "individuals will tend," "bargaining will be required," "collective action will result in," and so forth. The auxiliary "will" stands guard over the assertions, reminding the reader that they are hypothetical. The book is filled with "will" and "would" and "if" and "given." The authors seem more reluctant than some writers on the subject to use the least candid of the theorizing verbal forms, the gnomic present: "The basic structure *is* perfectly just when the prospects of the least fortunate *are* as great as they can be" (emphasis added).[12]

5. *"There might be one or more farmers whose personal preferences for road-repairing called for such large investment as to make the 'maximizing equilibrium' preferable to the 'Kantian median.'"*[13] The sentence is part of a footnote to a passage elaborating on the prisoner's dilemma for public goods. Precision in economics takes such a form, noting the exceptions and corner solutions. Doing so establishes one's character as a sharp economist, able to bend sharp curves with the best. If the reader has already accepted the excellence of the writer, the dotting of i's and crossing of t's will not be necessary. Older scholars have less need for careful footnotes, because their character has been established. The amount of arguing a scholar needs to do depends on the character he has in the minds of readers. Pierre de Fermat could set mathematicians on a three-hundred-year search for a proof by penciling a note in a margin; the ordinary Joe needs dozens of pages of explicitness to get any respect. The point is typical of rhetorical thinking. It says, "Note who the author is, in the eyes of his audience."

Limits of Modernism

So political economy uses rhetoric. But that is an imprecise way of putting the matter. Only partly do we "use" rhetoric. As Coleridge said somewhere, we do not speak the language; the language speaks us. There is no way to be "nonrhetorical," to stand entirely outside the traditions of argument and "use" rhetoric to "communicate" the "substance" of argument. Plato dreamed of a place beyond the cave, where at least the best of us could stand outside human discourse. He assaulted the professors of his day (by the name of sophists) because they said that man, not God, was the measure of man's sayings. His hostile portrait of the sophists, incidentally, is still widely credited by the sorts of readers who take their opinions about women and the Midwest from H. L. Mencken. But rhetoric, to repeat, is not merely the ornament one adds into the speech at the end, and it is not necessarily dishonest. It is the whole of argument—its logic, its arrangement, its appeals to authority, its passion, its pointed lack of passion, its audience, its purpose, its statistics, its poetry. It goes without saying that economics and politics, and therefore political economy, are rhetorical.

The tradition of rhetoric is the alternative to the all-pervading modernism of intellectual life. Modernism, briefly put, is the methodology of advanced thinkers from 1860 to 1960. Akin to their predecessors Descartes and Plato, modernists purvey the notion that narrowing the arguments of science is good for science, because it is closer to God's way of thinking. By contrast, sloppy old rhetoric— surviving academically in law schools, English departments, and programs in speech communication—says that arguments are not God's but man's. Science is measurement, to be sure; but man is the measure. Arguments are linguistic, not physical. The conversation in an academic subject takes place in a little society, not somewhere out in the cold night of absolute truth. We human beings say what is a good argument in economics—limited by our language of $2 + 2 = 4$ and the roundness of the earth, no doubt, but with room to argue.

We cannot see into God's mind and note what He thinks about voting studies or urban politics. We decide, together, more or less reasonably, for our own purposes. There is no Archimedean point outside our intellectual culture from which to lever up the intellectual world. It would be nice if there were. But there isn't. Intellectuals in the line of Plato, Descartes, and Bertrand Russell have labored for 2,500 years to develop a formula for that Archimedean point. Their labor has produced side benefits, for which we must be thankful; but unhappily its main object has not been achieved.

The limits of modernism, despite some noble successes, have become evident to many people of late. It is worth a little to know that modernism has been on the way out for a couple of decades and that a lot of reasonable people who have examined the matter think it moribund. One may, of course, after recognizing that modernism is an episode in Western intellectual life, wish nonetheless to adopt it, on its merits, with eyes open. Splendid. The point is to avoid adopting modernism unconsciously, in the mistaken impression that it is the only way of thinking.

The decline of modernism shows in the decline of its dichotomies: style and substance, form and content, analytic and synthetic, methods and findings, subjective and objective, values and facts, discovery and justification, and—a master dichotomy towering over them all— nonscience and science. A major project of modernism was to divide thought into nonscience and science. Unfortunately, the modernists did a better job of devising more and more elaborate demarcation criteria than in explaining why one would want to demarcate in the first place. The modernists considered it urgent to decide whether astrology or economics or history were sciences. They did not offer plausible reasons for caring. One might as well have devoted philosophical sweat to determining whether a particular field of knowledge was Christian or not. Come to think of it, holding thought up to a template of Christianity has more purpose to it—namely, personal salvation and the fulfillment of God's will on earth, both commendable purposes—than holding it up to the word "science."

There were plenty of bad reasons given or implied. For instance: Science earns a lot of money from governments and foundations, so I'd better claim to be scientific. Or, in a more dignified version: Science is prestigious, and therefore my field will not be prestigious unless I can claim it as a science. (The peculiarly English definition of science has led English speakers into extreme versions of this non sequitur. The study of politics has become economistic on such grounds. A century ago, the ordering of prestige was reversed.) Or, less selfishly: Science is the only progressive field of thought, and therefore if my field is to be progressive it must be made scientific. (Defining "progressive" as "looking like what I imagine physics looked like between 1600 and 1900" makes such an argument easy to sustain.) Or, returning to the lower motivations: Science produced our riches, and therefore we should make everything scientific. Besides being another non sequitur, the history on which it is based is a fairy tale. The common belief that science had much to do with the industrial revolution, modern levels of mortality, and the other betterments of our condition up to about 1930 is erroneous.

Or, most commonly in the 1930s and 1940s, modernism was claimed as a stroke against fascism:

> The most sinister phenomenon of recent decades for the true scientist
> . . . may be said to be the growth of Pseudo-Sciences . . . organized in
> comprehensive, militant and persecuting mass-creeds. . . . [The test-
> ability criterion is] the only principle or distinction . . . which will keep
> science separate from pseudoscience.[14]

In other words, an intolerant and hysterical version of modernism
was to be sent out to do battle against intolerance and hysteria. The
political analysis here—echoed even now in rearguard actions by
neomodernists[15]—was always weak, not least because it was the
modernists themselves (for example, Karl Pearson) who devised the
pseudosciences of which Hutchison speaks: eugenics, for example,
and racial anthropology—the sciences of the extermination camps.
The modernists shout angrily that open discourse leads to fascism.
Perhaps their anger defends them from their guilt.

Rhetoric and Logic

Rhetoric is a better protection against authoritarians. The other, official ways of dealing with arguments are too feeble to be of much use
in protecting us against fascists. St. Augustine asked, "Why should
[the faculty of eloquence] not be obtained for the uses of the good in
the service of truth?"—and the modernist cannot answer. Parsing arguments into Logical and Illogical, to cast out the illogical, is a good
idea on occasion. But it is not the universal technique that some philosophers and most laypeople who demand logic think it is. The difficulty is that most human arguments—some very good indeed—fall
outside the walls of the narrowly, syllogistically logical. Inference
from experiment, for instance, would be cast into the flames, as
Hume pointed out two centuries ago. Analogy, too, though it runs
our intellectual lives, resists reduction to syllogism. It is literally not
a syllogism to say: A market is a good deal like politics; votes in Congress are political; therefore votes in Congress can be analyzed as a
market.

It was Aristotle who first announced the dichotomy between syllogism (or logic) and enthymeme (or fractured syllogism, that is to
say, rhetoric). The dichotomy does not work, because the certainty to
which syllogism is supposed to lead does not exist. We are all rheto-
ricians. The mathematicians Phillip Davis and Reuben Hersh remark
that "the line between complete and incomplete proof is always

somewhat fuzzy, and often controversial."[16] The proof of the Pythagorean Theorem may be uncontroversial by comparison with the latest attempt to prove Fermat's Last Theorem, yet they differ only in degree. If standards of proof are debatable in mathematics, they are all the more so in political economy.

Not everyone has heard the news. The rhetoric against analogy, for example, is well exhibited by the mathematician A. Kaufman in *Introduction to the Theory of Fuzzy Subsets*:

> Writing, in the sense of the theory of ordinary sets, A resembles B, B resembles C, C resembles V, . . . V resembles L, therefore A resembles L . . . constitutes a sequence of deductions without validity . . . used . . . by political men to make the best of the stupidity of certain voters. The sophists have a particular habit of making us believe in the existence of transitivity when its existence may well be doubted.[17]

The rhetoric of professional philosophy is a little more subtle, but comes to the same conclusion, namely, that human reasoning not reducible to strict syllogism is wrong. A philosopher will offer to *repair* an analogical argument, saying something like this: "It is helpful [the philosopher, like the man from the government, wishes above all to be helpful] to recast the argument so that it is logically valid; then all questions about its soundness can focus on the truth of the premises." This would free the philosopher to supply the missing major or minor premise. Since these are unlimited in number, he can choose one that makes the resulting argument silly or sound, as he fancies. This is the usual rhetoric the philosophers apply to "fallacies" and other arguments that their methods do not illuminate: drag the argument under the streetlight, beating it into unrecognizable form along the way. Outsiders should worry when human reasoning is said to require such rough handling.

Frans H. van Eemeren and Rob Grootendorst have recently pointed out a contradiction in the philosophers' rhetoric.[18] They observe that repairing the allegedly incomplete argument in a hostile fashion will entail a contradiction—a contradiction at the level of the pragmatic rules necessary for speech to be possible. Speech presupposes "the maxim of cooperation" in speech, namely, that the argument can be made complete with fair ease. Yet the repaired and supposedly equivalent argument violates grossly "the maxim of quality"—that the argument is meant to be true. It violates the maxim of quality because, in being completed, the repaired version acquires a patently untrue premise—the one so helpfully supplied by the philosopher bent on exhibiting the fallacy.

The usual way of talking about logic, in other words, leaves most argument in fallacy. For instance, *a fortiori* arguments often involve the fallacy of a suppressed premise, a premise furthermore that formal logic disavows, namely, that the comparison of cases involves an increase in rigor from minor to major. In Talmudic argument, it is called *kal ve-chomer*, the relation of weighty to trivial, the first two rules of interpretation in the rhetoric of Hillel the Elder and of Rabbi Ishmael. Miriam spoke against her half-brother Moses, for which the Lord made her leprous. Moses prayed for her to be cured, and the Lord answered, "If her father had but spit in her face, would she not be ashamed seven days? [*A fortiori*, then, since she spoke against my servant Moses,] let her be shut from the camp seven days, and after that let her be received in again [freed of leprosy]."[19] As M. Mielziner notes, "Here an inference is being made from minor to major, namely, from a human father's to the Lord's disfavor." He quotes Coke on Littleton: "What has force in a minor matter will have force in a major matter; and what does not have it in a minor matter will not have it in a major."[20] The common law and the religious law are systems for making decisions on some reasonable basis, as are science and scholarship. They cannot depend solely on first-order predicate logic.

Furthermore, law, science, politics, and ordinary life— even ordinary academic life—are filled with "ethical appeals," that is, arguments from the *ethos* of the speaker, from his character as known by the community. Science depends heavily on appeals to expertise, and even the derived sense of "ethics" is necessary for good science. On first glance it would appear to be strange to say that a good mathematician needs to be a good person, or that—if economists are seen to be bad people—their economics will be doubtful. But ethical appeals are made repeatedly in legal proceedings and in science, as in life. Often it is not irrelevant that a Cretan witness is a well-known liar.

A related fallacy is even more popular. Humans somehow think that the number of witnesses count, and that the proportion of witnesses on each side matters even more. The *argumentum ad populum*, when a majority claims to be right because it is the majority, has no force in strict logic but great force in actual reasoning. Socrates chides Polus for his lawyerly ways:

> My gifted friend, [I reject your reasoning] because you attempt to re-
> fute me in rhetorical fashion, as they understand refuting in the law

> courts. For there, one party is supposed to refute the other when they bring forward a number of reputable witnesses. . . . But this sort of refutation is quite worthless for getting at the truth; since occasionally a man may actually be crushed by the number and reputation of the false witnesses brought against him.[21]

True, occasionally one may be crushed, as was Socrates. But it is also true that people sometimes lie in questionnaires and that the sun might not come up tomorrow. Considering that the quest for philosophical certainty begun by Socrates has not yet reached its object, it would seem legitimate in the meantime to make decisions with majorities and reputations as much as with syllogisms.

One could go on in this fashion. Take down a modern elementary textbook on logic—Copi's standard book, for example—and slowly read the section on fallacies. Try to ignore the authoritarian and dismissive rhetoric with which the philosopher treats "fallacies," and ask: Are these not in fact the usual forms of reasoning? Are they wholly evil, to be exiled from serious conversation? Or should we rather make distinctions between good analogies and bad, good arguments from authority and bad, good rhetoric and bad?[22]

The American Question

Rhetoric, then, gives a place to stand from which to watch the modernism in political economy and to watch how scholarly arguments actually evolve. It asserts that the categories for thinking about speaking and writing that developed in classical rhetoric (and more generally in the humanistic half of our culture) fit the scientific culture, too. Science uses metaphors and satisfying stories and appeals to authority. There is nothing wrong with doing so. To utter the word "rhetoric," we have noted, sounds like debunking. But a literary critic does not debunk Virgil when noting that Virgil used the Homeric stories as a frame. If an economist uses a metaphor of ice-cream stands along the beach to illuminate the ideological coloration of political parties, her metaphor may be apt or inapt, but she is not being unscientific.

Here is an epistemological example of what you can learn by standing in a rhetorical place. The metaphor of a game is prominent in the field of political economy. The game against nature, especially, has dominated thinking in the West since Francis Bacon. The physics model of science represents the scientist outwitting an unwitting nature, and was applied wholesale to economics and political science in the age of high modernism. But whatever the definition of political economy, its subject would seem to be the game against other human beings, not against insentient nature. Mixing up the two kinds of games has had lamentable results. For instance, economic policy in the 1960s treated the public as nature, against which the policy makers were playing. In the 1970s, of course, economists began to have second thoughts, the nub being that the public is not insentient nature but an audience. In becoming aware of audiences, the very theories of political economy have taken a rhetorical turn.

The turn has an epistemological use. Suppose that one believes the $500 Bill Axiom: that people pick up $500 bills and other opportunities sitting free for the taking on the sidewalk. The axiom implies the theorem that there are no $500 bills, or their equivalents in power or prestige, lying about untaken for long. The theorem suggests that any expert must answer to the American Question: If you're so smart, why aren't you rich? You, oh Expert, claim to foretell the future. Well, if you can predict the interest rate or the election outcome or the future of painting, why haven't you yourself made a million?

The upshot is that an expert in political economy cannot say certain things. In particular, she cannot claim the prediction and control that modernist science has long promised (without delivering, alas) and that some political economists still pursue. The American Question puts fundamental bounds on what humans can say about themselves. The bounds come from the saying, the rhetoric, itself. They limit mechanical models of human behavior. It does not make the mechanical models useless for interesting history or routine prediction; it just makes them useless for gaining a profitable edge on the future.

What is thrown into doubt by the American Question is a claim to systematic, justified, cheaply acquired, write-downable knowledge about profitable opportunities. The "profit" is to be broadly construed. The political economist's coin of profit need not be monetary. Political power is there on the sidewalk, too, waiting to be picked up if the 500,000 Vote Axiom is wrong. But of course the axiom is right: there is no simple way, to be written down in a book, for getting 500,000 votes. The American Question suggests that political scientists cannot predict elections in ways that would allow them to manipulate the outcome, doing better than the political artists they study. In truth, no one in political economy makes such lofty claims. It is over the border in economics that the chutzpah takes hold.

Notice the requirement of profitability. The political scientists can state true predictions all right: "A declared revolutionary socialist will not soon be elected to the House of Representatives from Orange County." But they cannot state valuable predictions: "Expenditure of $1 million on spot commercials on Channels 2, 5, and 8 during the three weeks before an election will assure ascension to the House." If two empires fight to the death, a great empire will fall. The valuable prediction is the impossibly difficult one: which empire will prevail. This is not to say that $1 million spent on television advertisements never won an election or that, after the election, a political scientist could not quite properly interpret the events as a victory for money and television. At one time, it was a bright new idea. After the combination won in the first congressional district, however, it would become routine in the second district and in the third and at length in the nth. If it were so easy to spot that a professor could say in a book how to spot it, the $500 opportunity already would have been picked up. The supernormal profits, as economists put it, would have been dissipated. The expected return from political advice, discounted for its uncertainty, should be approximately zero.

Similarly, prestige in the local saloon would be cheaply available if the American Question did not also cast doubt on predictions of sporting events. But it does. The lineaments of the sporting future apparent to the average fellow will be reflected in the sporting odds. (At the University of Iowa during the 1988 election campaign, a parimutuel betting system was operated, giving minute-by-minute odds on the outcome.) Only fresh details yield profits above average, measured in money or prestige. Fresh details are hard to come by. Information, like steel and haircuts, is costly to produce.

The American Question can be asked of all predictions in economics, journalism, sociology, political science, art, and political economy. It mocks the claims of predictors, social engineers, and critics of the social arts. The predictor who could get it usefully right would be a god incarnate, a seer and diviner.

The point is not that humans are too complicated or too changeable or too free. These humanistic criticisms of social science may be true, but they are not telling; they are easy to make and easy to answer. Such complexity is merely a matter of computer time. But the complexity arising from the very rhetoric of human prediction cannot be solved by another billion dollars of computation.

All manner of provision for the future is limited by the American Question. It is closely related to another rhetorical limit on prediction: that knowing science before it is known is impossible, which makes the planning of science impossible. The same holds for all manner of innovations. They cannot be planned for because in their nature they are unknowable—if they were knowable, they would be known already, and would not be innovations. The legal rule of first possession, for example, gives whoever gets there first the entitlement to land or a patent. It thus provides an incentive to throw away resources in races such as the one concluded a while ago between Kodak and Polaroid. The society would be better off if the outcome were properly discounted. The king could then auction off the entitlement to the highest bidder. But as David Haddock notes, "Where new knowledge is at issue, finding appropriate solutions becomes more complex. In such situations, one cannot define an entitlement because one cannot imagine what one has not imagined."[23]

Such questions, more than merely rhetorical, bring political economy face to face with itself. They connect science to practice, observation to understanding. As Anthony Giddens notes, "That the 'findings' of the social sciences can be taken up by those to whose behavior they refer is not a phenomenon that can, or should, be marginalized, but is integral to their very nature."[24] The economic theory that makes an economist's model plausible tells him that he cannot expect to predict from it profitably. That people pick up $500 bills, other things being equal, is an axiom in most economic models; it had better not be contradicted by any of them. The axiom need merely be applied to the analysis itself.

Science and Ethics

The rhetorical places to stand make it easier to see into other places. The ancient words are *koinoi topoi* in Greek and *loci communes* in Latin, "common places." These are the places humans have in common, from which to stand and hear their speech. The commonplaces are the locales of human reasoning, more capacious than the modernist parking garages that are supposed to serve for a scholarly life. To mention another example, much political economy, however defined, is storytelling; but people are usually not aware of it. The humanistic side of the scientific argument has been mislaid.

For instance, political economy in most versions is shallow ethically. The mention of ethics will be surprising if even after what we have said you nonetheless think of rhetoric as a fancy word for empty ornament and advertising. The rhetorical places encompass ethics, beginning in the scholar's study, with the ethics of inquiry.

This is to say that sciences are practices. They are governed by human decisions about propriety, honesty, good conduct, and so forth—in sporting terms, the rules and customs and excellent performances of the game. Alasdair MacIntyre defines a practice as "any coherent and complex form of socially established cooperative human activity." In his Aristotelian way, he argues that each practice creates standards of excellence, "goods internal to that form of activity." In defining the practice, these standards define also our wider notions of excellence, "with the result that human powers to achieve excellence, and human conceptions of the ends and goods involved, are systematically extended."[25] Excellence in basketball, defined by the practice of the Boston Celtics, extends our conception of excellence itself. So too in science and scholarship. The practices of recognized scientists provide standards for the Good Scientist. The Good Scientist contributes to our idea of the Good Person. As Emerson put it, the Thinking Man, a mere expert, becomes Man Thinking. Even the method of science, in other words, is saturated in ethics.

When economists and political scientists, having skimmed Karl Popper, say that their hypotheses should be falsifiable, they fancy it is sheer logic that guides them, not rhetoric or ethic. Yet they have *said* it; and they have used "should." The logicians reduce complex practices to a few incantations of Method. Yet the methodologists are calling on shared traditions, without realizing they are. The traditions of criticism in science make up its rhetoric.

Ethics used to be known as the practical science of communal life. The Greeks named it for its attention to *ethos,* character. "Ethical" is what pertains to the characteristic or habitual, as against the methodically intellectual. Rhetorically, as we have said, *ethos* is the character and disposition of a speaker, as impressed on the hearers by his speech. So ethics is what pertains to *ethos;* and rhetoric (as what pertains to the speaker or actor) is the consideration of what it is proper to say and do. In judging the relations of speaker to audience and actor to community, good rhetorics include ethics.

The trouble is that modern notions of morality reduce these issues of practical, communal judgment to abstractions. The model for ethical thinking is Kantian. The Kantians answer an ethical question with some rule that devalues the practical and the rhetorical. They attack rhetoric for introducing subtleties that confuse people—the subtleties of actual cases at law or actual decisions to send an expedition to Syracuse. Rhetoric, being practical, is said to be immoral and antiethical. But this is the reverse of the truth. Rhetoric is the study of the public side of *ethos,* the character revealed by speech. The Kantian program to found ethics on universal propositions has not made us any better, or better off. It has failed.

Recent students of rhetoric emphasize a further lesson: our sins and vanities of inference owe far less to flaws in the instruments or even the motivations of persuasion than to defects in the knowledge and character of their consumers. In our experiences, scholars who declare the standing of the scientist irrelevant to the merit of the paper are among the readers most swayed by implicit appeals to authority. Likewise, those who reject any proper role for rhetoric in science are among the scholars least sensitive to subtle abuses of statistics. Therefore, let the user of analogy or any speech be also the good person skilled at listening.

Political economy, in all its definitions, has tended to discount politics, and the wider moral discourse of which politics is a part, as mere talk—reducing it to something else. Some Marxists reduce politics to words and words to material interest, as do some bourgeois theorists. Others reduce politics to rationality, simply conceived, or to the nation emergent or to the balance of pluralistic interests. All these political economists want to get beyond mere words, which they view as ephemeral and false, to something more real underneath. The real, they think, can be manipulated, as the levers of power and history. But the distinctively political part is just words, and the words are just rhetoric.

The rhetoric is the main asset of a political culture, as durable as any of its goods and as consequential as any of its institutions. The institutions consist largely of agreements about how to talk—addressing all remarks to the Speaker of the House or submitting a military budget to arguments among civilians. This position is not antirealist. The world is still round, and the table still stands against the wall. But realism does not require that we attribute nothing to the ways we talk about politics. It is a naive realist who thinks that logic or science requires us to scorn ideas. Nor is the position unrealistic in the common sense of the word: evil still exists, and the con man still depends on his statistics. But realistic politics need not be *Realpolitik.*

The best protection against bad science is good scientists in good disciplines, aware of the rhetoric in their inquiry. Methods are no protection against misuse. That is why good rhetorics encompass the ethics of their practices. But rhetoric can exhibit the virtues as much as the vices of the modern academy. Better than modernism or scientism, rhetoric fits most visions of the good society. Political economists study machineries for making constitutions and revealing preferences, but their studies would lack point if honest rhetoric were rendered impossible. If all talk were perverse, all persuasion would be impossible. If no one could be persuaded, if everyone were motivated merely by the pocketbook or the voting booth, we would be entirely alone. We are not, and the way we talk politically to each other is rhetoric.

Nine

Viktor Vanberg and
James M. Buchanan

Rational Choice and Moral Order

The problem which science has to solve here consists in the expla-
nation of a social *phenomenon, of a homogeneous way of acting*
on the part of the members of a community for which public mo-
tives are recognizable, but for which in the concrete case individ-
ual motives are hard to discern.

—Carl Menger

A central theme of classical political economy has been the way the
character of a social and economic order depends on the framework of
rules and institutions within which individuals act and interact. It is a
theme that has gained renewed attention in modern economics.[1] One
of the persistent issues in this context is the tension between rational,
self-interested behavior—as postulated in economics—and the moral
order. The general benefits that a moral order generates are quite obvious; it is far less obvious how rational pursuit of self-interest should
induce the kind of conduct that a moral order requires.

Our purpose in this chapter is to discuss some of the fundamental conceptual and theoretical aspects of the "rational choice and
moral order" issue, an issue that, at least since Thomas Hobbes, has
plagued social theorists. In fact, it is often referred to as the "Hobbesian problem of social order" or simply the "Hobbesian problem." In
sociology, an influential theoretical program—associated with Emile
Durkheim and Talcott Parsons—is based on the claim that the
individualistic-utilitarian tradition of economics has not provided a
satisfactory solution to the Hobbesian problem, and that it is intrinsically unable to do so. Our purpose here is to argue the opposite: to

show how the Hobbesian question can be answered from an individualistic, rational-choice perspective.

The first two sections of this chapter analyze the "rational choice and moral order" issue in terms of the contrast between what we call constitutional interests on the one side and action interests or compliance interests on the other. We argue that the practical solution to the "problem of social order" consists in bringing people's action interests into congruence with their constitutional interests. The next two sections discuss the issue of how such congruence may be spontaneously brought about as a by-product of incentives that are naturally generated in the process of social interaction. Of particular interest in this context is the mechanism of reciprocity. The fifth and sixth sections are about a distinction between two kinds of rules, which we call trust rules and solidarity rules. The difference between these types of rules is crucial to the issue of spontaneous emergence of a moral order. The last section elaborates on some implications of our analysis.

Moral Rules, Constitutional Interests, and Action Interests

Explanatory accounts of moral rules are not always sufficiently careful to avoid the functionalist fallacy. This fallacy consists in assuming that by identifying the benefits that a moral code provides to a group (such as a community or social system), one has explained why the code is honored.[2] The functionalist fallacy is tempting because it seems natural to presume that the beneficial consequences of rules and institutions must have something to do with the fact that they exist and persist. The problem with the functionalist fallacy is not its focus on the beneficial consequences—in its own terminology, the *functions* that rules and institutions serve within a group. The problem is that the functionalist linkage provides no more than the illusion of an explanation; it distracts attention from the genuine challenge of identifying the actual processes that link the beneficial consequences with the effective causes of the rules and institutions.

In discussions of the rationale for and the effective causes of moral rules, the familiar contrasts between "individual and group interests," "private and common interests," or "individual and collective interests" are potentially misleading. These contrasts tend to suggest a conflict either between the interests of different entities (the individual versus the group) or between different interests within the behavioral calculus of a single person (a narrow self-interest ver-

sus a more noble common interest). We propose an alternative interpretation that differentiates between different levels of choice, and
between different kinds of interests related to these levels of choice.
In our framework, the issue is not one of conflicting preferences with
regard to the same kind of choice, but one of different kinds of choice
between different kinds of interests. We separate, define, and contrast two kinds of individual interests: constitutional or rule interests,
and operational or action interests.[3] An actor's constitutional interests are reflected in his preferences concerning alternative "rules of
the game" for the social group within which he operates. His constitutional interests influence those of his choices that pertain to the
kind of institutional order under which he is to live. Or, stated somewhat differently, they determine the preferences that would emerge
if he were to participate in choosing the constitution, in the broadest
sense, for his social community. By contrast, a person's action interests are reflected in his preferences concerning alternative courses of
action under given situational constraints, including the constraints
imposed by the existing rules and institutions.

Constitutional interests and action interests, as defined here, are
experienced by the same person, and possibly simultaneously; yet
there is no reason to expect that these interests will be either in natural harmony or in natural conflict. Trade-offs of the ordinary sort are
not relevant here, because these separate interests reflect an actor's
preferences concerning different kinds of alternatives. Constitutional
interests concern the imagined or real choice among alternative institutional environments; action interests concern alternative courses of
action within a given environment. Whether these two types of interests are in harmony—that is, whether a person prefers to comply
with a rule that he prefers constitutionally—is an empirical question.
A person's constitutional interests do not automatically translate into
corresponding action interests. My interest in living in a community
where promises are kept, for instance, does not in itself imply that I
must have an interest in always keeping my own promises. There is
nothing inconsistent in preferring a certain constitutional rule and at
the same time, given the existing situational constraints, violating the
rule in pursuit of one's action interests.[4]

Assuming that there are certain rules on which people's constitutional interests converge, a theory of social order has to deal with the
central issue of what social forces tend to bring constitutional interests and action interests into correspondence. Such correspondence is
needed in order for a generally preferred constitutional order to be

operative. Accordingly, the analytical focus has to be on why and under what conditions individuals can be expected to comply with rules that are in their constitutional interest.

Constitutional Interests and Moral Philosophy

The disjunction between people's constitutional interests and their action interests, though not stated in these terms, has long been a puzzling issue to moral philosophers. Kant's reflections on the "categorical imperative," for instance, can be interpreted as reflections about constitutional interests. Kant examines arguments that might guide people's preferences concerning rules that could qualify as general laws. He does not, however, examine the reasons that make people adopt as private maxims of behavior the general rules that they want to see practiced in the community. In our terms, Kant does not explain how people's action interests are supposed to come into congruence with their constitutional interests.[5]

David Gauthier has made a major effort to establish a rational choice link between constitutional and action interests. Gauthier analyzes moral choice in terms of "a choice among dispositions" rather than a series of separate choices in specific situations.[6] Gauthier's central argument is that the choice of a general disposition to be moral can be rational even if this choice occasionally results in missed opportunities to earn larger payoffs by nonmoral behavior. According to Gauthier, a moral disposition can be rational because it can permit access to cooperative arrangements, and to the potential gains from cooperation, from which persons without such a disposition would be excluded.[7]

In a later section, we develop a similar argument, but with one noteworthy difference. Gauthier's aim is to show that a correspondence between constitutional and action interests is implied by a proper conception of rationality. He seems to deny the possibility of a systematic gap "between rational compliance and rational agreement" when he claims that "agreement on a set of principles carries with it, in some manner, adherence to those principles."[8] In our view, Gauthier's attempt to establish a direct link between the rationality of constitutional agreement and the rationality of compliance is not successful, and it cannot be successful. Whether or not it is rational for persons to comply with rules that they constitutionally agree to is a matter of contingent, factual circumstances and not of general principles. It depends on the constraints that persons face after they have agreed to the rules. There is, to be sure, a rational link between constitutional agreement and compliance, but it is of an indirect nature, not the direct link suggested by Gauthier. If it is rational for persons to agree on rules, it is rational for them to see to it that compliance is rational. This means that the rules must be enforced where necessary, provided the costs of enforcement are warranted by the prospective cooperative gains.[9]

It has already been stated that our interest here is precisely in identifying the conditions under which compliance with agreed-on rules can be rational, and in analyzing the social mechanisms and processes that tend to bring about those conditions. There are two basic ways, complementary rather than mutually exclusive, in which a correspondence between constitutional interests and action interests can be brought about. One has been stressed by Thomas Hobbes in his theory of social order, where he argued that people whose constitutional interests coincide can rationally choose to modify the structure under which they act so as to bring about an explicit correspondence of constitutional and compliance interests (by deliberately changing the payoff structure of the generalized prisoner's dilemma matrix). In the Hobbesian conception, the correspondence between the two kinds of interests is viewed as a product of the rational capacity of individuals to implement their constitutional interests, to diagnose the problems they face, and to change the choice environment so as to make mutually preferred behavior individually rational.

The other solution to the "correspondence problem" is most often associated with David Hume, Adam Ferguson, Adam Smith, and other Scottish moral philosophers of the eighteenth century. These philosophers suggested that in some contexts of social interaction spontaneous forces may be present that will bring about a correspondence between constitutional and compliance interests, as if by an "invisible hand."[10] This conception focuses on the nonintentional nature of the linkage between the two kinds of interests. It holds that the constraints that make it rational to comply with constitutionally preferred rules are, at least to some extent, an unintentional (though systematic) by-product of actions taken in pursuit of immediate interests, without any explicit regard to constitutional preferences. It is this interpretation that has been at the heart of the "spontaneous order" tradition, of which a prominent contemporary advocate is F. A. Hayek.

The two views on how a correspondence between constitutional and action interests may be generated are by no means mutually exclusive. The invisible hand and the constitutional-constructivist principle may supplement each other and operate in combination. In the following sections we explore the potential range over which spontaneous forces may be expected to generate a correspondence between the two kinds of interests. We also attempt to determine the critical limits beyond which deliberate concerted effort becomes necessary. In other words, we examine the forces that spontaneously, as a by-product of ordinary social interaction, tend to generate compliance with constitutionally preferred moral rules.[11]

Coordination Rules and Prisoner's Dilemma Rules

The spontaneous-order tradition contains a certain ambiguity in its analytical approach to the rules and institutions issue. The ambiguity results from a failure to distinguish sufficiently between two different kinds of interaction problems: in the terminology of modern game theory, coordination problems and prisoner's dilemma problems.[12] There is a tendency throughout this tradition—from David Hume to Carl Menger to F. A. Hayek—to argue as if the kind of explanation that applies to coordination-type rules can be generalized to other kinds of rules as well, including those of the prisoner's dilemma type.

David Hume, for instance, in his discussion of a "theory concerning the origin of property, and consequently of justice," refers to the example of two men rowing a boat, as if the way oarsmen come to coordinate their activities illustrated the process by which people come to respect property and to follow the rules of justice.[13] In the same context Hume cites as further examples the ways in which "gold and silver are made the measures of exchange" or "speech and words and language are fixed." It is in the same sense that Hume refers to the example of the rules of the road when he talks about "the necessity of rules, wherever men have any intercourse with each other."[14] All these examples are, however, concerned with problems of the coordination type rather than with the prisoner's dilemma problems that typically form the basis of moral rules.[15] The "perverse incentives" that characterize prisoner's dilemma problems are absent in coordination problems; rules can therefore emerge and be maintained much more smoothly for coordination problems.[16] In recurrent coordination-problem situations, individuals' constitutional interests and action interests are typically in harmony, at least in the sense that there is little or no incentive for defection once a rule is established. Whether the coordination rule concerns rowing a boat, the use of a general medium of exchange, the use of language, or the rules of the road, there is generally no temptation to defect. Having a coordination rule established in a community can, in some sense, be considered a public good, but there is definitely no "free rider" problem. No person may hope to gain extra benefits by unilaterally defecting. Coordination rules are, in other words, largely self-enforcing.[17] Rules providing solutions to recurrent prisoner's dilemma–type problems are, by contrast, not usually self-enforcing. There is no natural harmony between constitutional and action interests, even if all members in a community agree about their constitutional interests. Rather, additional incentives—additional to the payoffs embodied in the payoff structure that defines the problem— have to be generated somehow in order to bring constitutional interests and action interests into harmony.[18]

The ambiguity in Hume's discussion of the "emergence of rules" issue is paralleled in Carl Menger's discussion of the same issue. Menger's explanation of the origins of money, which is commonly cited as the paradigmatic example for an invisible-hand explanation of rules and institutions, is apparently concerned with a coordination-type problem and has little direct relevance to prisoner's dilemma–type rules. It is misleading to list together, as Menger does, phenomena like law, language, the state, money, and markets as if all involved the same kind of explanatory problem.[19] The same criticism applies to F. A. Hayek when he talks about the spontaneous emergence of "useful institutions . . . such as language, morals, law, writing, or money." Such a list implicitly suggests that the emergence of moral rules can basically be explained along the same lines as the emergence of language or money.[20]

Since the spontaneous-order tradition fails to account adequately for the fundamental difference between coordination rules (such as rules of language or rules of the road) and prisoner's dilemma rules (such as rules of morality), it cannot be strongly enough emphasized that an explanation of one type of rule cannot be considered a model for an explanation of rules of the other type. This does not mean, however, that an invisible-hand explanation of the emergence of prisoner's dilemma–type rules is inconceivable. It only means that such an explanation will have to be stated in somewhat different terms; in particular, it will have to specify the forces or mechanisms that curb the ever-present, utility-maximizing temptation to defect.

Important suggestions for such an explanation have, in fact, been made within the spontaneous-order tradition. These suggestions embody the notion of reciprocity as a fundamental principle in human interaction.

Reciprocity and Cooperation

The prisoner's dilemma notion and the public goods notion are equivalent conceptual tools to characterize the incentive structure underlying the moral order. The public goods interpretation draws attention to the question of what incentives may induce an individual to contribute to the public good known as moral order. Typically, the individual's contribution is seen as a matter of compliance with the relevant rules; however, there is another way in which individuals can contribute to the moral order: by providing incentives for others to comply with the rules. An invisible-hand theory of how prisoner's dilemma–type moral rules come to be effective would have to show how, in the process of social interaction, selective incentives are spontaneously created that induce people to contribute, in the two ways mentioned, to the production of a moral order. The notion of reciprocity is a central one in this context; that is, the notion that when individuals repeatedly interact they are in a position to shape one another's behavior, to reward desirable and punish undesirable behavior. Reciprocity works as a spontaneous enforcement mechanism that encourages cooperative behavior. This observation has been stressed again and again throughout the history of social theory and across the various social sciences. It was central to the social theory of David Hume and other eighteenth-century Scottish moral philosophers, and it is central to the so-called exchange theory in modern sociology.[21]

In his book *The Evolution of Cooperation*, Robert Axelrod has added some interesting new aspects to the study of reciprocity.[22] Axelrod used a computer to simulate competition among the alternative behavioral strategies that actors may adopt in recurrent prisoner's dilemma–type interaction. Axelrod found that the simple strategy of tit for tat (the strategy of cooperating in the first move and thereafter doing whatever the opponent had done in his previous move) performed better than any of the other strategies that were included in the experiment. Tit for tat succeeded because it combined readiness to cooperate with readiness to punish defection. The willingness to cooperate (that is, to comply with moral rules) allows an actor to realize gains from cooperation in interactions with others who are equally willing. Being prepared to punish defection protects an actor against continuous exploitation.

Tit for tat obviously reflects the basic pattern of reciprocity. Though human reciprocating behavior is likely to be much more complex than tit for tat, Axelrod's results are of obvious relevance for the study of reciprocity as a spontaneous enforcement mechanism in everyday social life. Reciprocating behavior has been universally observed, and Axelrod's study illuminates an obvious reason why reciprocity can be expected to be a universal feature of human social conduct; it is likely to be adopted simply because it tends to be more successful than alternative behavioral strategies.[23] There are basically two forms that such adoption may take; that is, two mechanisms by which success can be expected to result in the behavioral pattern's diffusion: genetic evolution and individual learning. The observed patterns of human reciprocity can probably be best understood as the combined outcome of both mechanisms.

In his 1971 article, "The Evolution of Reciprocal Altruism," the biologist R. L. Trivers sought to explain reciprocating behavior in evolutionary terms. Trivers's analytical interest is in those behavioral patterns that produce some apparent benefit to another organism while involving some cost to the organism performing them.[24] As Trivers points out, beyond the relatively narrow limits of close kinship, where "kin selection" may allow for the evolution of genuinely self-sacrificing behavior, natural selection can be expected to favor helping patterns of behavior only where "in the long run they benefit the organism performing them"; this is typically the case where such behavior is reciprocated.[25] To the extent that reciprocity produces mutual net benefits, natural selection will tend to favor reciprocating behavior. Reciprocity allows the realization of benefits from mutual helping or cooperation, without being vulnerable to systematic exploitation by individuals who cheat, that is, who do not reciprocate.

The disposition to reciprocate is likely, to some extent, to be genetically "hard wired" into human nature.[26] On the other hand, the same behavioral tendencies can be learned; and learning accounts for some of the extraordinary complexities that characterize human reciprocity.[27] The interaction of learned and genetically inherited traits appears to be exemplified by what Trivers calls "moralistic aggression."[28] Since rewarding and punishing others are costly to the actor, such activities will be learned only to the extent that they also generate beneficial consequences for the actor himself. Moralistic aggression may be learned as successful behavior in settings where the initiator and the recipient of the aggression are likely to meet again—where the shadow of the future provides a rationale for incurring the costs of the aggression. There are, however, instances of moralistically aggressive behavior that do not seem to fit such a description, because the aggressor cannot reasonably expect the recipient's future behavior to generate benefits to the aggressor that will outweigh the costs of his punishing act. Anger may cause people to reciprocate, that is, to retaliate, against defectors even where the potential payoffs from such behavior are outweighed by the costs incurred.[29]

The seemingly irrational readiness of an angry person to punish others is difficult to account for in terms of individual learning. An evolutionary explanation might, however, be constructed in terms of potential advantages from such behavior in the very long run. To be disposed to punish defectors even when the costs seem excessive may well be beneficial in the longer run by providing better protection from other actors' exploitative inclinations. To be perceived as somebody who is willing to hurt himself for the sake of revenge may be a most effective deterrent.[30]

Trust Rules and Solidarity Rules

To the extent that the production of moral order involves the same problems as the production of public goods in general, rational self-seeking actors cannot be expected to contribute unless there are selective incentives, that is, benefits that are contingent on the actors' own contributions. The principle of reciprocity can be expected to generate such selective incentives, at least to some extent. In terms of our earlier analysis, reciprocity can be expected to bring people's action interests into congruence with their constitutional interests in recurrent prisoners' dilemma–type interactions. The role that reciprocity may play in this respect requires, however, some qualification.

Reciprocity seems likely to emerge and to be effective as a behavioral pattern only in small group settings, where individuals are known to one another and expect to have further dealings within the same group. The question becomes one of identifying the conditions under which persons are likely to form small groups, or cooperative clusters, that internally secure rule following through reciprocity. In this regard it is useful to distinguish between two types of rules, which we shall call trust rules and solidarity rules.

Trust rules are rules such as "keep your promises," "tell the truth," or "respect others' property." Trust rules are significant in dealings with known persons. By his compliance or noncompliance with trust rules, a person selectively affects specific other persons. Because compliance and noncompliance with trust rules are thus "targeted," the possibility exists of forming cooperative clusters: any subset of actors, down to two individuals, can realize cooperative gains by following those rules in their dealings with one another. Adoption of and compliance with trust rules offer differential benefits to any group or cluster, independently of the behavior of other persons in the wider community or population. Even in an otherwise totally dishonest world, any two individuals who start to deal with each other honestly—by keeping promises, respecting property, and so on—would fare better than their fellows because of the gains from cooperation that they would be able to realize. To be sure, they would be even better off if all their fellow human beings could be trusted to act honestly; but the gains from rule compliance can be realized within any subset, however small, without any need for wider compliance. It is precisely the possibility of forming and benefiting from such cooperative clusters that makes the mechanism of reciprocity effective in enforcing trust rules.

Solidarity rules are rules such as "don't litter in public places," "respect waiting lines," "don't drive recklessly," "pay your fair contribution to joint endeavors," and "don't shirk your duties in a team." In contrast to trust rules, compliance or noncompliance with solidarity rules cannot be targeted at particular persons. There is always a predefined group all members of which are affected by their individual rule-related behavior. Whether the relevant group is a work team (as in case of the shirking problem) or the world population (as in case of certain pollution problems), a person cannot avoid affecting, by his compliance or noncompliance with the applicable solidarity rule, all members of the predefined group. For solidarity rules it is not true, as it is for trust rules, that any two individuals can form a cooperative cluster that would allow them to realize differential gains from which outsiders are excluded. Solidarity rules require adherence by the whole group before they provide mutual benefits from which noncompliant individuals are excluded.

Since solidarity rules do not allow clustering, or allow it only in a restricted sense, reciprocity is a much less effective mechanism of spontaneous enforcement for those rules.[31] This crucial difference between trust rules and solidarity rules is reflected in the differences between Axelrod's 1984 study on the "evolution of cooperation" and his 1986 study on the "evolution of norms."[32] Though this is not an explicit part of Axelrod's own interpretation, the 1984 study can be said to be about the spontaneous emergence of trust rules, whereas the 1986 study is an attempt to explain the spontaneous emergence of solidarity rules (the example that Axelrod uses in this study is the norm "don't cheat on exams"). The notion of clustering is central to the first study, but plays no role whatsoever in the second. Instead, the second study makes use of assumptions about vengefulness as an inherent emotional energy that makes people willing to incur some cost in order to punish not only those whom they observe cheating but also—and this turns out to be central to Axelrod's account of the evolution of norms—to punish others who fail to punish observed defections.

Clustering and Compliance

Where individuals repeatedly interact with one another, there are direct personal gains to be made by obeying rules like "keep your promises" and by punishing others for defecting. The shadow of the future, the expected effects of one's own current behavior on the other person's future behavior, is crucial for one's current behavioral choices.[33] In dealing with reciprocating opponents one cannot expect to be able to get away with cheating; the only way to secure their ongoing cooperation is to play by the rules. It is in an individual's direct interest to behave in such a way that he is perceived by others as an honest, trustworthy person. Being trustworthy makes one an attractive partner for cooperation and thus increases one's prospects of realizing cooperative gains.[34] On the other hand, the interest in protecting oneself against exploitation provides an immediate incentive for punishing cheaters. The most obvious and least costly form of punishment is simply to exclude a cheater from cooperation until he makes up for his dishonest behavior and proves himself to be a trustworthy person. But an individual may very well have an incentive to take stronger punitive measures, even though they are more costly to himself. Such behavior sends a message to one's direct opponent as well as to third parties. It indicates that one is prepared to retaliate whenever one is being cheated. In addition, by signaling to other members of the group that the opponent is a cheat, one is able to inflict—at little cost to oneself—an even more effective punishment, as others will be more reluctant to deal with the defector in the future.

The mechanism of reciprocity can create a private interest in observing trust rules and in punishing others for violating the rules. Moral order will be generated, at least to some extent, spontaneously through reciprocity. This might be taken as an example of how a public good may be a by-product of the individual pursuit of purely private interests. It should be noted, though, that as far as trust rules are concerned, moral order can be considered a public good in a limited sense only. To be sure, living in a community of honest people confers benefits that are genuinely public. Consequently there appear to be opportunities for defectors to free ride on these benefits by taking advantage of an environment where people are generally honest and expect others to be generally honest. But the mechanism of reciprocity does not allow for someone systematically to free ride on other persons' compliance with trust rules. Defectors will be inevitably excluded from those benefits that can only be realized in ongoing cooperative relations.

For solidarity rules it is obviously true—as it is for prisoner's dilemma–type rules in general—that a rational actor's constitutional interests in such rules do not, per se, generate compliance. Separate, selective incentives are required for bringing action interests into harmony with constitutional interests. The way in which such selective incentives can be expected to be generated is different for solidarity rules and for trust rules. The two types of rules differ in the extent to which the benefits from obeying and enforcing the rules are genuinely public goods that spill over among a large number of nonexcludable recipients. Obeying and enforcing solidarity rules tends to generate more public and fewer private elements than obeying and enforcing trust rules. In fact, the distinction between trust rules and solidarity rules may be viewed, not as a dichotomy, but as a continuum along which particular rules may be located according to the "publicness" of the benefits obtained by obeying the rules.

The incentives for complying with trust rules and for punishing others who defect derive from the expected effects of one's own actions on other actors' future behavior. First, there are the effects on the future behavior of one's direct opponents: the gains one can expect from making them more inclined to cooperate and less inclined to defect in future interactions. Then there are the indirect effects on third parties: to be perceived as a trustworthy but vengeful person increases one's prospects of realizing gains from cooperation and, at the same time, makes one an unsuitable target for exploitation.[35] Both the direct and the indirect effects on other persons affect their future behavior towards the actor himself. The actor thus has a private incentive for complying with trust rules and for punishing defectors. The same cannot be said for solidarity rules. By complying with rules like "don't shirk your duties in a team," a person generates benefits that are public to the relevant group. These benefits cannot be selectively allocated in order to affect the behavior of particular members within the group. On the other hand, by punishing others who defect, a person may make their future compliance more likely; nevertheless, he will share the benefits from such improved behavior with all members of the group, without selective rewards to himself. In other words, by complying with solidarity rules and by punishing others for not complying, a person is producing a genuine public good, that is, a benefit that is shared by all members of some predefined group and that does not qualify as a selective incentive.

The above arguments do not imply that there are no selective incentives at all for individuals to comply with solidarity rules and to punish defectors. Such incentives may exist, for instance, where a person's behavior toward solidarity rules affects his reputation. His behavior may be perceived by others as a signal about what type of person he is; and this perception may affect their future behavior toward the person.[36] A person's revealed willingness to comply with solidarity rules may be interpreted by (direct or indirect) observers as indicative of his general trustworthiness. A similar interpretation may be placed on a person's revealed willingness to contribute to the enforcement of solidarity rules. In addition to these kinds of selective incentives, the emotional factors that we have discussed under the label "moralistic aggression" can also be expected to contribute, to some extent, to a spontaneous enforcement of solidarity rules. In fact, as mentioned before, it is these emotional factors that play a crucial role in Axelrod's model of the evolution of norms.[37]

From Hobbesian Anarchy to Moral Order

A major implication of our analysis for the Hobbesian problem of social order is that the clustering option that exists for trust rules makes the leap out of the Hobbesian anarchy somewhat less difficult than the usual public-goods interpretation of moral order suggests. As far as trust rules are concerned, individuals do have means, even in large group settings, to orchestrate privately the transition from anarchy to moral order. The first step towards a normative order is taken when any two inventive individuals realize that they can fare better by dealing honestly with each other, by following certain rules. Such a two-person cooperative cluster can get the order-creating process started because the differential success of the initial cooperators can be expected to provide incentives for others, either to join the existing cluster or to copy the successful cooperative arrangement. Reciprocity will, at least to some extent, protect existing cooperative clusters against invasion by defectors: reciprocating actors will allow only those actors to be included in their cooperative network who are willing to submit to the rules.

Since the possibility of discriminating between cooperators and defectors is critical for the stability of cooperative clusters, there appear to be limits to the size of the group within which the principle of reciprocity may serve as a workable mechanism of spontaneous rule enforcement. But a gradual process seems possible, by which a segmented moral order may emerge that extends beyond the limits of single cooperative clusters existing as scattered islands within a Hobbesian world. Such an extended, but still largely spontaneous, moral order might be achieved through a second-order clustering process. Just as on the individual level any two actors can profit from forming a cooperative cluster, on the group level any two groups can realize additional cooperative gains by entering some kind of mutual collective surety arrangement. If each group collectively accepts responsibility for its members' rule compliance in dealing with members of the other group, the intragroup enforcement mechanism can be extended to between-groups dealings. Mutually profitable transactions can then be carried out beyond the limits of the original cooperative clusters. The requirements for the emergence of such second-order cooperative clusters are just as parsimonious as the requirements for the initial emergence of cooperative clusters. It takes no more than two groups that are inventive enough to realize the gains that can be made by such a surety arrangement; and, once a "model" exists, other groups have an incentive to participate in or to imitate such arrangements.[38]

A more general conclusion concerning the relation between group size and the prospects for a spontaneously created moral order is implied in our analysis. Discussions on this issue commonly assume an inverse relation between group size and the likelihood that a moral order will emerge spontaneously and be sustained. It is typically argued that, in the absence of deliberately organized enforcement, people's willingness to contribute to the production of moral order will decrease as group size increases. The reasons given for this decrease are familiar from discussions on the significance of group size for the production of public goods.[39] First, the individual will have less and less reason to expect that his own contribution (his own compliance and his punishing of defectors) will be decisive for the persistence of moral order. Second, the informal, spontaneous mechanisms of enforcement will be less effective in larger and more anonymous groups.

Our analysis of the differences between trust rules and solidarity rules suggests that the standard diagnosis concerning the relevance of group size to the existence of a moral order needs to be qualified. It should be apparent that solidarity rules and trust rules are not affected in exactly the same way by an increase in group size; in particular, that trust rules are much less vulnerable to increasing numbers than solidarity rules. The formation of cooperative clusters, which is possible with regard to trust rules, makes rules like "keep your promises" much more robust and resistant to the detrimental effect of increasing numbers. So far as trust rules are concerned, individuals do have means, even in large group settings, to start building a moral order; these means are not available in the same way where solidarity rules are concerned.

To the extent that different kinds of social settings can be meaningfully arrayed along the trust rules–solidarity rules spectrum, the arguments that we have elaborated have implications for our understanding of the working principles of these different settings. The fundamental Hayekian distinction between two kinds of social order—between spontaneous order and directed social order, or more specifically, between market order and organization—comes to mind in this context.[40] The rules of the game that characterize market-type orders are apparently trust rules rather than solidarity rules, whereas the opposite is true for organization-type orders—a fact that has implications for the relative robustness of these two kinds of orders. Markets possess the great advantage over other types of social arrangements, that they are based ultimately on two-party transactions. It is this feature that makes reciprocity effective as a compliance-inducing device. It is not at all surprising that the eighteenth-century economists who discovered the self-enforcing characteristics of market order were excited. The Hobbesian problem of order had been, in large part, resolved. Recognition of the same reciprocity characteristic of market interaction led David Gauthier to call the idealized market a "moral-free zone."[41]

All this is not to suggest, of course, that the self-enforcing capacity inherent in markets would make the constructed arms and agencies of the law dispensable. Nevertheless, it seems clear that markets are particularly robust social arrangements.

Ten

Epilogue: Philosophical
Issues in Political Economy

I recently heard an economist reproach his interlocutor for knowing as little about economics as he, the economist, knew about political philosophy. In that case the reproach missed the mark; had it been addressed to me, it would have been true: I do not know anything about economics. Abundant modesty aside, I would like to offer my credentials, theoretical and practical, to comment on political economy. Donald McCloskey and John Nelson's chapter raised the question—which is the American Question—"If you're so smart, why aren't you rich?" Well, I am now. Before the publication of *The Closing of the American Mind* in 1987, I could not have said that. The lack of modesty in my statement of course must be somewhat chastened by the reflection that my competitor on the bestseller list, Bill Cosby, made $84 million that year. Since he is much richer than I, he must be much smarter.

Having been trained at the University of Chicago, though not in economics, I could six months ago have been carted out here by one of the Chicago economists as a perfect example of a lower-class personality, unable to delay gratification in order to hoard my resources, invest them properly, and so on. I was the despair of my economics-trained students. In this regard I taught only by negative example. Today I have invested my intellectual capital at the right time, so I have been thoroughly rational according to economic models. Abram

Shulsky has refined this analysis by pointing out that when interest rates were low and taxes high, I was in debt, and that I chose the narrow window of the lowest tax rate in years in which to make some money. As the economic man, therefore, I fit here.

Furthermore, and more important, as a young man at the University of Chicago, I saw and listened to—indeed, I lived in a world that was permeated by—such men as Frank Knight, Friedrich Hayek, the young Milton Friedman, and George Stigler. There was an Olympus, as it were, of a certain kind of economics around me.

The rich and impressive chapter by Viktor Vanberg and James Buchanan is perhaps characteristic of political economy: it tries to assert that economics *is* political philosophy. I mean that it addresses the greatest traditional questions. Political economy is an old tradition, in some sense founded by Adam Smith but actually much older. In the older understanding, of course, economics was the servitor of politics, which was the grander science and dealt with the comprehensive good. Under its governance, guided by it, economics served the secondary interests of wealth—secondary to the great national goals and also, surely, not superior to those of religion, education, and so on.

The problem of political economy is that economics seceded—but seceded in the way, say, that the automobile business seceded from the carriage-making trade. Economics is strong, healthy, self-confident; and one has to ask oneself why one is impressed. One is impressed by economists, in the first place because in some sense they claim to have a science. Political scientists can hardly claim to have a science these days. Second, I think, simply because economists are the only social scientists whose very science provides them with a place in government. You don't have to be a political scientist to be secretary of state. You do have to be an economist to be chairman of the Council of Economic Advisers. Economists carry a certain force with them. They are the ones with the winds of history in their sails, and I usually see them going by with their sails billowing.

What is particularly charming about this volume, and endlessly fascinating to me, is how wonderful the economists have been, in their various ways, in putting themselves out on the line—the dividing line between their discipline and the rest of the world. This has been very impressive. What comes especially to light is that in the course of this secession, economics has been left with a problem, one that is sensed very strongly in the chapter by Vanberg and Buchanan. The problem is that within the perspective of economics, justice is usually in quotation marks. And yet, when economics becomes or tries to comprise political science, the larger goal of politics—call it the question of justice or the question of the common good, if you like—keeps coming back in one or another frustrated way.

Given my external perspective and psychological taste, when it comes to these questions I cannot help asking myself why people do economics. Economists don't talk like politicians or political scientists, and I have to ask myself why anybody would talk like this. A conversation, I think, illustrates the same issue. Two rational-choice theorists disagreed about how one should talk to a student who has cheated. One said, "I say it's bad." I think he could only say that personally, and not economically; this is my assertion, which has something to do with the problem posed by Vanberg and Buchanan's chapter. The other said he never says, "It's bad." Instead, he tells the student that it is not in his best interest to cheat.

At that point I shouted out like a person from the mob, "That's not true!" And I think it is clearly not true, at least not on the grandest level. If students read the lives of the heroes, of Napoleon or Alexander the Great or Caesar, they will find that these men were not famous for their truthfulness. Who was the most successful, impressive political figure in the world since the Second World War? De Gaulle, who did nothing but lie his entire life. He was able to deceive the French people repeatedly. Having started a revolution himself, he put people to death for doing the same thing. That's politics; and in a way that's life.

There is a real problem here, which I think Professors Vanberg and Buchanan are addressing by asking this question: How can we go from the rational, selfish individual to some respect for the common good? I cannot put their question any other way (although perhaps they would disagree with my formulation). Their notion of constitutional rules, their trying to move from individuals to small collaborations to the larger group—all this seems to be an attempt to find some way, somehow, of deriving out of selfishness some concern for the common good. In some sense, it seems to me, they are trying to reinvent the wheel. But unlike most such inventors, they have a good reason for doing it: the wheel no longer exists.

I do not, however, think they are looking back sufficiently at the old models of the wheel; I will return to this issue later. If I may mix up my metaphor, I'd also say that they are trying to square the circle. Rousseau put the problem with human relations like this. Everybody cares most about himself; everybody loves himself most. This is perfectly all right. But everybody wants everybody else to love him as much as he loves himself. That is simply impossible. In a way, the political problem is close to being insoluble. The old problem—perhaps not the oldest way of formulating the problem, but certainly the old problem within our tradition—is that of the individual and society.

I assert that it is impossible to go from atomic individuals to caring for the common good. What is impressive about Vanberg and Buchanan's chapter, however, is that it states the difficulty with great clarity and tries to fill the gap that is there. In a way it reduces that gap and shows where one has to leap. I think the authors have leapt, but I am not sure they reached the other side. They understand that there is some threat to a moral constitutional order; the criminal personality poses a problem, but the authors have no scheme in which they can prove that breaking those rules is bad for the criminal.

Vanberg and Buchanan propose a series of ways to bridge the problem of individuality and community. They touch on the possibility that perhaps a certain genetic history builds in some kind of communal sentiment or caring. They mention Adam Smith's moral sentiments without telling much about them. They suggest that small groups, starting with two people, could develop effective rules. On these lines of thought, clearly, two people can agree on such rules more easily than a small group, and a small group more easily than an entire society. But the group of ten or twelve persons that the authors outline is the perfect prescription for a street gang. Will the members not quickly learn that their cooperation in exploiting others will be profitable? An old joke tells of a man who stops in Maine and asks for road directions to Boston and is told, "You can't get there from here." The problem with the authors' suggestion is that you can't get there from here. Certainly you can construct groups, but the moral basis of those groups is no different from that of a band of thieves. The small-group approach, and then building out of small groups, will not suffice.

The question I keep asking myself is, Why begin this way? Why suppose that the real human being is this kind of atom, this individual, concerned only about himself and his series of preferences? (The preferences themselves are taken to have no rational basis, but man can use reason, once he has somehow chosen reason, to select the best means to satisfy them, and also, perhaps, to evaluate the various ends against one another in relation to a higher or more comprehensive end.) I do not understand that postulation. Human beings are not evidently like that, for the person we see in society is, for example, very frequently a religious believer. Why should we not think of the human being we see as a being in the image of God (or a being toward death, as Heidegger says), rather than a selfish, maximizing, or satisficing, being? Each of these formulas has its plausibility, and I do not understand why the authors choose one to the exclusion of the others.

I believe economists to be very moral men—and I know that they would consider that an insult. (I also find economists the most cheerful of the social scientists; anthropologists, for example, tend to be rather gloomy.) Professor Craig Stubblebine has remarked that locks on houses prove that we do not trust people. Hobbes, in making exactly this observation, noted that even fathers put locks on their chests to keep their sons from stealing. What does that say about our trust in human nature? The individualistic system is thus proved, in a way, by the fact that for all our good wishes, our love of family and of our wonderful children, we still lock the chest. Upon hearing this, Professor Buchanan remarked, "God save us!" If we get to the point where we have to depend upon such extremes. . .

Now I know that was just a turn of phrase, but I think it revealed very well something that I observed in the old University of Chicago economists: the notion that a decent society requires a certain amount of trust, that the model of mutual exploitation is in some sense only a model, and that one tries to prevent that extreme situation which in a way Professor Stubblebine was accepting as a sort of happy proof. What I mean to say about the economists' being very moral is something said over and over but nonetheless, I believe, true: that despite their tough-guy stance they believe a harmonious end will emerge where everybody will profit even though nobody has to go through the efforts of morality. I think one can state the gist of Professor Buchanan's famous article on the Good Samaritan as being that he too was somehow selfish, that his goal was to be a good Samaritan, which somehow made him feel good. If he had full understanding, he would be willing to apply such sanctions as would make the recipient of his good deeds behave and not just be a freeloader. One could call this an attack on the moral man in the name of morality. Such a characterization gives some indication of what I mean. One could say I am trying to identify what kind of person accepts this nonmoral beginning point. I think it is the kind of person who hates hypocrisy, who wants to accept human beings not as they actually are or most deeply are, but as we see them every day.

Another remark surely fits here; it was repeated by Professor Buchanan and agreed to by Professor Gauthier: those economists who take the rational, individualist approach don't want anything from outside. In other words, they are trying to devise effective rules that rest only on rational agreement among individuals, without any appeal to outside criteria or higher authority. The question is whether one can avoid using anything from outside—whether the attempt to do so does not require elaborate contortions.

I mentioned the University of Chicago professor Frank Knight earlier. I knew him fairly well—he obviously was not my teacher; I would know a lot more if he had been. But I saw him a great deal—I remember his coming to my doctoral exam. He was somewhat different from most economists. In the first place he was always a professor of philosophy and economics. Philosophy came first, I think, for Frank Knight. Even if it did not, one thing is certain: he was God-obsessed. He spent his life thinking about God. As he got older it became ever more apparent—he would be seen at every session or lecture that might deal with that question. My understanding of this is as follows: He was an old Voltairean and somehow he knew that this was the crucial issue. He was an atheist very explicitly, but he was an atheist who was not sure. That is not the same thing as an agnostic. He knew he had placed his chips, but he did not know where the wheel was going to stop. In a way his economics depended upon God not existing; if God did exist, there was something outside, and this meant conduct could be shameful and sinful. And he knew that this wasn't so clear.

I remember the first time I saw him. Arnold Toynbee (who was a kind of pious fraud, he was so famous) was visiting, and everybody was sitting there, so thrilled to see the great man. Frank Knight came stalking in late and sat down noisily. Toynbee was saying, "Now, we men are all brothers and that's because there is the fatherhood of God." Finally, Knight said—just loudly enough for everybody to hear—"Where do you get that shit?" He really cared about the issue, whereas Milton Friedman is indifferent to it. To Friedman, whether to believe in God or not to believe in God is a preference. For Frank Knight it was clearly *the* question. Somehow I feel a little of Frank Knight in Professor Buchanan.

I turn now to an attempt to understand where the economists begin, what they start from. I am impressed that throughout this volume the name of Hobbes keeps coming up—that although Hobbes did not found political economy, somehow his model was closer than anything else to what we would like. I think that Hobbes is not a bad beginning point for economists, because I really do consider him an essential source. He is thought to reason so closely and in a way that is so useful to economists, I think, because he was indeed the first to argue through this kind of individualism. I am very struck, in contrast, by a silence concerning Locke. If economists want to use Hobbes, however, they are going to have trouble establishing the notion of a free market; for it seems to me that in crucial respects Smith followed Locke, not Hobbes.

I want to say a few words about Hobbes, because in my view the contributors to this book have done a good thing in bringing, if not political science and economics, at least political philosophy and economics back together—and of course Hobbes understood himself to be a political philosopher. The study of what he actually said is of great importance to us, because economists treat him a little too much as they do Adam Smith, as simply a forerunner of what economists are now doing. I would suggest, however, that a man who so clearly defined the problem at the beginning may have also thought it through more deeply and coherently than his successors. At least I think we have to open up that possibility.

Let me raise a question that modern economists do not talk about but to which I think Adam Smith gave serious thought. Hobbes insisted that man originally was in a state of nature. That very important point means that man was this way naturally. There is a nature, in which man had a nature. One could say that the critical difference between the way Hobbes describes man and what economists say goes on in man is that economists today talk about preferences, whereas Hobbes talked about passions. Passions are real, natural things. Hobbes maintained, of course, that one had to get some kind of ordering of the passions, that fear was objectively a passion that all men share, and that precisely that passion could be the ground of a social contract. A very powerful common passion is what could provide the connection. That passion, fear of death, was really the beginning of society. Hobbes is the founder of the social contract teaching (and Locke and Adam Smith continue that approach). Professors Vanberg and Buchanan really are talking about establishing a social contract. Hobbes argued, however, that if you do not have an objective, common passion—as opposed to kaleidoscopic preferences—there is no possibility of a contract.

Hobbes was really the model for social contract thinking, at least for thinking that the social contract doctrine could work or be satisfying intellectually. (I am of course arguing, unfortunately, that I do not think Professors Buchanan and Vanberg have been satisfying intellectually.)

A central part of Hobbes's endeavor consists of the careful attention he devotes to handling the problems connected with anger. Vanberg and Buchanan talk about anger in their chapter to some extent; but this, I believe, is a place where their analysis falls short.

They recognize anger as a problem and suggest several lines of approach to it. In some sense they appear to argue that from the standpoint of individual rationality that they are using, anger really should not be there. On the other hand, they suggest that it may be utilitarian if it provides the passion that leads one to punish and therefore to make the game work; that is, if it produces retaliation. They obviously have a problem with the real phenomenon of anger, which is an absolutely dominant, overwhelming thing. I want to mention Homer in this connection. Anger is a central theme of Greek psychology, beginning with Homer's *Iliad*, whose first word is "anger"; Achilles was the angry man. Any study of Plato or Aristotle will show that anger is a central and good part of the soul, although problematic, to be sure, as everything is. (Both Plato and Aristotle had this in common with rational-choice theorists: they believed that man has problems with getting himself in order.) Anger is, objectively, a strange, dark passion, but it is also connected with the noblest things. I mean, simply, that it is the only passion in man, the only power that can explain his willingness to die for something. And it seems to me that the willingness to die for something always mucks up rational-choice theory. I may be wrong, but I think an example of this is our foiled strategy during the Vietnam War. The willingness of the North Vietnamese to die meant that they were willing to pay a great deal more than anybody, certainly than economists, believed they would. I do not find rational-choice theory very helpful, either, in explaining extreme actions such as those of the Ayatollah Khoemeini. Usually they are the extreme actions of angry men. The notion that extremes of angry behavior could be fine-tuned by genetics is highly questionable to me.

Hobbes's whole argument is that we have to cut anger, and everything that goes with it, out of the soul—both the ugly vengefulness and the nobility connected with anger. That is the foundation stone for a great deal of modern psychology. And of course, if one is frightened enough, one does not get angry; that in a way shows the power of fear in the soul. Here lies the basic source of the criticism made on all sides of bourgeois man, or the man of the capitalist order, or the rational individualist. Perhaps the best known example is Hegel's definition of the bourgeois as the man motivated by fear of violent death. This excision, as it were—it is almost an operation—of anger from the soul, took away much of the soul's nobility, but also made it possible to have a modern economy.

Since Hobbes says that the natural condition of man is war, one first has to understand war and its causes, and only then understand that a market is a continuation of war by other means (if I may misappropriate Clausewitz). One of Hobbes's predecessors tells us what real selfishness is and what one has to do really to put a market in order and to change from warlike to peaceful selfishness—and that is Machiavelli, whose basic theme, of course, is force and fraud. Hobbes developed his own thought in this continuous tradition. This is one of the things I have in mind in suggesting that, despite sounding like tough guys, economists are really not warriors. My thought—my exhortation or invitation—is that we really must go back and read Hobbes with great care, and likewise Adam Smith. By this I do not mean treating Smith as, for instance, George Stigler does, taking just the elements that suit him. Rather, I mean reading with a serious attention and an openness that permit us really to learn from the text, to be disciplined by it.

Professor Gauthier's chapter discusses Ulysses' choices when he sailed past the island of the Sirens. One critical aspect of Ulysses' choice is not mentioned, however. Ulysses' sticking wax in the ears of his sailors reflects his judgment that he should hear and they should not. It would be absurd to take that risk if these were just ice cream cones that the Sirens were offering. The story concerns the knowledge of something very powerful that may not be good or tolerable for everybody but that a ruler may need or want. A real issue is involved in Ulysses' choice, which rational-choice analysis wrings out until it loses its human vitality. My fear is that the market model, although obviously very useful in ways that Professor Rhoads, among others, describes, begins with such a thin picture of man and such a thin picture of reason that it contributes to the terrible growth of irrationalism that Professor Gauthier mentions.

As a younger man I discussed this issue with Charles E. Lindbloom for hundreds and hundreds of hours. I once said to him, "Aren't you in danger of simplifying man for your model?" He replied, "I'd love to simplify him so I could predict him." That is fine for the model, but the question is, What would that have to do with life? Moreover, if one started making policy on this basis, without a clear notion of human nature as something that is inviolable, would one not be transforming man, or possibly deforming him? I believe we need a reengagement of these issues with all the experience that we have had. All that unhappy experience with predictions, plans, and policies that allows us to be theoretical—we would not be theoretical if we succeeded in all that; we would be too happy.

I also think we must study Hobbes, since he speaks to the ancients; in this respect I am thinking about the chapter of Professors McCloskey and Nelson. In one sense I am very worried about a loss of understanding of man's depth, his freedom; but I am equally disturbed, or perhaps more so, by the eradication, proposed by Professor McCloskey, of the distinction between sophist and philosopher. In a way that is equivalent to the loss of the distinction between education and propaganda. I think we will have to take seriously how Socrates presents the sophists to consider whether indeed his depiction might be true and whether some such distinction might not indeed hold. These are the kinds of issues that we need to address. I will end by asking, What do we need? We need history of political philosophy; let us get to work.

Editors' Note: What follows is an edited version of a discussion among James Buchanan, Viktor Vanberg, and Allan Bloom.

BUCHANAN: First of all, I appreciate your reference to Frank Knight, and I basically agree with your characterization and interpretation of him. I'm reminded of an old University of Chicago saying that was current when I was there in the forties that there is no God, and Frank Knight is His prophet.

I think your comments were quite perceptive, although I think that you're ambiguous on some points and perhaps misunderstand our position on some points. I start with the individual as he exists, largely because I don't know where else to start. That's all there is in my view. I start with the individual; I build up, then, from the individual. That's not the same thing as taking a methodologically individualist position. And, to some extent, taking a normative individualist's position is different from attributing to an individual a set of economic motives. The *homo economicus* assumption is a quite different assumption. Individuals can all seek their own version of the good, the true, and the beautiful. All of my logic follows as long as individuals don't universally agree. As long as individuals differ in what they prefer or what they desire, everything follows in a contractarian sort of logic. Many noneconomists tend to confuse that and think that being an individualist is the same thing as applying a *homo economicus* description of the individual. That's something, I think, that may slip a little bit into your discussion.

Early in your discussion you pose the question—and you express some doubt whether we would accept your formulation, but I surely do—How do we move from individuals with identifiable, separate, differing interests, whatever these might be? How do we move from that which generates a Hobbesian conflict to a situation where individuals will behave in furtherance of something that you called a common good and that, in slightly different terminology, I will call their more general, shared interest? How do we get over this problem of complying with the set of rules or with the social order that they would all be involved in? How do we construct that bridge? And how we construct that bridge is the whole exercise that David Gauthier, I, and many other people are involved in. That's where justice comes in, and in this connection I want to take issue with the criticisms to which John Rawls was subjected [during discussion at the conference]. I feel a great deal of affinity for the whole Rawlsian exercise because that's precisely what Rawls is up to—trying to build this bridge from individual, identifiable interests that differ, to something in the general interest. The mode of construction is to step back behind some kind of veil and then try to agree, or talk about the possibility of agreeing on some principles of justice; justice is not brought in from the sky. I'm unwilling to bring in justice from the sky—that's the key difference here.

Now, this brings me to two final points that I'm not sure about. Let me relate my first point not to your discussion here but to your book *The Closing of the American Mind*. I share your prejudices almost completely.

BLOOM: I thought they were truths.

BUCHANAN: Your comment on rock music and the sixties is wonderful, and I wish I had written it, it was so good. I completely agree with it, but what I find finally disturbing about the book, and I find it also true of your present discussion, is something you don't quite come out with. You're not quite willing to say it, but underneath there is a kind of moral absolutist position that I can't go along with. You bring your attack to bear on a lot of cultural and value relativism. I can share most of that, but underneath it all there is a kind of moral absolutism that you don't quite come out front with.

BLOOM: That's what Frank Knight said at my doctoral dissertation defense. I feel like I'm reliving my youth.

BUCHANAN: I am, I think, a relatively absolute absolutist. And that can be true of moral as well as other values. But underneath it all you seem to be wanting to go and pull down something from on high. That's basically our difference.

BLOOM: It's such a civil and interesting response for me. I don't think you get to the social contract, but you get to the intellectual contract very easily. I would not say that my quest is for absolutes, but you can't simply say that the fundamental things are merely prejudices or preferences. One has to get to the big issues, and in order to get to the big issues one has to be able to dismiss some. I mean, for example, the issue for Knight was somehow the market versus God, and he really didn't worry about people who were interested in odd entertainments or perversities. It is in that sense that the intellectual discussion, in order to be seriously engaged, cannot simply be a market phenomenon. I would be open—I wouldn't be absolutely certain there's nothing on high—and that's the key difference. But I didn't say that I'm looking for something on high.

VANBERG: I would like to add a bit to the arguments to which Professor Buchanan already alluded. Your central question as I understood it is, Why do you begin where you begin?—with an individualistic conception and a notion of the self-interested individual? Basically my answer is the same as Professor Buchanan's: Where else do you want to begin? If you can provide an alternative perspective that allows us to make better sense of what we observe around us, then I am certainly the person who's most interested in learning about it. Our assumption is first that among the alternatives that we know of, it's the most truthful and most powerful perspective, which allows us to make sense of our observations of revealed behavior. And second, it seems to us to be the most fruitful perspective for approaching the question of how should we organize our social life.

You somehow implied—and this is a classical assumption in much of political philosophy—that if you start off with the assumption of self-interested individuals, then the problem of political and social order cannot be solved. We tried to show that it can be solved; that is, for people to be able to live in a mutually beneficial, peaceful social order, it's not necessary that they have a concern for the public good. Self-interested people who are capable of diagnosing the problem situation they are in—in the way that Hobbes did, and the way we do by depicting these prisoners' dilemma kinds of structures—such people are well able to identify their interests in being mutually constrained by certain rules, and they can find ways to make workable such systems of rules as they can agree on. And in order for those systems of rules to be workable, no transformation and no public concern is necessary. David Hume got it, in my understanding, perfectly right when he said that the whole problem is that it is an illusion to expect that we can change something in our nature. We can't transform ourselves into angels; we are the way we are. All we can hope for, and all we can do, is to change the constraints under which we act, so as to get a framework that allows us to carry out a peaceful and mutually beneficial social life.

Let me add just one more point. You mentioned the problem of passions—anger and such things—and how they relate to a rational-choice perspective. I'm quite willing to concede that these types of behavior don't lend themselves so readily to rational-choice explanation; that we should be aware of these things; and that we might have to add something to our theories. But the question is, What can we add? And how can we expand our explanation in a systematic way, and not just say that there are these additional things? But the point that I really wanted to make is that even with regard to those things—anger and other passions—rationality is not totally excluded. There is a famous cartoon in which a raging wife and husband throw china at each other. Now I would predict, and rational-choice theory would predict, that if a raging person knows that one piece of china is extremely valuable and one is cheap, the person will pick up and throw the cheap piece.

BLOOM: That raging person is not Achilles. He took the biggest Chinese vase he could find. Now, just two or three words on the other side. My position, of course, is that I don't think you predict; and that would be the issue of the debate. I don't think you have persuasively bridged the gap. If I did, I would of course immediately give in. Second, when you quoted Hume, you mentioned human nature. I don't find that economists talk much about human nature. In a way, that is the issue: what human nature is. If that is the question, then human nature might prove to be fundamentally social or fundamentally individualist. I don't know.

I believe it's not true that you begin the argument with human beings as they actually are. Just think of Hobbes, who mounted an enormous rhetoric to persuade people that the things they thought mattered *don't* matter. Many of them thought they believed in God, believed in an afterlife, thought that their social institutions were solid. And he engaged in a powerful act of rhetoric to describe the state of nature, where the life of man is solitary, poor, nasty, brutish, and short. He sought to persuade people, that this is the fundamental situation. That's not the way our society looks and indeed I'm even less persuaded that that's the way other societies look, because our society is partly already a creation of that economics. In a way, you see, I'm accusing that economics of being a project of very intelligent men who made us the way we are. And then we say, "Aha! Look! We're that way."

Notes

Chapter 1   Introduction: Political Economy and the Problems of Political Philosophy

1. Adam Smith, *An Inquiry into the Nature and Causes of the Wealth of Nations*, ed. Edwin Cannan (Chicago: University of Chicago Press, 1976), vol. 1, p. 449.

2. Aristotle, *The Politics*, trans. Carnes Lord (Chicago: University of Chicago Press, 1984) p. 51 (Chapter I. xi.1259a35–36).

3. Smith, *Wealth of Nations*, vol. 1, p. 144.

4. Smith, *Wealth of Nations*, vol. 1, p. 437.

5. Thomas L. Pangle, *The Spirit of Modern Republicanism* (Chicago: University of Chicago Press, 1988), p. 308 n.6.

6. Smith, *Wealth of Nations*, vol. 1, p. 449 (emphasis supplied).

Chapter 2   The Concept of Private Property in the History of Political Economy

The spelling and capitalization have been modernized in all quotations.

1. Adam Smith, *An Inquiry into the Nature and Causes of the Wealth of Nations* (New York: Modern Library, 1937), Book IV, Introduction, p. 397.

2. For Smith, the security of private property is the true ground of prosperity, regardless of the particular regulations to which commerce is subjected:

The security which the laws in Great Britain give to every man that he shall enjoy the fruits of his own labor, is alone sufficient to make any country flourish, notwithstanding [the corn laws] and twenty other absurd regulations of commerce. *Wealth of Nations*, Book IV, Chap. V, p. 508.

Nevertheless, he does not make an explicit defense of private property on these grounds.

3. This may seem a paradoxical statement, given all the argumentation Smith provides in favor of the system of "natural liberty" as opposed to the systems of agricultural preference or mercantilism. Smith, however, is arguing that the system of natural liberty is preferable in terms of its practical results; he allows that natural liberty, however intrinsically good it may be and however much its protection may be the purpose of government, may be infringed when the public necessity requires. (Consider, for example, his discussion of imprudent Scottish banking practices and the resulting need to regulate bank notes, even in violation of the "natural liberty" of individuals to accept in payment such notes as they see fit. *Wealth of Nations*, Book II, Chap. II, p. 308.) Thus, he must discuss the systems opposed to natural liberty at great length to show that they do not produce the public benefits that their supporters claim for them; if one of them did, the fact that it infringed on natural liberty might not, for Smith, be a sufficient argument against adopting it.

4. Adam Smith, *Lectures on Jurisprudence*, ed. R. L. Meek, D. D. Raphael, and P. G. Stein (Oxford: Clarendon Press, 1978), pp. 6–7, cited by Marc F. Plattner in "Natural Rights and the Moral Presuppositions of Political Economy," in this volume.

5. This and similar references in the text refer to the numbered sections of John Locke, *Second Treatise of Government*. I have used the Library of the Liberal Arts edition (Indianapolis: Bobbs-Merrill, 1952).

6. Since the "state of nature" is characterized by the absence of an authoritative power competent to judge disputes among individuals, it is not synonymous with primitive conditions or times; a breakdown of political authority in a highly developed society will return human beings to the state of nature.

7. In fact, as will become somewhat clearer below, it is not certain that these really are two separate limitations. Typically, Locke argues as if there were a sort of natural rationing: by not allowing anything to "perish uselessly in one's possession," one in fact leaves "enough and as good" for others. This line of argument will be readily recognizable, if not totally persuasive, to anyone who as a child was encouraged to eat his oatmeal by being told to think of the starving children in Europe. In any case, when the chips are down, it is only the spoilage limitation that is operative.

8. Aristotle, *The Politics*, I.viii.1256b15–20. I have used the Carnes Lord translation (Chicago: University of Chicago Press, 1984).

9. For Aristotle, it must be remembered, economics (*oikonomike*) is, along with ethics and politics, part of an overarching practical science directed toward "living well"; thus, it is not surprising to see that an "economic" question, such as whether wealth can be accumulated indefinitely,

cannot be adequately discussed without reference to concepts which take us beyond the boundaries of economics as ordinarily understood.

10. Throughout the discussion of the spoilage limitation, Locke emphasizes its legal rather than its practical aspect. Consider the following examples: "Whatever is beyond [the amount which can be made use of before it spoils] is more than his share and belongs to *others*" (sect. 31; emphasis supplied); "If the fruits rotted or the venison putrefied before [the gatherer or hunter] could spend it, he offended against the common law of nature and was liable to be punished" (sect. 37).

11. Strictly speaking, they are identical only in the case of a natural plenty, which Locke at first assumes to exist. If, however, the original state is one of penury, then one's absolute duty to preserve oneself must override one's conditional duty to preserve others. One's obligation to preserve the rest of mankind applies only when "[one's] own preservation comes not in competition" (sect. 6).

12. Locke explains how money "solves" the problem of making use of the product of a vast extent of land; he does not explain how such a property could be worked. Since Locke does not argue, as Aristotle did, that there are "natural slaves" who would be incapable of the forethought necessary to farm on their own, Locke must have assumed that, after the first division of the land into private holdings, there remained landless persons who would be available to farm the land of others.

13. See Leo Strauss, *Natural Right and History* (Chicago: University of Chicago Press, 1953), pp. 246–47, for a discussion of Locke's rhetorical intention in using such phrases.

14. This helps explain why Locke emphasized the dishonesty rather than the foolishness of accumulating more food than could be consumed before it spoiled; to judge by the discussion in this section, substituting the accumulation of gold and silver for the accumulation of food would be, from the point of view of reasonableness, jumping from the frying pan into the fire.

15. The "law of nature . . . wills the peace and preservation of all mankind" (sect. 7). According to the "fundamental law of nature, man [is] to be preserved as much as possible when all cannot be preserved" (sect. 16). Locke even implies that there is a duty to be charitable: everyone "when his own preservation comes not in competition, ought . . . , as much as he can, to preserve the rest of mankind" (sect. 6). In the primitive situation of the state of nature, it is not clear that this injunction to be charitable ever becomes effective; there is either a natural plenty, in which case there is no need for charity, or a natural scarcity, in which case one's own preservation always "comes in competition." In any case, since the "fundamental law of nature" commands the preservation of the human race ("as much as possible," to be sure) but not its comfort or convenience, we understand why the unequal accumulation of useful, durable goods, as discussed above, is not a problem for Locke.

16. Of course, in the England of Locke's time, there was no longer land available for the taking. Nevertheless, Locke asserts that "even to this day" there is still unused land in the world ("in some inland, vacant places of

America") where an individual might claim land without prejudicing the interests of others (sect. 36).

17. "It is true, in land that is common in England or any other country where there are plenty of people under government who have money and commerce, no one can enclose or appropriate any part without the consent of all his fellow commoners; because this is left common by compact, i.e., by the law of the land, which is not to be violated" (sect. 35).

18. As we have seen, of the two original criteria for deciding the amount of accumulation of property that is lawful, the spoilage criterion is determinative in case of conflict.

19. It should be noted that this is only true with respect to the members of a particular commonwealth; the commonwealth's right, with respect to foreigners, to regulate the property within its own boundaries would still depend on its members' right, under natural law, to claim title to property without the express consent of "all the commoners," that is, the rest of humanity. As Locke makes clear in section 120, when an individual enters civil society he subjects both himself and his possessions to the government of the commonwealth.

20. Locke's general position would seem to be that the natural-law prohibition on waste is not valid in civil society. See Leo Strauss, *Natural Right and History* (Chicago: University of Chicago Press, 1953), p. 241. However, given that the "fundamental law of nature" is that all, or as many as possible, are to be preserved, one wonders if this could hold true in a case in which the wasting of food implied the death of someone who could otherwise have been preserved. In this case, would the starving person not be the victim of a violation of natural law to vindicate which, there not being any appeal to the civil law, he would have the right, for all the good it would do him, to appeal to heaven?

21. 1 Tim. 6:17. In context, the quoted phrase implies that human beings should concern themselves not with worldly riches, but with spiritual ones.

22. Indeed, the mainstream of Locke scholarship has taken this view of his relationship with Christian natural-law thinkers such as Hooker, with whom Locke claims a special affinity.

23. James Madison, *Federalist* 10, in Alexander Hamilton, John Jay, and James Madison, *The Federalist* (New York: Modern Library), p. 55.

24. John Locke, *Some Considerations of the Consequences of the Lowering of Interest and Raising the Value of Money,* p. 60, reprinted in John Locke, *Several Papers Relating to Money, Interest and Trade, etc.* (New York: August M. Kelley Publishers, 1968).

25. This quotation and the two that follow are from a letter from Thomas Jefferson to the Rev. James Madison (a cousin of the future president), October 28, 1785, *The Life and Selected Writings of Thomas Jefferson,* ed. Adrienne Koch and William Peden (New York: Modern Library, 1944), pp. 388–90.

26. Locke, *Some Considerations,* pp. 1–12.

27. Locke, *Second Treatise of Government,* sect. 42.

28. See H. R. F. Bourne, *The Life of John Locke* (1876; Scientia Verlag Aalen, Darmstadt, West Germany, 1969), vol. 2, pp. 363–72, for Locke's proposal to

establish the linen trade in Ireland; and pp. 377–90, for his scheme for reforming the Poor Laws.

29. In contrasting this motive of human behavior with the desire for pleasure, Smith notes that it is less intense but, given that it acts at all times, more reliable. "The principle which prompts to expence, is the passion for present enjoyment; which, though sometimes violent and very difficult to be restrained, is in general only momentary and occasional. But the principle which prompts to save, is the desire of bettering our condition, a desire which, though generally calm and dispassionate, comes with us from the womb, and never leaves us till we go into the grave." *Wealth of Nations*, Book II, Chap. III, p. 324.

30. See James M. Buchanan, "Is Economics the Science of Choice?" in *What Should Economists Do?* (Indianapolis: Liberty Press, 1979), pp. 41–46, for a careful explanation of how homo economicus emerges from an abstract consideration of the logic of choice, once certain very general assumptions are made about what "utility" means to an individual faced with alternatives.

31. See, for example, George J. Stigler, "The Development of Utility Theory," in *Essays in the History of Economics* (Chicago: University of Chicago Press, 1965), pp. 66–165, for a discussion of the changes in utility theory.

32. John Locke, *Essay Concerning Human Understanding* (New York: Dover, 1959), vol. 1, p. 332 (Book II, Chap. XXI, §31).

33. Ibid., vol. 1, p. 342 (Book II, Chap. XXI, §45).

34. "Men may choose different things, and yet all choose right; supposing them only like a company of poor insects [without immortal souls]; whereof some are bees, delighted with flowers and their sweetness; and others beetles, delighted with other kinds of viands." Ibid., vol. 1, pp. 351–52 (Book II, Chap. XXI, § 56).

35. Ibid., vol. 1, p. 356 (Book II, Chap. XXI, §65). Stigler describes positive time preference as "a simple myopia with respect to future needs" but that does not appear to have a direct impact on the notion of consumer rationality. However, he regards it as unproved that "there is any strong tendency for the society as a whole" to undervalue (or, for that matter, to overvalue) "future consumption relative to present consumption." *The Theory of Price*, 3d ed. (New York: Macmillan, 1966), p. 280. Thus there would be, in any case, no need for governmental action to counteract the effects of positive time preference.

36. *Some Thoughts Concerning Education,* §33, cited in Nathan Tarcov, *Locke's Education for Liberty,* (Chicago: University of Chicago Press, 1984), p. 87.

37. See note 3, above.

38. If so, the bank was forgoing the interest it could have earned by loaning out the money; the key point seems to be that the bank was not a private, profit-making venture, but rather a public institution established to facilitate the city's trade. Even so, once the "universal article of faith" was firmly established in the minds of those who traded in Amsterdam,

the bank may have been tempted to cheat by loaning some of the deposited funds and thus earning interest on them.

39. See note 25, above.

40. "Parties," an essay published in the *National Gazette*, January 23, 1792, reprinted in *The Writings of James Madison*, ed. Gaillard Hunt (New York: Putnam's Sons, 1901–1910), vol. 6, p. 86, as cited in David F. Epstein, *The Political Theory of the Federalist* (Chicago: University of Chicago Press, 1984), p. 75.

41. Epstein, in *The Political Theory of the Federalist*, pp. 59–110, discusses this distinction in detail in the course of a masterly exegesis of *Federalist* 10.

42. Ibid., p. 108.

Chapter 3   Natural Rights and the Moral Presuppositions of Political Economy

Significant portions of this chapter previously appeared in Marc F. Plattner, "Capitalism," in *Confronting the Constitution*, ed. Allan Bloom (Washington, D.C.: American Enterprise Institute, 1990).

The spelling and capitalization have been modernized in all quotations.

1. Adam Smith, *An Inquiry into the Nature and Causes of the Wealth of Nations*, ed. Edwin Cannan (Chicago: University of Chicago Press, 1976), vol. 1, p. 449 (Book IV, Introduction).

2. Adam Smith, *The Theory of Moral Sentiments*, ed. D. D. Raphael and A. L. Macfie (Oxford: Oxford University Press, 1976), p. 342.

3. Adam Smith, *Lectures on Jurisprudence*, ed. R. L. Meek, D. D. Raphael, and P. G. Stein (Oxford: Clarendon Press, 1978), pp. 6–7.

4. In an "Advertisement" to the sixth edition (1790) of *The Theory of Moral Sentiments*, Smith notes that "various occupations" have prevented him from writing the discourse on jurisprudence promised at the conclusion of this work, and states, "In the *Inquiry Concerning the Nature and Causes of the Wealth of Nations*, I have partly executed this promise: at least so far as concerns police, revenue, and arms." The inclusion of "arms" must refer to the discussion "Of the Expense of Defense," Part I of Chapter I of Book V ("Of the Revenue of the Sovereign or Commonwealth") of *The Wealth of Nations*. A similar brief discussion "Of the Expense of Justice" also appears under the heading of revenue (in Book V), though Smith does not refer to it in the Advertisement. See*Theory of Moral Sentiments*, p. 3.

5. Smith, *Lectures on Jurisprudence*, p. 331

6. Smith, *Theory of Moral Sentiments*, p. 341.

7. *The Laws of Plato*, trans. Thomas L. Pangle (New York: Basic Books, 1979), pp. 126–133 (740a–745b).

8. Jean-Jacques Rousseau, *Discours sur les sciences et les arts* (First Discourse) in *Oeuvres completes* (Bibliothèque de la Pleiade: Paris, 1964), vol. 3, p. 19. Cf. Montesquieu, *The Spirit of the Laws*, III, 3. Rousseau wrote the article on "Political Economy" in the *Encyclopedie*. Given Rousseau's adherence to the ancient view that subordinated wealth to virtue, it is not surprising that Joseph Schumpeter concludes that this article "contains next to no economics." Joseph A. Schumpeter, *History of Economic Analysis* (New York: Oxford University Press, 1954), p. 139.

9. Smith, *Wealth of Nations*, vol. 2, p. 208 (Book IV, Chap. IX).

10. Ibid., vol. 1, p. 493 (Book IV Chap. II). Cf. vol. 2, pp. 48–49 (Book IV, Chap. V).

11. Ibid., vol. 2, pp. 49–50 (Book IV, Chap. V).

12. Ibid., vol. 1, p. 367 (Book II, Chap. III).

13. Ibid., vol. 1, pp. 362–65 (Book II, Chap. III). These conclusions must to some extent be qualified in the light of Smith's discussion of the need for publicly sponsored education as a means of combating the cowardice and "gross ignorance and stupidity" that, in a commercial society, afflict the great body of the people "unless government takes some pains to prevent it." Ibid., vol. 2, pp. 282–338 (Book V, Chap. I, Part III, Articles II and III). Yet the vehemence of Smith's critical comments in these passages does not lead him to call into question his advocacy of commercial society; and the measures he recommends to counteract the corrupting aspects of commercial society fall into the category not of traditional moral or religious education but of "enlightenment": elementary instruction in reading, writing, and mathematics for the common people; the encouragement of public diversions to "correct whatever was unsocial or disagreeably rigorous in the morals" of popular religious sects; and learning in science and philosophy ("the great antidote to the poison of enthusiasm and superstition") for the middle and upper classes. Moreover, it should be noted that Smith's discussion of education comes under the heading of "revenue" rather than "police." That is, education is treated not in terms of the ends of political society, but as an expense of a kind legitimately borne by the sovereign "because the profit could never repay the expense to any individual or small number of individuals, though it may frequently do much more than repay it to a great society." Ibid., vol. 2, p. 209 (Book IV, Chap. IX). In short, the theoretical framework in which Smith's discussion of education appears already presupposes the desirability of extending the sphere of private commercial enterprise as far as it may effectively go.

14. John Locke, *Two Treatises of Government*, ed. Peter Laslett (New York: New American Library, 1965), II, 42, p. 340.

15. Smith, *Wealth of Nations*, vol. 2, pp. 230–31 (Book V, Chap. I, Part I).

16. John Locke, *A Letter Concerning Toleration*, ed. Patrick Romanell (New York: Bobbs-Merrill, 1950), p. 48.

17. Locke, *Two Treatises*, II, 124, p. 395.

18. Thomas Hobbes, *Leviathan* (New York: Bobbs-Merrill, 1958), Part I, Chap, XIII, p. 108.

19. Thomas Hobbes, *De Cive* (New York: Appleton-Century-Crofts, 1949), Epistle Dedicatory, p. 5.

20. Locke, *Two Treatises*, II, 27, pp. 328–29. All quotations in the following five paragraphs are also drawn from *Two Treatises*, II, Chap. V, sections 25–51.

21. Ibid., I, 42, p. 206.

22. Ibid., II, 34, p. 333.

23. Locke, *A Letter Concerning Toleration*, p. 47.

24. *The Laws of Plato*, p. 129 (741e).

25. Aristotle, *Nicomachean Ethics*, trans. H. Rackham (Cambridge, Mass.: Harvard University Press, 1962), p. 195 (1120b).

26. Aristotle, *The Politics*, Book I (1256 a–b).

27. Montesquieu, *The Spirit of the Laws*, trans. Thomas Nugent (New York: Hafner, 1949), 20:2, p. 317.

28. Hobbes, *De Cive*, Book XIII, p. 150 (italics supplied).

29. *The Federalist Papers* (New York: New American Library, 1961), 8, p. 69.

30. Locke, *Two Treatises*, II, 182, p. 437.

31. Ibid., II, 177, p. 434.

32. John Stuart Mill, *Principles of Political Economy* (London: Longmans, Green & Co., 1909), p. 208.

33. Ibid., p. 881.

34. Smith, *Lectures on Jurisprudence*, pp. 315–325, 401–404. Cf. David Hume, "Of the Original Contract," in *Political Essays*, ed. Charles W. Hendel (Indianapolis: Library of Liberal Arts, 1953), pp. 43–61, and *A Treatise of Human Nature*, ed. L. A. Selby-Bigge (Oxford: Clarendon Press, 1896), III, viii–x.

35. Hume, *A Treatise of Human Nature*, III, ii.

36. Smith, *Lectures on Jurisprudence*, pp. 105, 399, 401, 458, 398.

37. Jeremy Bentham, "A Fragment on Government," in *The Works of Jeremy Bentham*, ed. John Bowring (New York: Russell and Russell, 1962), vol. 1, pp. 261–72, and "Anarchical Fallacies," *Works*, vol. 2, p. 501.

38. Alfred Marshall, *Principles of Economics*, 8th ed. (New York: Macmillan, 1949), Appendix B, p. 760. Lionel Robbins also expresses the view that Bentham's influence on subsequent economic thought has generally been underestimated. *The Theory of Economic Policy in English Classical Political Economy* (London: Macmillan, 1952), pp. 38–39. Robbins, it should be added, includes David Hume along with Adam Smith among the "English classical economists," and emphasizes the disjunction between this utilitarian school and the natural rights school of political economy represented by the physiocrats. Ibid., pp. 2, 46–9.

39. Albert Venn Dicey, *Lectures on the Relation Between Law and Public Opinion in England* (London: Macmillan, 1948), p. 309. See also pp. 171–75.

40. Jeremy Bentham, *Principles of the Civil Code,* in *Works,* vol. 1, pp. 302, 305.

41. Marshall, *Principles of Economics,* p. 760.

42. Bentham, *Principles of the Civil Code,* pp. 307–12.

43. Mill, *Principles of Political Economy,* p. 115.

44. Ibid., p. 697. See also pp. 881ff.

45. Ibid., p. 780. See also p. 938.

46. Ibid., pp. 211–12.

47. Ibid., p. 805.

48. Dicey, though he asserts that laissez-faire was "practically the most vital part of Bentham's legislative doctrine," recognizes that "laissez-faire is not from a logical point of view an essential article of the utilitarian creed." Indeed, he devotes a short chapter on "The Debt of Collectivism to Benthamism" to showing that British socialists of the early twentieth century adopted and redirected Benthamite principles. *Law and Public Opinion in England,* pp. 146–47, 303, 310.

49. Joseph A. Schumpeter, *History of Economic Analysis* (New York: Oxford University Press, 1954), p. 531.

50. Henry Sidgwick, *The Principles of Political Economy,* 3d ed. (London: Macmillan, 1901), p. 516. The first edition was published in 1883.

51. Frank Hyneman Knight, *The Ethics of Competition* (Chicago: University of Chicago Press, 1935), p. 56n.

52. F. A. Hayek, *The Constitution of Liberty* (Chicago: Regnery Gateway, 1972), p. 441.

53. Knight, *Ethics of Competition,* p. 56.

54. Arthur M. Okun, *Equality and Efficiency: The Big Tradeoff* (Washington, D.C.: Brookings Institution, 1975), p. 44.

55. John Rawls, *A Theory of Justice* (Cambridge, Mass.: Harvard University Press, 1971), p. 15.

56. Ibid., p. 101. It is worth noting that although Rawls purports to be returning to the tradition of individual rights and the social contract, his teaching is closer in some crucial respects to the utilitarian tradition of the economists. The clearest evidence of this is his rejection out of hand of the idea of a right to the fruits of one's labor.

57. Locke, *Two Treatises of Government,* II, 27, pp. 328–29. See also II, pp. 340–41.

58. The Lockean justification of economic inequality, shared by the American Founders, does not demand laissez-faire or preclude government policies aimed at assisting the needy. It is incompatible, however, with government policies explicitly aimed at redistribution of income. For an analysis of the redistributionist doctrines of Okun and Rawls, and of the dangers redistributionism poses for liberal democracy, see Marc F. Plattner, "The Welfare State vs. the Redistributive State," *The Public Interest* 55 (Spring 1979).

59. See Hayek, *The Constitution of Liberty,* pp. 89, 93–95; and Milton Friedman, *Capitalism and Freedom* (Chicago: University of Chicago Press, 1962), pp. 164, 166.

60. Hayek, *The Constitution of Liberty*, pp. 93–100; Friedman, *Capitalism and Freedom*, pp. 161–66.

61. Hayek, *The Constitution of Liberty*, p. 85 ff; Friedman, *Capitalism and Freedom*, p. 195. Note that the titles of these two works call attention to the central place their authors give to freedom.

62. Hayek, *The Constitution of Liberty*, p. 100. For a further discussion of the views of Hayek, Friedman, and other free-market economists on questions of economic justice, see Marc F. Plattner, "The New Egalitarianism," in *Modern Capitalism*, ed. Peter Berger, vol. 1, *Capitalism and Equality in America* (Lanham, Md.: University Press of America, 1987).

Chapter 4   Competing Conceptions of Political Economy

1. Sir James Steuart, *An Inquiry into the Principles of Political Economy*, ed. Andrew S. Skinner (Chicago: University of Chicago Press, 1966), p. 15.

2. Ibid., pp. 16, 17.

3. John Stuart Mill, "On the Definition of Political Economy; And on the Method of Investigation Proper to It," in *Essays on Some Unsettled Questions of Political Economy* (1844; London School of Economics and Political Science, 1948), p. 123.

4. Adam Smith, *An Inquiry into the Nature and Causes of the Wealth of Nations* (New York: Modern Library, 1937), p. 397.

5. Ibid., p. 651.

6. J. S. Mill, "Definition of Political Economy," pp. 123, 124.

7. Ibid., p. 138.

8. Ibid., p. 139.

9. Ibid., p. 140.

10. Henry Sidgwick, *The Principles of Political Economy* (London: Macmillan, 1883).

11. Alfred Marshall, *Principles of Economics*, 8th ed. (1890; London: Macmillan, 1920), p. 1.

12. John Maynard Keynes, *Essays and Sketches in Biography* (New York: Menider Books, 1956), p. 89.

13. Marshall, *Principles of Economics*, pp. 32, 34.

14. Ibid., p. 35.

15. Ibid., p. 36.

16. A. C. Pigou, *Economics of Welfare*, 4th ed. (London: Macmillan, 1948), p. 11.

17. Lionel Robbins, *The Nature and Significance of Economic Science* (London: Macmillan, 1932), p. 16.

18. Ibid., p. 17.

19. Ibid., p. 35.

20. Gary Becker, *The Economic Approach to Human Behavior* (Chicago: University of Chicago Press, 1976), pp. 3–14.

21. Alan Peacock, *The Economic Analysis of Government* (Oxford: Martin Robertson, 1982), p. 68.

22. Sumner Myrdal, *The Political Element in the Development of Economic Theory*, trans. Paul Streeten (New York: Simon & Schuster, 1969), p. 22.

23. *Review of Radical Political Economics* (New York: Union of Radical Political Economics, May 1969). Emphasis supplied. Quote taken from inside the front cover.

24. Ibid.

25. Tom Bottomore, *A Dictionary of Marxist Thought* (Cambridge, Mass.: Harvard University Press, 1983), p. 375.

26. Ibid. Emphasis supplied.

27. James Buchanan and Gordon Tullock, *The Calculus of Consent* (Ann Arbor, Mich.: University of Michigan Press, 1962). Emphasis in the original.

28. Dennis C. Mueller, *Public Choice* (Cambridge, England: Cambridge University Press, 1979), pp. 1, 2.

29. S. K. Nath, *A Reappraisal of Welfare Economics* (Clifton, N.J.: Augustus M. Kelley Publishers, 1969).

30. Joseph Cropsey, *Political Philosophy and the Issues of Politics* (Chicago: University of Chicago Press, 1980), p. 37.

31. Leo Strauss, *What Is Political Philosophy?* (Chicago: University of Chicago Press, 1959), p. 12.

32. Arthur. M. Okun, *Equality and Efficiency* (Washington, D.C.: Brookings Institution, 1975).

Chapter 5   Economists on Tastes and Preferences

I would like to thank James Ceaser, William Johnson, Donald McCloskey, Edgar Olsen, Maurice Scott, and John Whitaker for their helpful comments on an earlier draft. Several of these readers will disagree with parts of the final version and are in no way implicated in its shortcomings. This chapter gives an incomplete impression of my views on normative economics. For a discussion of its many virtues, see parts 1 and 2 of Steven E. Rhoads, *The Economist's View of the World: Government, Markets, and Public Policy* (Cambridge, England: Cambridge University Press, 1985).

1. "Political economy" is a term used to describe many dissimilar bodies of literature. What follows will be principally concerned with economists who are "political" in the sense that their work centers on public policy and public institutions—those who might be called welfare, public finance, benefit-cost, or public choice economists. Though public choice economists differ from the others in many ways, they share a belief in the normative principles set forth in this paragraph.

2. Ezra J. Mishan, *Cost-Benefit Analysis* (New York: Praeger, 1976), p. 318.

3. William Baumol, *Welfare Economics and the Theory of the State* (Cambridge, Mass.: Harvard University Press, 1969), p. 29.

4. Rhoads, *The Economist's View of the World,* especially chapter 9; and "Do Economists Overemphasize Monetary Benefits?" *Public Administration Review* (November/December 1985): 815–820.

5. For example, one article that purported to make "welfare comparisons of policies concerning information and regulation" concluded by noting that "proper evaluation requires considerable information on consumer tastes which is difficult to acquire, not only in practice but even in principle." Claude S. Colantoni, Otto A. Davis, and Malati Swaminuthan, "Imperfect Consumers and Welfare Comparisons of Policies Concerning Information and Regulation," *Bell Journal of Economics and Management Science* 7 (Autumn 1976): 613. See also Schwartz and Wilde, "Intervening in Markets on the Basis of Imperfect Information: A Legal and Economic Analysis," *University of Pennsylvania Law Review* 127 (1979): 668; Walter Y. Oi, "The Economics of Product Safety," *Bell Journal of Economics and Management Science* 4 (Spring 1973); Victor Goldberg's critique of Oi's paper and Oi's rejoinder in *Bell Journal of Economics and Management Science* 5 (Autumn 1974): 683–95. Despite the fancy mathematical models used, the empirical situation is so unclear that Oi ended this exchange of opinion by referring to his own preference for throwaway pop bottles even though he knew they were more likely to explode.

6. Kenneth J. Arrow, "Risk Perception in Psychology and Economics," *Economic Inquiry* (January 1982): 1–9.

7. New York Times/CBS Poll, *The Charlottesville Daily Progress*, April 15, 1986.

8. U.S. Council on Environmental Quality, *Public Opinion on Environmental Issues* (1980), pp. 33–36.

9. Hannah Pitkin, *The Concept of Representation* (Berkeley: University of California Press, 1967), chap. 7.

10. James C. Miller III, "A Program for Direct and Proxy Voting in the Legislative Process," *Public Choice* 7 (Fall 1969): 107–13, reprinted in *The Economic Approach to Public Policy,* ed. Ryan Amacher, Robert Tollison, and Thomas Willett (Ithaca, N.Y.: Cornell University Press, 1976), p. 373.

11. Ryan Amacher and William Boyes, "Cycles in Senatorial Voting: Implications for the Optimal Frequency of Elections," *Public Choice* 33 (1978): 5–13.

12. T. C. Schelling, "The Life You Save May Be Your Own," in *Problems in Public Expenditures Analysis,* ed. Samuel Chase, Jr. (Washington, D.C.: Brookings Institution, 1968), p. 161.

13. Pitkin reports that surveys that asked questions such as "Do you believe that a congressman should vote on any question as the majority of his constituents desire or vote according to his own judgment?" and "Should members of Congress vote according to their own best judgment or according to the way the people in their districts feel?" brought results ranging "from two-thirds in favor of constituency feelings to more than half in favor of the representative's judgment." *Concept of Representation,* pp. 277–78.

14. Sidney Schoeffler, "Note on Modern Welfare Economics," *American Economic Review* 42 (1952): 883, 887.

15. Kelvin Lancaster, "A New Approach to Consumer Theory," *Journal of Political Economy* 74 (April 1966): 149–50. For an example of economists building on Lancaster's work see Colantoni, Davis, and Swaminuthan, "Imperfect Consumers and Welfare Comparisons," cited in note 5 above.

16. George Stigler and Gary Becker, "De Gustibus Non Est Disputandum," *American Economic Review* 67 (March 1977): 89.

17. Gary Becker, *The Economic Approach to Human Behavior* (Chicago: University of Chicago Press, 1976), p. 145.

18. Becker and Stigler, "De Gustibus Non Est Disputandum," p. 83.

19. *Washington Post*, August 25, 1987.

20. Becker, *The Economic Approach to Human Behavior*, pp. 147–48.

21. Jerome Rothenberg, "Welfare Comparisons and Changes in Tastes," *American Economic Review* 43 (1953): 887.

22. Becker, *The Economic Approach to Human Behavior*, p. 145.

23. Plato, *Gorgias* and *The Republic*, trans. Allan Bloom (New York: Basic Books, 1968), chaps. II and IV and Bloom's interpretive essay, especially pp. 348, 375.

24. Robert Jastrow, *The Enchanted Loom* (New York: Simon and Schuster, 1981), pp. 132–33.

25. *Charlottesville Daily Progress*, May 30, 1981. Note also a recent study of psychiatrists that found that a majority of the small minority of therapists who repeatedly had sexual intercourse with patients believed that their conduct "was bad for both therapist and patient." *Washington Post*, Sept. 1, 1983.

26. Thomas Schelling, "The Intimate Contest for Self-Command," *The Public Interest* 60 (Summer 1980): 110.

27. "Tobacco and Liquor Taxation" (Fall 1964, Mimeographed).

28. The first set of figures were reported in a Louis Harris poll in the *Washington Post*, September 18, 1978; the second from a Harris poll in the *Washington Post*, May 23, 1977. Other polls have found that far more Americans think we are less happy because of increased affluence than think we are happier. Low-income respondents do not equate happiness with economic well-being any more than do high-income respondents. Jennifer Hochschild, "Why the Dog Doesn't Bark: Income, Attitudes and the Redistribution of Wealth," *Polity* (Summer 1979): 509.

29. Tibor Scitovsky, *The Joyless Economy* (Oxford: Oxford University Press, 1978), pp. 163–64. Scitovsky is an economist, and this is a good place to acknowledge the existence of an economic literature that is not open to much of the criticism offered here. Sen, Yeager, and Arrow, discussed briefly above, have also contributed much to it. It tends to be written disproportionately by economists educated outside the United States. For other theoretical works see C. C. Von Weizsacker, "Notes on Endogenous Change of Tastes," *Journal of Economic Theory* 3 (1971): 345–72; R. Thaler and H. M. Shefrin, "An

Economic Theory of Self-Control," *Journal of Political Economy* 89 (1981): 392–406; R. Pollak, "Endogenous Tastes in Demand and Welfare Analysis," *American Economic Review, Papers and Proceedings* 68 (May 1978): 374–79; Jon Elster, *Ulysses and the Sirens* (Cambridge, England: Cambridge University Press, 1979). For more applied work that in part challenges consumer sovereignty, see J. E. Meade, *An Introduction to Economic Analysis and Policy* (London: Oxford University Press, 1937), especially pp. 119–23; I. M. D. Little and J. A. Mirrlees, *Project Appraisal and Planning for Developing Countries* (London: Heinemann Educational Books, 1974), especially pp. 24–25, 224–25; United Nations, *Guidelines for Project Evaluation* (New York, 1972), pp. 32–33. These authors, together with most radical or Marxist economists (e.g., H. Gintis, "Welfare Criteria with Endogenous Preferences: The Economics of Education," *International Economic Review* 15 [June 1974]: 415–30), treat tastes and preferences differently than most mainstream economists, as Pollak acknowledges: "Economists have traditionally been suspicious of changing tastes. . . . Taste formation and change pose more difficult problems for welfare analysis. Variable tastes undermine the normative significance of the fundamental theorem of welfare economics" (p. 374).

30. Arnold Weinstein, "Individual Preference Intransitivity," *Southern Economic Journal* 34 (1968): 336. See also Arthur Maass, "Benefit-Cost Analysis: Its Relevance to Public Investment Decisions," *Quarterly Journal of Economics* 80 (May 1966): 216; Duncan MacRae, "Normative Assumptions in the Study of Public Choice," *Public Choice* 16 (Fall 1973), especially pp. 32–33; Amartya Sen, "Behavior and the Concept of Preference," *Economics* 40 (August 1973): 214–59.

31. James Buchanan, "Individual Choice in Voting and the Market," *Journal of Political Economy* 62 (August 1954): 336.

32. See also Kenneth Arrow, *Social Choice and Individual Values* (New York: Wiley, 1963), especially pp. 17–18. But note MacRae's discussion of Arrow in "Normative Assumptions in the Study of Public Choice," pp. 32–33.

33. Sen, "Behavior and the Concept of Preference," p. 257.

34. A. Myrick Freeman III, *The Benefits of Environmental Improvement* (Baltimore: John Hopkins University Press, 1979), p. 97. For an economist who disagrees with his colleagues' frequent unwillingness to use questionnaires or self-testimony as a route to understanding, see Donald McCloskey, "The Rhetoric of Economics," *Journal of Economic Literature* (June 1983): 481–517.

35. Since the federal cigarette tax has not been raised in many years and since soaring health care costs are making the external costs of smoking loom larger, the present tax may soon be justified on externality grounds alone.

36. Mishan, *Cost-Benefit Analysis*, p. 386. Arthur Okun seems to support Mishan's view. See *Equality and Efficiency* (Washington, D.C.: Brookings Institution, 1975), p. 78. See also Mishan, *Welfare Economics: An Assessment* (Amsterdam: North Holland, 1969), pp. 36–37.

37. Kenneth Arrow, "Political and Economic Evaluation of Social Effects and Externalities," in *The Analysis of Public Output*, ed. Julius Margolis (New York: Colombia University Press, 1970), p. 16; Kenneth Arrow, *Social Choice*

and Individual Values (New York: Wiley, 1963), p. 18; Amartya Sen, *Collective Choice and Social Welfare* (San Francisco: Holden-Day, 1970), p. 82; Leland Yeager, "Pareto Optimality in Policy Espousal," *Journal of Libertarian Studies* 2 (1978): 203–204.

38. Leonard Merewitz and Stephen Sosnick, *The Budget's New Clothes* (Chicago: Markham, 1971), p. 78.

39. Mishan, *Cost-Benefit Analysis*, p. 387.

40. Friedrich Hayek, *The Constitution of Liberty* (Chicago: University of Chicago Press, 1960), p. 145.

41. This fact is commented on in Dennis Mueller, *Public Choice* (Cambridge, England: Cambridge University Press, 1979), p. 205, and Charles Rowley, "Market 'Failure' and Government 'Failure,'" in *The Economics of Politics*, by James Buchanan et al. (West Sussex, England: Institute for Economic Affairs, 1978), p. 36. For citations to the entire literature on the subject, see Amartya Sen, "Liberty, Unanimity and Rights," *Economics* 43 (August 1976): 217–45.

42. James S. Duesenberry, *Income, Saving and the Theory of Consumer Behavior* (New York: Oxford University Press, 1967), pp. 100–101; Geoffrey Brennan, "Pareto Desirable Redistribution: The Case of Malice and Envy," *Journal of Public Economics* 2 (1973). See also William Breit and Roger Ransom's discussion of Veblen in *The Academic Scribblers* (New York: Holt, Rinehart & Winston, 1971), p. 42.

43. Mishan, *Cost-Benefit Analysis*, pp. 314–15.

44. David Long, Charles Mallar, and Craig Thornton, "Evaluating the Benefits and Costs of the Job Corps," *Journal of Policy Analysis and Managment* 1 (Fall 1981): 61.

45. To be sure, some economists are embarrassed by what their model produces in the criminal justice field. Richard Nelson, for example, correctly notes that this view of the costs of crime will seem "clearly absurd" to most of us. But Nelson offers only a few brief sentences setting forth his "biases" on legitimate interests. Richard Nelson, *The Moon and the Ghetto* (New York: Norton, 1977), p. 151. Some economists have noted that additional crime may lead to other societal costs in the form of additional expenditures to protect oneself from crimes; James Buchanan, *The Limits of Liberty* (Chicago: University of Chicago Press, 1975), p. 122.

46. Timothy Hannon, "The Benefits and Costs of Methadone Maintenance," *Public Policy* 24 (1976): 200–201; Gary Becker, "Crime and Punishment: An Economic Approach," *Journal of Political Economy* 76 (1968): 169–217; Richard Posner, *Economic Analysis of the Law* (Boston: Little, Brown, 1972), pp. 357–59. My discussion here has produced contrasting criticisms. One public administration student thought it unfair to suggest that most economists would count the benefits to thieves in their cost-benefit work since he could not believe "that most economists would go this far." An economist reader could not believe that I would exclude all benefits to thieves. He reminds me that the thief could be a mother stealing from the rich to feed her children.

47. Jeffrey Sedgwick, "Welfare Economics and Criminal Justice Policy" (Ph.D. dissertation, University of Virginia, 1978), pp. 156–57.

48. *Chicago Tribune,* September 1, 1974.

49. Joseph Cropsey, "What is Welfare Economics?" *Ethics* 65 (January 1955): 124. See also Walter Berns, "The Behavioral Sciences and the Study of Political Things: The Case of Christian Bay's The Structure of Freedom," *American Political Science Review* 55 (1961): 550–59.

50. James Q. Wilson and George Kelling describe some interesting psychological experiments that have shown this mushrooming effect. "Broken Windows," *Atlantic Monthly* (March 1982): 29–38. See also Wilson's *Thinking About Crime* (New York: Basic Books, 1975), especially chap. 2; Peter Singer, "Altruism and Commerce: A Defense of Titmuss Against Arrow," *Philosophy and Public Affairs* 2 (1973): 319; Derek Wright, *The Psychology of Moral Behavior* (London: Penguin, 1971), pp. 133–39; Peter Skerry, "The Charmed Life of Head Start," *The Public Interest* 73 (Fall 1983): 18–40.

51. *Charlottesville Daily Progress,* October 17, 1982 and March 14, 1982.

52. See John Hospers's discussion of Bentham in *Human Conduct: Problems of Ethics* (New York: Harcourt Brace Jovanovich, 1961), p. 145.

53. David Collard, *Altruism and Economy* (Oxford: Martin Robertson, 1978), p. 63. Collard notes that Marshall did not in fact devote any substantial part of his analytical attention to this supreme aim.

54. Burton Weisbrod, "Comparing Utility Functions in Efficiency Terms or, What Kind of Utility Functions Do We Want?" *American Economic Review* 67 (1977): 991–95.

55. James Tobin, "On Limiting the Domain of Inequality," *Journal of Law and Economics* 13 (1970), reprinted in *The Economic Approach to Public Policy,* ed. Ryan Amacher, Robert Tollison, and Thomas Willet (Ithaca, N.Y.: Cornell University Press, 1976), p. 290.

56. Economists involved in carrying out the income maintenance experiments acknowledged this fact in telephone interviews I conducted for research on social experiments.

57. *Washington Post,* December 13, 1985.

58. *Washington Post,* May 21, 1987.

59. Edgar Browning and Jacquelene Browning, *Public Finance and the Price System* (New York: Macmillan, 1979), pp. 110–11. Later editions omit the provocative mention of the possibilities of drug and alcohol expenditures, but the underlying philosophy is unchanged. See also George Stigler and Gary Becker, "De Gustibus Non Est Disputandum," pp. 80–81.

60. Mishan, *Cost-Benefit Analysis,* chap. 11. See also Browning and Browning, *Public Finance and the Price System,* 1983 edition, p. 273.

61. David Ellwood and Lawrence Summers, "Is Welfare Really the Problem?" *The Public Interest* (Spring 1986): 57–78.

62. See, for example, Glen Loury "The Moral Quandary of the Black Community," *The Public Interest* (Spring 1985): 9–22.

63. Ellwood and Summers, "Is Welfare Really the Problem?" p. 78.

64. Robert Lehreman, "Generating Poverty: Why Do Young Men Become Absent Fathers?" (Paper delivered at Eighth Annual Research Conference, Association for Public Policy and Managment, October 30–November 1, 1986).

65. Richard Freeman and Harry Holzer "Young Blacks and Jobs—What We Now Know," *The Public Interest* (Winter 1985): 18–31.

66. Browning and Browning, *Public Finance and the Price System,* 1987 edition, pp. 256, 288.

67. Joseph Stiglitz, *Economics of the Public Sector* (New York: W. W. Norton, 1986), pp. 256, 288.

68. Adam Smith, *The Theory of Moral Sentiments* (Indianapolis: Liberty Classics, 1976), Part I, Sec. III, Chap. II.

69. Social scientists find that the primary source of human self-esteem is a sense of accomplishment. Robert Lane, "Government and Self Esteem," *Political Theory* 10 (1982): 5–31. On the subject of self-respect and welfare, see Clifford Orwin, "Welfare and the New Dignity," *The Public Interest* 71 (Spring 1983): 85–95.

70. Allan Bloom, *The Closing of the American Mind* (New York: Simon and Schuster, 1987), p. 345.

71. Ibid., p. 370.

72. Allan Bloom, "The Democratization of the University," in *How Democratic is America?* ed. R. Goldwin (Chicago: Rand McNally, 1969), p. 117.

73. Jacques Barzun, *The American University* (New York: Harper and Row, 1968), p. 215.

74. Nevitt Sanford, "Education for Individual Development," in New Dimensions in Higher Education, ed. Everett H. Hopkins, Department of Education Series no. 31, 1967, p. 14.

75. *Washington Post,* November 28, 1976.

76. Mancur Olson and Christopher Clague have called the treatment of consumer tastes "the Achilles heel of neoclassical economics." Mancur Olson and Christopher Clague, "Dissent in Economics: The Convergence of Extremes," *Social Research* 38 (Winter 1971), reprinted in *The Economic Approach to Public Policy,* ed. Ryan Amacher, Robert Tollison, and Thomas Willett (Ithaca, N.Y.: Cornell University Press, 1976), p. 86. See also Steven Kelman, *What Price Incentives? Economists and the Environment* (Boston: Auburn House, 1981), pp. 19–20.

77. U.S. Department of Health, Education and Welfare, *Toward a Long-Range Plan for Federal Financial Support for Higher Education* (Washington, D.C.: Government Printing Office, January 1969), p. 38.

78. Roger Bolton, "The Economics and Public Financing of Higher Education: An Overview," in *The Economics and Financing of Higher Education in the United States,* a compendium of papers submitted to the Joint Economic Committee, U.S. Congress (Washington, D.C.: Government Printing Office, 1969), p. 33. For a thoughtful discussion of "groping upward" and higher

values by an economist (writing on the environment) who would disagree with Bolton, see Robert Dorfman, "An Afterword: Humane Values and Environmental Decisions," in *When Values Conflict: Essays on Environmental Analysis, Discourse and Decision,* by Lawrence Tribe et al. (Cambridge, Mass.: Ballinger, 1976), pp. 155–73.

79. For a more extended discussion see Rhoads, *The Economist's View of the World,* pp. 174–78.

80. Stigler and Becker, "De Gustibus Non Est Disputandum," p. 79.

81. Martin Bronfenbrenner, "Poetry, Pushpin and Utility," *Economic Inquiry* (January 1977), p. 95.

82. Ibid., p. 98.

83. Ibid., pp. 96–99.

84. Ibid., p. 108.

85. Ibid., p. 108.

86. John Stuart Mill, *Utilitarianism,* p. 13. See also Mill's "Civilization," in *Dissertations and Discussions: Political, Philosophical and Historical,* 3 vols. (Boston: Wm. V. Spencer, 1864), vol. 1, pp. 186–231.

87. See Rhoads, *The Economist's View of the World,* especially chap. 9.

88. The words are Smart's in J. J. C. Smart and Bernard Williams, *Utilitarianism: For and Against* (Cambridge, England: Cambridge University Press, 1973), p. 24.

89. David Ricci, *The Tragedy of Political Science* (New Haven: Yale University Press, 1984).

90. Donald McCloskey, *The Rhetoric of Economics* (Madison: University of Wisconsin Press, 1985).

91. Ezra Mishan, *The Cost of Economic Growth* (New York: Praeger, 1967).

Chapter 6   Economic Man and the Rational Reasoner

1. See Amartya Sen, "Rational Fools: A Critique of the Behavioral Foundations of Economic Theory," *Philosophy & Public Affairs* 6 (1977): 317–44, and Herbert A. Simon, *Models of Man* (New York: John Wiley and Sons, 1957), especially pp. 204–206. In satisficing, an agent sets a threshold of "satisfactoriness" and chooses the first option to come to her attention that exceeds the threshold.

2. D. M. Winch, *Analytical Welfare Economics* (Harmondsworth, England: Penguin, 1971), p. 25.

3. Ibid.

4. Kenneth J. Arrow, *Social Choice and Individual Values,* 2nd ed. (New York: John Wiley and Sons, 1963), p. 21. Originally published in 1951.

5. See Immanuel Kant, *Critique of Pure Reason,* trans. Norman Kemp Smith (New York: St. Martin's Press, 1965), pp. 151–75, "Deduction of the Pure Concepts of the Understanding." Translation first published in 1929 by Macmillan.

6. Michael Laver, *The Politics of Private Desires* (Harmondsworth, England: Penguin, 1981), p. 26.

7. See David Hume, *A Treatise of Human Nature*, ed. L. A. Selby-Bigge (1739; Oxford: Clarendon Press, 1888), Book II, Part III, Sec. III, p. 416.

8. See Jon Elster, *Ulysses and the Sirens* (Cambridge, England: Cambridge University Press, 1979), chap. 2, "Imperfect Rationality: Ulysses and the Sirens." The appropriate quotation (from the *Odyssesy*) appears at the head of R. H. Strotz, "Myopia and Inconsistency in Dynamic Utility Maximization," *Review of Economic Studies* 23 (1955–56): 165. See also Edward F. McClennen, "Prisoner's Dilemma and Resolute Choice," in *Paradoxes of Rationality and Co-operation*, ed. Richmond Campbell and Lanning Sowden (Vancouver: University of British Columbia Press, 1985), especially pp. 98–103.

9. For the distinction between myopic and sophisticated choice, see Peter F. Hammond, "Changing Tastes and Coherent Dynamic Choice," *Review of Economic Studies* 43 (1976): 162.

10. See my *Morals by Agreement* (Oxford: Clarendon Press, 1986), especially pp. 167–70.

11. See Thomas C. Schelling, *The Strategy of Conflict* (Cambridge, Mass.: Harvard University Press, 1960), especially p. 18, and Derek Parfit, *Reasons and Persons* (Oxford: Clarendon Press, 1984), especially pp. 12–13.

12. See Edward F. McClennen, *Rationality and Dynamic Choice: Foundational Explorations* (Cambridge, England: Cambridge University Press, 1990), and "Constrained Maximization and Resolute Choice," *Social Philosophy and Policy* 5 (1988): 95–118, reprinted in *The New Social Contract: Essays on Gauthier*, ed. E. F. Paul et al. (Oxford: Basil Blackwell, 1988).

13. McClennen "Constrained Maximization and Resolute Choice" p. 111.

14. Ibid.

15. Ibid., p. 112.

16. Ibid., pp. 112–13.

Chapter 7 Economic Experiments

This chapter draws heavily, in parts, upon Nathan Rosenberg and L. E. Birdzell, Jr., *How the West Grew Rich* (New York: Basic Books, 1986). That book provides extensive documentation for many of the assertions made here concerning the history of Western capitalism. This is also an appropriate place to acknowledge an intellectual debt to L. E. Birdzell, Jr., from whom I have learned a great deal.

The spelling has been modernized in all quotations.

1. Engels offered a succinct periodization, in which handicraft technology represented the pre-1500 technology of feudalism, manufacturing represented the post-1500 technology of early capitalism, and modern industry

represents the post-1750 industrial technology: "We divide the history of industrial production since the Middle Ages into three periods: (1) handicraft, small master craftsmen with a few journeymen and apprentices, where each laborer produces the complete article; (2) manufacture, where greater numbers of workmen, grouped in one large establishment, produce the complete article on the principle of division of labor, each workman performing only one partial operation, so that the product is complete only after having passed successively through the hands of all; (3) modern industry, where the product is produced by machinery driven by power, and where the work of the laborer is limited to superintending and correcting the performances of the mechanical agent." Friedrich Engels, *Socialism: Utopian and Scientific* (Chicago: Kerr, 1910), pp. 12–13.

2. Karl Marx and Friedrich Engels, *The Communist Manifesto*, in *Selected Works*, vol. 1 (Moscow: Progress Publishers, 1969), p. 109.

3. Marx and Engels, *Communist Manifesto*, pp. 111–13.

4. For an extended discussion of this point, see Nathan Rosenberg, "Karl Marx on the Economic Role of Science," *Journal of Political Economy* (July–August 1974), reprinted in *Perspectives on Technology* (New York: Cambridge University Press, 1976).

5. Richard Nelson, *The Moon and the Ghetto* (New York: W. W. Norton and Co., 1977) provides a valuable discussion of some of these issues.

6. Karl Marx, *Capital*, vol. 3 (Moscow: Foreign Languages Publishing House), p. 103.

7. Insofar as Marx may be said to have dealt with the trade-off between equity and efficiency, he did so by assigning to capitalism the historical role of providing efficiency and to a later socialism the role of delivering equity.

8. These matters are discussed in detail by Nathan Rosenberg and L. E. Birdzell, Jr., *How the West Grew Rich* (New York: Basic Books, 1986), especially chapters 4–8.

9. Of the regulated companies, which controlled so much of foreign trade even in the late eighteenth century, Adam Smith made the sardonic observation: "To be merely useless, indeed, is perhaps the highest eulogy which can ever justly be bestowed upon a regulated company." Adam Smith, *An Inquiry into the Nature and Causes of the Wealth of Nations* (New York: Modern Library, 1937), p. 693.

10. The last two paragraphs are drawn, with only slight modification, from Rosenberg and Birdzell, *How the West Grew Rich*, pp. 234–35.

11. U.S. Department of Commerce, Bureau of the Census, *Statistical Abstract* (Washington, D.C.: Government Printing Office, 1979): 813–14, table 1429.

12. See Nathan Rosenberg and Claudio Frischtak, eds., *International Technology Transfer: Concepts, Measures, and Comparisons* (New York: Praeger Publishers, 1985).

13. It has been a deliberate policy in the Soviet Union in the past to limit the number of models of a given product and the frequency of model changes. For a discussion of the impact of this policy, see Joseph Berliner, *The*

Innovation Decision in Soviet Industry (Cambridge, Mass.: MIT Press, 1976), pp. 195–98.

14. One important by-product of supplier unreliability is an incentive to vertical integration in order to achieve greater control over the supply of inputs and thereby to reduce dependence upon others. This translates, of course, into another incentive to increase the size of the firm.

15. Janos Kornai, *Anti-Equilibrium* (Amsterdam: North Holland, 1971), pp. 288–89.

16. See Leon Smolinski, "The Scale of Soviet Industrial Establishment," *American Economic Review Papers and Proceedings* (May 1962). Smolinski asserts that giantism began with the first of the Five Year Plans in 1928. Giantism "started in 1929 when the original draft of the First Five Year Plan was scrapped as being too conservative, and both the output goals and the size of the new projects, from which the bulk of the additional output was to come, underwent a series of drastic upward revisions. The sky was soon the limit. Coal mines of 10 million tons annual capacity were being designed (some 4 times larger than the world's largest mine and some 150 times larger than an average Soviet mine then in operation), the world's largest cement works of 930,000 tons, steam condensing power stations of 1 million kilowatts, etc. At the same time, hundreds of smaller projects included in the original draft were being dropped, even when they were complementary to the 'giants' themselves. Giantism reached its peak around 1932, was condemned in 1938, and revived, in a modified form, in 1950" (pp. 139–40).

17. Karl Marx, *Capital*, vol. 1 (New York: Modern Library), p. 686.

18. "In a large factory with one or two central motors the cost of these motors does not increase in the same ratio as their horse power and, hence, their possible sphere of activity. The cost of the transmission equipment does not grow in the same ratio as the total number of working machines which it sets in motion. The frame of a machine does not become dearer in the same ratio as the mounting number of tools which it employs as its organs, etc. Furthermore, the concentration of means of production yields a saving on buildings of various kinds not only for the actual workshops, but also for storage, etc. The same applies to expenditures for fuel, lighting, etc. Other conditions of production remain the same, whether used by many or by few." Marx, *Capital*, vol. 3, p. 79.

19. "If we now fix our attention on that portion of the machinery employed in the construction of machines, which constitutes the operating tool, we find the manual implements reappearing, but on a cyclopean scale. The operating part of the boring machine is an immense drill driven by a steam-engine; without this machine, on the other hand, the cylinders of large steam-engines and of hydraulic presses could not be made. The mechanical lathe is only a cyclopean reproduction of the ordinary foot-lathe; the planing machine, an iron carpenter, that works on iron with the same tools that the human carpenter employs on wood; the instrument that, on the London wharfs, cuts the veneers, is a gigantic razor; the tool of the shearing machine, which shears iron as easily as a tailor's scissors cut cloth, is a monster pair of scissors; and the steam hammer works

with an ordinary hammer head, but of such a weight that not Thor himself could wield it." Marx, *Capital*, vol. 1, p. 421.

20. "The general requirements for the reemployment of these 'excretions' are: large quantities of such waste, such as are available only in large-scale production; improved machinery whereby materials, formerly useless in their prevailing form, are put into a state fit for new production; scientific progress, particularly chemistry, which reveals the useful properties of such waste." Marx, *Capital*, vol. 3, p. 100.

21. Smolinski, "The Scale of Soviet Industrial Establishment," p. 141.

22. Socialist problems with respect to agriculture have been compounded by a powerful commitment to industrialization. In pursuit of industrialization, socialist societies have typically shifted the terms of trade systematically against the agricultural sector. They have forced the farmers to deliver their products at artificially low prices—the compulsory delivery of agricultural products to state purchasing agencies has usually been at prices well below those that would prevail in a free market. This has drastically weakened the incentive of farmers to generate marketable surpluses of their products. At the same time, these practices have seriously damaged the incentives to farm efficiency by disrupting the close link between personal effort and individual reward that prevails on small-scale, privately owned farms (who will sit up all night with a sick cow?). Finally, and not least important, the collectivization of agriculture has largely eliminated one of the main sources of savings in the economy—the frugal farmer.

23. Joseph Berliner, *The Innovation Decision in Soviet Industry* (Cambridge, Mass.: MIT Press, 1976), pp. 33–34. Some more recent World Bank data show a much greater concentration of industrial enterprises at the high end of the spectrum, with respect to number of employees, in Yugoslavia and Hungary as compared to South Korea and Japan. Mainland China occupies an intermediate position, reflecting the large number of small rural enterprises:

Size and Distribution of Industrial Enterprise (percentage)

Size of Enterprise	China (1982)	So. Korea (1981)	Japan (1972)	Yugoslavia (1981)	Hungary (1981)
5–33 employees	59.2	70.6	80.2	6.6	2.2
33–75 employees	19.5	14.4	10.7	15.8	4.8
75–189 employees	12.2	9.2	6.1	32.1	18.7
189–243 employees	8.5	1.5	0.8	12.0	9.2
More than 243 employees	0.6	4.3	2.2	33.5	65.1

SOURCE: World Bank, as reported in "China's Economy Survey," *Economist*, August 1, 1987, p. 10.

24. Of course, firms of different sizes are likely to differ with respect to the kinds of innovative activity in which they are most competent to engage. Given the different requirements of different classes of innovation, it would be natural to expect patterns of specialization based upon size. Moreover, many innovations actually carried out by large firms, such as du Pont, have been based upon inventions originally made in small firms. For a suggestive analysis of the role of firm size in innovation, see Kenneth Arrow, "Innovation in Large and Small Firms," in *Entrepreneurship,* ed. Joshua Ronen (Lexington, Mass.: D.C. Heath and Co., 1983), chap. 1. Arrow's conclusion is "that there is likely to be a tendency toward specialization—less costly and more original innovations will come from small firms, and those involving higher development costs but less radical departures in principle will come from larger firms" (p. 16).

25. Within each ministry, there is a separation between R&D and production. "The decision was taken early in the development of Soviet economic institutions to pursue the presumed advantages of scale and specialization, and to concentrate R&D within branch institutions rather than to have individual R&D departments at each enterprise. This separation of R&D units from production units extends to the separate subordination of each to different channels of planning, finance, and supply. This has proved a considerable barrier to the transfer of new technology from the laboratory to production. Similar Western experience clearly demonstrates how important it is to maintain a close linkage between the management of production and that of R&D, to coordinate the two activities, and to ensure that the new technology is compatible with the technical production procedures and organizational characteristics and needs of the adopting enterprise." Herbert Levine, "On the Nature and Location of Entrepreneurial Activity in Centrally Planned Economies: The Soviet Case," chap. 9, in *Entrepreneurship,* pp. 249–50.

26. See Masahiko Aoki and Nathan Rosenberg, "The Japanese Firm as an Innovating Institution" (paper delivered at International Economic Association Roundtable Conference, Tokyo, September 15–17, 1987).

Chapter 8   The Rhetoric of Political Economy

1. G. R. Boynton, "Telling a Good Story: Models of Argument, Models of Understanding in the Senate Agriculture Committee," *Argument and Critical Practices,* ed. Joseph W. Wenzel (Annandale, Va.: Speech Communication Association, 1987), pp. 429–38.

2. Max Black, *Models and Metaphors* (Ithaca, N.Y.: Cornell University Press, 1962), p. 236.

3. John Nelson, Allan Megill, and Donald McCloskey, eds., *The Rhetoric of the Human Sciences* (Madison: University of Wisconsin Press, 1987).

4. Brian Barry, *Political Argument* (London: Routledge and Kegan Paul, 1965), p. 1. Quote first appeared in Jacob Viner, "The Intellectual History of Laissez Faire," *The Journal of Law and Economics* (October 1960).

5. Gary Becker and George Stigler. "De Gustibus Non Est Disputandum," *American Economic Review* 67 (March 1977): 76–90.

✓ 6. Albert Hirschman, *Rival Views of Market Society* (New York: Viking Press, 1986), and Pierre Bourdieu, *Distinction*, trans. Richard Nice (Cambridge, Mass.: Harvard University Press, 1984).

7. Richard Posner, *Economic Analysis of Law* (Boston: Little, Brown, 1972), pp. 98–99.

8. James M. Buchanan, and Gordon Tullock, *The Calculus of Consent: Logical Foundations of Constitutional Democracy* (1962; Ann Arbor: University of Michigan Press, 1967), p.20.

9. Ibid., p. 62.

10. Ibid., p. 92.

11. Ibid., p. 211.

12. John Rawls, "Distributive Justice." Reprinted in E. S. Phelps, ed., *Economic Justice* (Harmondsworth, England: Penguin), 1973, p. 328.

13. Buchanan and Tullock, *The Calculus of Consent*, p. 351.

14. Terence Hutchison, *The Significance and Basic Postulates of Economic Theory*, 2nd ed. (1938; New York: Kelley, 1960), pp. 10–11.

15. David Stove, *Popper and After: Four Modern Irrationalists* (Oxford: Pergamon Press, 1982).

16. Philip J. Davis and Reuben Hersh, *The Mathematical Experience* (Boston: Houghton Mifflin, 1981), p. 34; cf. p. 40.

17. Quoted in David Levy, "The Plausibility of Preference Axioms over Commodity Space," Center for the Study of Public Choice, (October 1987).

18. Frans H. van Eemeren and Rob Grootendorst, *Speech Acts in Argumentative Discussions* (Dordrecht, Netherlands and Cinnaminson, N.J.: Foris Publications, 1983), pp. 179 ff.

19. Num. 12:14.

20. Moses Mielziner, *Introduction to the Talmud*, (New York: Bloch, 1968), pp. 181, 260. 4th ed.

21. Plato, *Gorgias* (Cambridge, Mass.: Harvard University Press, 1967), pp. 471e–472a.

22. Douglas N. Walton, *Arguer's Position: A Pragmatic Study of Ad Hominem Attack, Criticism, Refutation, and Fallacy* (Westport, Conn.: Greenwood, 1985), and Wayne Booth and Marshall W. Gregory, *The Harper and Row Rhetoric: Writing as Thinking, Thinking as Writing* (New York: Harper and Row, 1987), especially chap. 13.

23. David Haddock, "First Possession versus Optimal Timing: Limiting the Dissipation of Economic Value," *Washington University Law Quarterly* (Fall 1986): 789.

24. Anthony Giddens, *The Constitution of Society* (Cambridge: Polity Press, 1984), p. 228.

25. Alasdair MacIntyre, *After Virtue* (Notre Dame, Ind.: University of Notre Dame Press, 1981), p. 175.

Chapter 9   Rational Choice and Moral Order

We thank David Schap for helpful comments on an earlier draft.

The epigraph is from Carl Menger, *Investigations into the Method of the Social Sciences with Special Reference to Economics* (New York and London: New York University Press, 1985).

1. Geoffrey Brennan and James M. Buchanan, *The Reason of Rules: Constitutional Political Economy (Cambridge, England: Cambridge University Press, 1985).*

2. Instances of the functionalist fallacy can be found in sociology and anthropology, in particular in the functionalist schools within these disciplines. Economics, because of its individualistic orientation, has been less susceptible, though not perfectly immune. The fallacy appears, for example, in some of the analysis concerning the emergence of "efficient" institutions.

3. A similar distinction is made by Douglas D. Heckathorn, *Collective Incentives and the Creation of Prisoner's Dilemma Norms* (University of Missouri at Kansas City, 1987, Mimeographed), who uses the terms "inclinations" and "regulatory interests" to distinguish between the interests ("inclinations") that make rational actors in prisoner's dilemma situations choose the mutually destructive strategy and their ("regulatory") interests in having the choice situation regulated in a way that would allow them to realize the mutually advantageous cooperative outcome.

4. The "practice what you preach" argument is inappropriate if it is based on the assumption that it would be inconsistent not to do so. It is not necessarily inconsistent to advocate a social rule while at the same time behaving differently from the way that that rule requires.

5. In his writings on the philosophy of law (*Metaphysik der Sitten*), Kant is well aware of the difference between the two kinds of interests. Immanuel Kant, *The Philosophy of Law* (Edinburgh: T. & T. Clark, 1887), pp. 91ff., 155ff., 163ff. (we owe these references to Hartmut Kliemt).

6. David Gauthier, *Morals by Agreement* (Oxford, England: Oxford University Press, 1986), p. 183. For a discussion of the "rationality of morality" issue in terms of a choice of dispositions rather than case-by-case choices, see also Viktor Vanberg, *Morality and Economics: De Moribus Est Disputandum* (New Brunswick: Transaction Books, 1988).

7. Gauthier, *Morals by Agreement*, p. 183: "The essential point in our argument is that one's disposition to choose affects the situations in which one may expect to find oneself." Gilbert Harman, *Moral Agent and Impartial Spectator* (Department of Philosophy, University of Kansas. Lindley Memorial Lecture, 1986) identifies the same kind of argument in David Hume's basing moral behavior on self-interest: "Self-interest is involved because, if you cannot be trusted to tell the truth, keep your promises, or avoid injuring your associates, people will not join up with you in common enterprises and you

will lose out in comparison with other people who do tell the truth, keep their promises, and avoid injury to associates."

8. David Gauthier, *Morality, Rational Choice, and Semantic Representation: A Reply to My Critics* (University of Pittsburgh, 1987, Mimeographed), p. 8. Gauthier sees a shortcoming of John Rawls's contractarian conception in the fact that Rawls shows why it is rational for persons to agree on certain principles, but "does not show, or attempt to show, the rationality of their compliance with the agreed principles."

9. In fact, Gauthier's argument is not always perfectly unambiguous in this respect. In some places, he apparently assumes the de facto existence of conditions under which compliance can be expected to be in a person's interest; for example: "So what we suppose is that I find reason to comply with constraining principles in the benefits that accrue to me through the response of my fellows." *A Reply to My Critics,* p. 14.

10. The paradigmatic notion is, of course, that of the spontaneous order of markets. It should be kept in mind, though, that the spontaneous coordination within markets and the enforcement of the legal institutional framework of markets are different issues. The notion of spontaneous market coordination can very well be combined with a more constructivist view on the institutional framework.

11. See James M. Buchanan, *The Limits of Liberty: Between Anarchy and Leviathon* (Chicago: University of Chicago Press, 1975); *Freedom in Constitutional Contract* (College Station and London: Texas A & M University Press, 1977); and *Economics: Between Predictive Science and Moral Philosophy* (College Station: Texas A & M University Press, 1988) for a discussion that puts more emphasis on the constitutional-constructivist perspective.

12. In terms of the typical payoff structure in a two-by-two matrix, the two kinds of interaction problems can be characterized as follows:

Coordination Problem:

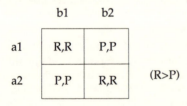

	b1	b2	
a1	R,R	P,P	
a2	P,P	R,R	(R>P)

Prisoner's Dilemma Problem:

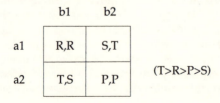

	b1	b2	
a1	R,R	S,T	
a2	T,S	P,P	(T>R>P>S)

13. David Hume, *A Treatise of Human Nature* (1940; Oxford: Clarendon Press, 1967), p. 490; and *Enquiries Concerning Human Understanding and Concerning the Principles of Morals* (Oxford: Clarendon Press, 1975), pp. 306, 307. In the setting that Hume obviously has in mind—namely, the two men on different sides of the boat pulling one oar each—the oarsmen are clearly facing a pure coordination problem. There exists, in such setting, simply no opportunity for cheating. The situation is different, of course, if the oarsmen are pulling two oars each, one sitting behind the other.

14. Hume, *Enquiries*, p. 210. In the context from which the quotation is taken, Hume draws a comparison between rules for the conduct of ordinary games and the "rules of justice, fidelity, and loyalty" upon which a society is based. After emphasizing that the comparison is in several ways "very imperfect," Hume states: "We may only learn from it the necessity of rules, wherever men have any intercourse with each other. They cannot even pass each other on the road without rules. Waggoners, coachmen, and postillions have principles, by which they give the way" (ibid.).

15. The relation between moral rules and prisoner's dilemma problems is stressed in Gauthier's *Morals by Agreement*. On Gauthier's argument, see James Buchanan, "The Gauthier Enterprise" (1987, Mimeographed), pp. 8–9; Viktor Vanberg, *Morality and Economics: De Moribus Est Disputandum*, Social Philosophy and Policy Center Original Papers Series (New Brunswick: Transaction Books, 1988), pp. 3–4.

16. The two kinds of problem situations and the respective kinds of problem-solving rules are discussed in more detail in Vanberg, "Spontaneous Market Order and Social Rules: A Critical Examination of F. A. Hayek's Theory of Cultural Evolution," *Economics and Philosophy* 2 (1986) : 75–100.

17. Their self-enforcing character has the disadvantage that a spontaneous transition from some established coordination rule (e.g., driving on the right side of the road) to a different one may be unlikely or even impossible, even though the other rule may be preferable in terms of people's constitutional interests. In this sense, and only in this sense, people's constitutional interests and their action interests may be in disharmony even for coordination rules. But such potential disharmony is, of course, a totally different issue from the typical disjunction between constitutional and compliance interests in the case of prisoner's dilemma–type moral rules—the issue that we are interested in here.

18. See the different rankings of payoffs in note 12.

19. Carl Menger, *Investigation into the Method of the Social Sciences with Special Reference to Economics* (New York and London: New York University Press, 1985), p. 147: "Law, language, the state, money, markets, all these social structures in their various empirical forms and in their constant change are to no small extent the unintended result of social development. The prices of goods, interest rates, ground rents, wages, and a thousand other phenomena of social life in general and of economy in particular exhibit the same peculiarity. Also, understanding of them . . . must be analogous to the understanding of unintentionally created social institutions. The solution of

the most important problems of the theoretical social sciences in general and of theoretical economics in particular is thus closely connected with the question of theoretically understanding the origin and change of 'organically' created social structures."

20. Friedrich A. Hayek, "Kinds of Order in Society," *New Individualist Review* 3 (1964): 5.

21. The role of the reciprocity notion in social theory, in particular with regard to the Scottish moral philosophy, to anthropology, and to exchange sociology, is discussed in Viktor Vanberg, *Die zwei Soziologien: Individualismus und Kollektivismus in der Sozialtheorie*, ed. Paul Siebeck (Tübingen: J. C. B. Mohr, 1975), pp. 15 ff., 55 ff.; and *Markt und Organisation*, ed. Paul Siebeck (Tübingen: J. C. B. Mohr, 1982), pp. 129 ff.

22. Robert Axelrod, *The Evolution of Cooperation* (New York: Basic Books, 1984).

23. It has been occasionally argued (e.g., by Alvin W. Gouldner, "The Norm of Reciprocity," *American Sociological Review* 25 [1960]: 161–78) that people's disposition to reciprocate reflects a "norm of reciprocity" which requires such behavior as "proper" conduct. Though it is certainly true that normative expectations are often attached to reciprocating behavior (concerning gratitude as well as revenge), the universality of such behavior strongly indicates that those normative expectations are a secondary, phenomenon, that they are a consequence rather than the cause of the general behavioral tendency to reciprocate.

24. Robert L. Trivers, "The Evolution of Reciprocal Altruism," *The Quarterly Review of Biology* 46 (1971): 35, labels such behavior "altruistic": "Altruistic behavior can be defined as behavior that benefits another organism, not closely related, while being apparently detrimental to the organism performing the behavior, benefit and detriment being defined in terms of inclusive fitness." The terms "altruistic" and "altruism" are probably not the best to describe the behavior under investigation, since these terms tend to presuppose certain assumptions about the "underlying motivation." It would seem preferable to use a term that is purely descriptive of the behavior to be explained, and that is neutral about how it is to be explained. Jack Hirshleifer, "Competition, Cooperation, and Conflict in Economics and Biology," *The American Economic Review Papers and Proceedings* 68 (1978): 240, suggests the term "helping behavior," a term that does not presuppose what the "determinants of helping behavior" are. He points out: "The patterns of helping are grouped by biologists into three categories: those associated with *kinship;* those merely *incidental* to selfish behavior; and those involved in *reciprocal* interaction."

25. Trivers, "The Evolution of Reciprocal Altruism," 35.

26. John Rawls, *A Theory of Justice* (Cambridge, England: Cambridge University Press, 1971), pp. 494–95, refers to such a "hard-wired" tendency to reciprocate as a crucial ingredient in the "capacity for a sense of justice": "The basic idea is one of reciprocity, a tendency to answer in kind. Now this tendency is a deep psychological fact. Without it our nature would be very different and fruitful social cooperation fragile if not impossible. . . . Beings

with a different psychology either have never existed or must soon have disappeared in the course of evolution. A capacity for a sense of justice built up by responses in kind would appear to be a condition of human sociability."

27. Robert L. Trivers refers to some of those complexities when he argues: "Because human altruism may span huge periods of time, a lifetime even, and because thousands of exchanges may take place, involving many different 'goods' and with many different cost benefit ratios, the problem of computing the relevant totals, detecting imbalances, and deciding whether they are due to chance or to small-scale cheating is an extremely difficult one." "The Evolution of Reciprocal Altruism," *The Quarterly Review of Biology* 46: 35–57. For an interpretation of reciprocity as learned behavior, see, for example, George C. Homans, *Social Behavior: Its Elementary Forms* (New York: Harcourt Brace Jovanovich, 1974), pp. 51ff.

28. Trivers, "The Evolution of Reciprocal Altruism," p. 49.

29. An analogous argument applies to "positive" emotions like gratitude, which sometimes seem to make people reciprocate the helping behavior of others in situations where there is little prospect of future benefits to outweigh the cost of the act of gratitude; see Ulrich Witt, "Evolution and Stability of Cooperation without Enforceable Contracts," *Kyklos* 39 (1986): 245–66.

30. On the role of emotional behavior for the enforcement of rules in social communities, see John Mackie, "Morality and the Retributive Emotions," in *Persons and Values* (Oxford: Clarendon Press, 1985), pp. 206–19.

31. It is certainly possible for subgroups within a given community to realize differential gains from internally practicing solidarity rules. For instance, a work team whose members refrain from shirking will be more productive than teams whose members are "morally unconstrained." The crucial point, however, is that with solidarity rules not *any* subset can realize differential gains from rule compliance. There always exists a group, defined by the nature of the collective good that rule compliance produces, for which some inclusive rule compliance has to be secured.

32. Robert Axelrod, "An Evolutionary Approach to Norms," *American Political Science Review* 80 (1986): 1095–1111.

33. Axelrod, *The Evolution of Cooperation*, p. 12: "What makes it possible for cooperation to emerge is the fact that the players might meet again. This possibility means that the choices made today not only determine the outcome of this move, but can also influence the later choices of the players. The future can therefore cast a shadow back upon the present and thereby affect the current strategic situation."

34. The point has been nicely articulated by William Graham Sumner, *The Forgotten Man and Other Essays*, ed. A. G. Keller (New Haven: Yale University Press, 1918), p. 95: "Some say that a man cannot afford to be honest unless everybody is honest. The truth is that, if there was one honest man among a lot of cheats, his character and reputation would reach their maximum value. . . . If a man . . . does right, the rewards of doing right are obtained. They are not as great as could be obtained if all did right, but they are greater than those enjoy who still do wrong."

35. It should be added, though, that being perceived as a vengeful person may involve a certain trade-off. While providing protection from exploitation, it may also decrease, to some extent, one's attractiveness as a potential partner for cooperation because others may worry about the risk of being vengefully prosecuted if they should ever inadvertently defect or if they should be mistaken for defectors.

36. Axelrod, "An Evolutionary Approach to Norms," p. 1107: "An important, and often dominant, reason to respect a norm is that violating it would provide a signal about the type of person you are. . . . This is an example of the signaling principle: a violation of a norm is not only a bit of behavior that has a payoff for the defector and for others, it is also a signal that contains information about the future behavior of the defector in a wide variety of situations."

37. Axelrod, "An Evolutionary Approach to Norms." As indicated above, Trivers' arguments on "moralistic aggression" imply that a certain disposition to retaliate is likely to be selected for a disposition that is relatively (though, of course, not totally) independent of the prospective costs and benefits involved in particular retaliatory acts.

38. Evidence for real-world examples of such collective responsibility or surety arrangements are in fact provided by legal historians and anthropologists. On the Anglo-Saxon frankpledge system, see William Alfred Morris, *The Frankpledge System* (New York: Longmans, Green and Co., 1910) and the references in Leonard P. Liggio, "The Transportation of Criminals: A Brief Political-Economic History" in *Assessing the Criminal: Restitution, Retribution, and the Legal Process*, ed. R. E. Barnett and J. Hagel III (Cambridge, Mass.: Ballinger, 1977), pp. 273–74. Anthropological evidence is reported in Sally Falk Moore, *Law as a Process: An Anthropological Approach* (London: Routledge and Kegan Paul, 1978), chap. 3, "Legal Liability and Evolutionary Interpretation: Some Aspects of Strict Liability, Self-help, and Collective Responsibility." D. D. Heckathorn's discussion on the role of "collective sanctions" is also of interest in this context. See *Collective Incentives and the Creation of Prisoner's Dilemma Norms*, mimeographed (Kansas City: University of Missouri, 1987).

39. The classical contribution on the general significance of group size for the provision of public goods is, of course, Mancur Olson, *The Logic of Collective Action* (Cambridge, Mass.: Harvard University Press, 1965). Buchanan, "Ethical Values, Expected Values, and Large Numbers," *Ethics* 76 (1965), vol. 76, pp. 1–13, (reprinted in *The Limits of Liberty: Between Anarchy and Leviathan* [Chicago: University of Chicago Press, 1977], pp. 151–68) discusses the issue with specific regard to the problem of moral order. For a more recent discussion, see Michael Taylor, *Community, Anarchy, and Liberty* (Cambridge, England: Cambridge University Press, 1982) and Werner Raub, *Problematic Social Situations and the "Large-Number Dilemma": A Game-Theoretical Analysis* (University of Nuernberg, 1986 Mimeographed), (to appear in *Journal of Mathematical Sociology*).

40. See Hayek, "Kinds of Order in Society," and Hayek, *Law, Legislation and Liberty*, vol. 1 of *Rules and Order* (London: Routledge and Kegan Paul, 1973), p. 35. See also Vanberg, *Markt und Organisation*, especially pp. 88 ff.

41. Gauthier, *Morals by Agreement*, pp. 83 ff.

Contributors

Allan Bloom is professor in the Committee on Social Thought at the University of Chicago, where he also codirects the John M. Olin Center for Inquiry into the Theory and Practice of Democracy. His books include *The Closing of the American Mind*, *Shakespeare's Politics* (with Harry V. Jaffa), and translations and interpretations of Rousseau's *Letter to d'Alembert*, Plato's *Republic*, and Rousseau's *Émile*.

James M. Buchanan, recipient of the 1986 Nobel Prize in economic science, is Harris University Professor of Economics and advisory general director of the Center for Study of Public Choice at George Mason University in Fairfax, Virginia. He is the author of numerous articles and many books, including *Calculus of Consent* (with G. Tullock); *Cost and Choice*; *The Limits of Liberty*; *Democracy and Deficit* (with R. Wagner); *Freedom in Constitutional Contract*; *The Power to Tax* (with G. Brennan); *Liberty, Market, and State*; *The Reason of Rules* (with G. Brennan); *Economics: Between Predictive Science and Moral Philosophy*; and *Explorations into Constitutional Economics*.

David Gauthier is Distinguished Service Professor of Philosophy at the University of Pittsburgh. His principal interests include the relationship of morality to rational choice and moral and political thought in the seventeenth and eighteenth centuries. Among his writings are *The Logic of Leviathan*, a study of Thomas Hobbes, and *Morals by Agreement*, a systematic development of a contractarian moral theory.

Donald N. McCloskey is John F. Murray Professor of Economics and Professor of History at the University of Iowa. He has written six books and edited or coedited six others in economics, economic history, and the rhetoric of the social sciences. His most recent book is *If You're So Smart: The Narrative of Economic Expertise*. He codirects with John Nelson the Project on Rhetoric of Inquiry.

John S. Nelson teaches political science at the University of Iowa. He specializes in political theory, economy, and communication, and codirects the Project on Rhetoric of Inquiry. He has edited three volumes of essays: *What Should Political Theory Be Now?*, *Tradition, Interpretation, and Science*, and *The Rhetoric of the Human Sciences*. His current studies include postmodern culture, political myth, human rights, and diverse rhetorics.

James H. Nichols, Jr., is professor of government at Claremont McKenna College and Avery Fellow at the Claremont Graduate School. He is author of *Epicurean Political Philosophy: The De Rerum Natura of Lucretius*, of a translation and interpretation of Plato's *Laches,* and of articles on human rights and pragmatism.

Marc F. Plattner is counselor at the National Endowment for Democracy and editor of the *Journal of Democracy*. He is the author of *Rousseau's State of Nature* and the editor of *Human Rights in Our Time.* He has written a number of articles on issues relating to capitalism and economic justice.

Steven E. Rhoads is a professor of government and foreign affairs at the University of Virginia. His most recent book is *The Economist's View of the World: Government, Markets and Public Policy.* He is currently writing a book about comparable worth in the United States, England, and Australia.

Nathan Rosenberg is Fairleigh Dickenson, Jr., Professor of Economics at Stanford University. He is the author of several books, including *How the West Grew Rich* (with L. E. Birdzell, Jr.) and *Technology and the Pursuit of Economic Growth* (with David C. Mowery).

Abram N. Shulsky is a senior fellow at the National Strategy Information Center in Washington, D.C., where he is writing a book on intelligence and national security. His Ph.D dissertation in political science from the University of Chicago concerned the treatment of economic issues in Aristotle's *Politics*. He has taught at the University of Chicago, Cornell University, and the Catholic University of America.

Viktor Vanberg is editorial director, Center for Study of Public Choice, and professor of economics, George Mason University. Before coming to the United States in 1983, he taught sociology at several universities in Germany. He has published on the individualist tradition in social theory, on the theory of institutions and organizations, and, more recently, in the area of constitutional economics. He is coeditor of the new journal *Constitutional Political Economy*. His more recent publications include *Morality and Economics—De Moribus est Disputandum*, "Hayek as Constitutional Political Economist" in *Wirtschaftspolitische Blätter*, "Carl Menger's Evolutionary and John R. Commons' Collective Action Approach to Institutions: a Comparison," *Review of Political Economy*, and (coauthored with J. M. Buchanan) "Interests and Theories in Constitutional Choice" in the *Journal of Theoretical Politics*.

Colin Wright is Frances and Norwood Berger Professor of Economics and Society at Claremont McKenna College, and was formerly dean of faculty at Claremont McKenna College and director of the Lincoln Institute at Claremont Graduate School. He has published articles in the area of urban economics and pollution control, such as "Residential Location in a Three-Dimensional City" in the *Journal of Political Economy* and "Pigovian Margins and Pollution Control" (*Economica*, with Chris Archibald). Since leaving academic administration his work has focused chiefly on political economy.

Index

Amacher, Ryan, 82, 218n5.11
Anger as passion, 200, 205
Aoki, Masahiko, 229n7.26
Aristotle, 207n1.2, 208n2.8,
  207–8n2.9, 214nn3.25–26
  on accumulation of wealth, 25, 46
  defines political science and
    political economy, 2–3
  on economics, 16–17, 46, 58
  modes of, and limits to,
    acquisition of, 18–19
  on syllogism and enthymeme, 165
Arrow, Kenneth, 81, 89, 105,
  218n5.6, 220n5.32, 220–21n5.37,
  224n6.4, 229n7.24
Axelrod, Robert, 234n9.22,
  235nn9.32–33, 236nn9.36–37
  reciprocity concept of, 182, 186, 188

Barry, Brian, 156, 157, 229n8.4
Barzun, Jacques, 98, 223n5.73
Baumol, William J., 79, 218n5.3
Becker, Gary S., 100, 157, 221n5.46,
  222n5.59, 224n5.80, 230n8.5
  on changing tastes, 83–85,
    219nn5.16, 18, 20, 22
  definition of economics, 65,
    216n4.20

Bentham, Jeremy, 214n3.37,
  215nn3.40, 42
  on altruism, 93
  on principle of utility, 49, 50
  on security and equality, 50–51
Berliner, Joseph, 226–27n7.13,
  228n7.23
Best prior plan, 115–19, 123
Birdzell, L. E., 226nn7.8, 10
Black, Max, 156, 229n8.2
Bloom, Allan, 98, 223nn5.70–72
Bolton, Roger, 100, 223n5.778
Booth, Wayne, 230n8.22
Bottomore, Tom, 217nn4.25–26
Bourdieu, Pierre, 157, 230n8.6
Bourne, H. R. F., 210–11n2.28
Boyes, William, 82, 218n5.11
Boynton, G. R., 156, 229n8.1
Brennan, Geoffrey, 231n9.1
Bronfenbrenner, Martin, 100–102,
  224nn5.81–85
Browning, Edward, 97, 222n5.59,
  223n5.66
Browning, Jacquelene, 97,
  222n5.59, 223n5.66
Buchanan, James M., 71–72, 73, 88,
  211n2.30, 217n4.27, 220n5.31,
  230nn8.8–11, 13, 231n9.1,
  232n9.11, 233n9.15